499 WORDS EVERY *COLLEGE* STUDENT

SHOULD KNOW

A PROFESSOR'S HANDBOOK ON WORDS ESSENTIAL TO GREAT WRITING & BETTER GRADES

Skyhorse Publishing

Dedication

This book is dedicated to my dear former students, all of whom now (I hope) know what "abrogate" means

Copyright © 2017 by Stephen Spignesi

All rights reserved. No part of this book may be reproduced in any manner without the express written consent of the publisher, except in the case of brief excerpts in critical reviews or articles. All inquiries should be addressed to Skyhorse Publishing, 307 West 36th Street, 11th Floor, New York, NY 10018.

Skyhorse Publishing books may be purchased in bulk at special discounts for sales promotion, corporate gifts, fund-raising, or educational purposes. Special editions can also be created to specifications. For details, contact the Special Sales Department, Skyhorse Publishing, 307 West 36th Street, 11th Floor, New York, NY 10018 or info@skyhorsepublishing.com.

Skyhorse® and Skyhorse Publishing® are registered trademarks of Skyhorse Publishing, Inc.®, a Delaware corporation.

Visit our website at www.skyhorsepublishing.com.

10 9 8 7 6 5 4 3 2

Library of Congress Cataloging-in-Publication Data is available on file.

Cover design by Rain Saukas

Print ISBN: 978-1-5107-2387-0
Ebook ISBN: 978-1-5107-2388-7

Printed in the United States of America

Acknowledgments

Special thanks to Mike Lewis, John White, Rachel Montgomery, Lee Mandato, and Janet Spignesi Daniw, as well as Mike Campbell and all the fine folks at Skyhorse Publishing, word lovers all, who have always been helpful, generous, and supportive.

Also, especial gratitude to all the fine folks at these websites for doing an extraordinary job and for making their efforts available to the world:

1. CollinsDictionary.com
2. DailyBeast.com
3. Definition.org
4. Dictionary.Cambridge.org
5. Dictionary.com
6. Fun-with-Words.com
7. IMDB.com
8. LiteraryDevices.net
9. MacmillanDictionary.com
10. MerriamWebster.com
11. NYTimes.com
12. OxfordDictionaries.com
13. Quodb.com
14. TheFreeDictionary.com
15. Thesaurus.com
16. Vocabulary.com
17. WordsinaSentence.com
18. YourDictionary.com

...as well as the myriad dictionary and thesaurus sites online, many of which were extremely helpful in the compiling of this book.

Foreword

Words equal credibility.

The more articulate a person is in their writing and speaking, the more seriously they will be taken—by everyone.

This book teaches 499 words every student should know and focuses on the classroom-tested *Trinity of Vocabulary Use*: For each word, the vocabulary-enriched and educated student should be able to:

- understand the word when they *read it* or *hear it*
- use the word in their *speaking*,
- make good use of the word in their *writing*

I tried to provide easy-to-understand, informative and, on some occasions, humorous explanations of every word, and explore how to use them in sentences, and in proper context. The majority of these words were chosen because they are fairly commonplace in media, books, online, and elsewhere, and students need to be able to understand them. I come across many of these words all the time.

A student came into class one day and said, "You taught my father something last night." He explained that he was watching cable news with his father and the commentator remarked that a particular candidate was a demagogue. His father asked, "What's a demagogue?," and because we had just learned the word in class, my student was able to explain it to him so that he understood what the cable anchor was saying. This was a wonderfully gratifying moment for me.

Thus, the idea for this book. The people who know these words and use them routinely are intelligent and eloquent. Their communication is also coherent because they know the right word to express the right message. In the Oxford English Thesaurus, there are 380 synonyms for "good." Knowing which synonym describes precisely what the writer is trying to express is the product of knowing vocabulary words. Words are a tool and a good craftsman possesses and uses quality tools.

For each word, the following information is provided:

- **Correct spelling** of the word.
- **What the word is**; i.e., verb, noun, adjective, etc.
- **Pronunciation**: This book uses "real-world pronunciation" rather than traditional linguistic pronunciations (y'know, with the upside down "e" and all that.) The syllables are spelled out the way they sound, and the syllable that gets the emphasis is in italics.
- **A few informative facts** about the word that are both instructive and entertaining, which also provide some context when relevant. They appear in gray sidebars next to the word.
- Several examples of the word **Used in Context**, often citing pop culture sources such as TV shows and movies, as well as classic literature, encyclopedias, and contemporary writings.
- **A few synonyms** for the word.

Regarding Citations

Movies are in *italics*;

Books are in *italics*, followed by the author;

Newspaper, Web, and Magazine Articles are in "quotes," followed by the author;

TV Shows are in *italics*, followed by the title of the episode in "quotes."

Stephen Spignesi
New Haven, Connecticut

Words transform both speaker and hearer; they feed energy back and forth and amplify it. They feed understanding or emotion back and forth and amplify it.
—Ursula K. Le Guin

Handle them carefully, for words have more power than atom bombs.
—Pearl Strachan Hurd

Don't ever diminish the power of words. Words move hearts and hearts move limbs.
—Hamza Yusuf

Good words are worth much, and cost little.
—George Herbert

If we understood the awesome power of our words, we would prefer silence to almost anything negative.
—Betty Eadie

The 499 Words

1.	Abdicate	28.	Agnostic	55.	Arrogate
2.	Aberration	29.	Alacrity	56.	Assiduous
3.	Abhor	30.	Alienate	57.	Assuage
4.	Abjure	31.	Allegory	58.	Atheist
5.	Abridge	32.	Alleviate	59.	Atrophy
6.	Abrogate	33.	Allusion	60.	Attenuate
7.	Abstemious	34.	Altruism	61.	Augur
8.	Abstract	35.	Ameliorate	62.	Avarice
9.	Abstruse	36.	Amenable	63.	Aversion
10.	Accede	37.	Anachronism		
11.	Accretion	38.	Analogy	64.	Begrudge
12.	Acerbic	39.	Anathema	65.	Beguile
13.	Acquiesce	40.	Annul	66.	Beleaguer
14.	Acrimony	41.	Anomaly	67.	Bemoan
15.	Acuity	42.	Antagonist	68.	Bemused
16.	Acumen	43.	Antecedent	69.	Benevolent
17.	Addled	44.	Anticlimax	70.	Besmirch
18.	Adduce	45.	Antipathy	71.	Bifurcate
19.	Adroit	46.	Antithesis	72.	Bilingual
20.	Adulation	47.	Aphorism	73.	Bilious
21.	Adumbrate	48.	Apocryphal	74.	Binary
22.	Advocate	49.	Apprise	75.	Bipartisan
23.	Aesthetic	50.	Approbation	76.	Bipolar
24.	Affectation	51.	A priori	77.	Blasphemy
25.	Affinity	52.	Apropos	78.	Blithe
26.	Aggrandize	53.	Arcane	79.	Bombastic
27.	Aggregate	54.	Archetype	80.	Bona fide

81.	Bravado	116.	Collegial	150.	Devolve
82.	Broach	117.	Colloquy	151.	Dialectic
83.	Brusque	118.	Comity	152.	Dichotomy
84.	Bulwark	119.	Commensurate	153.	Didactic
85.	Bumptious	120.	Comport	154.	Diffident
86.	Bureaucracy	121.	Concatenation	155.	Digression
87.	Buttress	122.	Conciliate	156.	Dilatory
		123.	Condescending	157.	Diminution
88.	Cacophony	124.	Conflate	158.	Disclaim
89.	Cadence	125.	Conformist	159.	Disconcerting
90.	Cadre	126.	Consanguineous	160.	Discordant
91.	Cajole	127.	Consensus	161.	Discredit
92.	Callous	128.	Contemporane-	162.	Discursive
93.	Canard		ous	163.	Disenfranchise
94.	Canon	129.	Contentious	164.	Dishearten
95.	Cantankerous	130.	Contiguous	165.	Disinclined
96.	Capacious	131.	Convergence	166.	Disingenuous
97.	Capricious	132.	Convivial	167.	Disparity
98.	Caricature	133.	Culpable	168.	Dispassionate
99.	Carpe diem			169.	Disputatious
100.	Castigate	134.	Dearth	170.	Dissemble
101.	Catalyst	135.	Debase	171.	Dissolute
102.	Catatonia	136.	Declaim	172.	Divergent
103.	Catharsis	137.	Decorous	173.	Doppelganger
104.	Causal	138.	Decry	174.	Duplicity
105.	Caveat	139.	De facto		
106.	Censorious	140.	Deferential	175.	e.g.
107.	Censure	141.	Deign	176.	Ebullient
108.	Chagrin	142.	Deleterious	177.	Eclectic
109.	Chauvinism	143.	Delineate	178.	Edify
110.	Chicanery	144.	Demagogue	179.	Efficacy
111.	Chide	145.	Denigrate	180.	Effrontery
112.	Chimera	146.	Deplorable	181.	Effusive
113.	Circuitous	147.	Despoil	182.	Egalitarian
114.	Circumspect	148.	Desultory	183.	Egregious
115.	Codicil	149.	Deus ex machina	184.	Ellipsis

390.	Precursor	424.	Rostrum	458.	Treacly
391.	Predilection	425.	Ruminate	459.	Trope
392.	Prevaricate			460.	Truculent
393.	Probity	426.	Sagacious	461.	Truism
394.	Profligate	427.	Salient		
395.	Promulgate	428.	Salutary	462.	Ubiquitous
396.	Propagate	429.	Sanguine	463.	Umbrage
397.	Propitiate	430.	Sardonic	464.	Unabashed
398.	Prosaic	431.	Satiate	465.	Unassailable
399.	Proselytize	432.	Scintilla	466.	Unconscionable
400.	Provenance	433.	Scurrilous	467.	Unctuous
401.	Puerile	434.	Seditious	468.	Unequivocal
402.	Punctilious	435.	Semantics	469.	Unilateral
403.	Purview	436.	Simile	470.	Unmitigated
404.	Pusillanimous	437.	Sine qua non	471.	Untenable
		438.	Specious	472.	Usurp
405.	Qualm	439.	Spurious		
406.	Quell	440.	Stasis	473.	Vacillate
407.	Querulous	441.	Stoical	474.	Vacuous
408.	Quiescent	442.	Subjugate	475.	Vagary
409.	Quintessential	443.	Supercilious	476.	Valorous
410.	Quixotic	444.	Superfluous	477.	Vapid
411.	Quotidian	445.	Surreptitious	478.	Venal
		446.	Sycophant	479.	Verisimilitude
412.	Raison d'etre	447.	Syllogism	480.	Verity
413.	Rancorous	448.	Symbiotic	481.	Vicarious
414.	Recalcitrant	449.	Syntax	482.	Vicissitude
415.	Recompense			483.	Vilify
416.	Rectitude	450.	Tautological	484.	Virulent
417.	Redoubtable	451.	Temerity	485.	Visceral
418.	Remonstrate	452.	Tenable	486.	Vitiate
419.	Reproach	453.	Theist	487.	Vociferous
420.	Reprobate	454.	Tonally	488.	Volition
421.	Requisite	455.	Torpor	489.	Voluble
422.	Res ipsa loquitur	456.	Transcendent		
423.	Risible	457.	Transient	490.	Waffling

A

1. Abdicate
verb (ab•dih•kate)

To give up a royal title; to fail to satisfy a responsibility

Used in Context

"I refused to **abdicate** and declared that I would gather troops together and return with them in order to help the Government to maintain order in the land."—*The Kaiser's Memoirs*, Wilhelm II

"Phillipe knew that my firstborn, his brother Pierre, wanted to **abdicate**, which he did, eventually, to join the church."—*The Princess Diaries*

"Should your brother continue to ignore the advice of His Government, He must **abdicate**."—*The King's Speech*

King Edward VIII abdicated the British throne in 1936 in order to marry Wallis Simpson.

A common topic of discussion in the United Kingdom is whether or not Queen Elizabeth II will ever abdicate and turn the crown over to her son Charles. The Queen's biographer said the monarch would never abdicate because she feels it's her duty to remain Queen until her death.

"On behalf of my country, and in the name of the other leaders of the world with whom I have today consulted, I hereby **abdicate** all authority and control over this planet to General Zod."—*Superman II*

Synonyms: abandon, abjure, abnegate, cede, relinquish, renounce, resign, retire, step down, surrender, vacate

2. Aberration
noun (ab•uh•*ray*•shun)

An event that is not normal or not what is expected

Abnormal chromosomes are known as aberrations.

The fantasy role-playing game *Dungeons & Dragons* has creatures known as "aberrations." They have bizarre anatomies and paranormal abilities.

A cardiac aberrancy is an aberration of the electrical function of the heart.

Used in Context

"The heatwave that has already killed hundreds across Eastern Europe is no **aberration**."—*New Scientist*, August 3, 2007

"No, it is no **aberration**. The behavior of these particles is quite unmistakable. Dust is flowing into this man, through his dæmon."—*The Golden Compass*

"The police commissioner defended the rising tide of crime as a statistical **aberration** tied to growing unemployment."—*Gone Baby Gone*

"I'm hoping to prove that within every normal system there exists an **aberration**. Something different."—*Angus*

Synonyms: abnormality, anomaly, deviation, disfigurement, impairment, irregularity, mutation

3. Abhor
verb (ab•*hor*)

To strongly dislike something, often verging on hatred

Used in Context

"You, my creator, **abhor** me; what hope can I gather from your fellow creatures, who owe me nothing?"—*Frankenstein*, Mary Shelley

"I **abhor** the use of violence."—*Hellboy*

"They have a similar philosophy in India. They **abhor** violence."—*The Outer Limits*, "Alien Shop"

> It is a very powerful statement to say you abhor something, or that something is abhorrent to you.

"I loathe and **abhor** this place."—*Strike!*

Synonyms: abominate, be down on, despise, detest, hate, have no use for, loathe, scorn

4. Abjure
verb (ab•*jer*)

To give up a firmly held belief; to renounce something

Used in Context

"Obama is right to be realistic and to **abjure** bombastic rhetoric."—"Obama's Realism Doctrine," Richard Cohen, *The Washington Post*, May 10, 2009

"You have the authority to bind me. Speak the name, **abjure** and command me and I will be removed from this body."—*Babylon 5*, "The Lost Tales"

"But at the age of eighty, I seek quiet, and **abjure** contention."—*The Domestic Life of Thomas Jefferson Compiled From Family Letters and Reminiscences*, Sarah N. Randolph

"I absolutely and entirely renounce and **abjure** all allegiance and fidelity to any foreign prince, state or sovereignty, of whom or which I have heretofore been a subject or citizen."—*Ugly Betty*, "Nice Day for a Posh Wedding"

Synonyms: abandon, deny, disavow, disown, foreswear, give up, recant, reject, relinquish, renounce, repudiate

5. Abridge
verb (uh•*brij*)

To shorten a book or other writing by removing sections of text, words, or sentences

One of the synonyms for "abridge" is abbreviate and a general rule for using abbreviations in your writing is: don't. If sprinkled throughout with discretion, abbreviations can be okay, but you're not a Founding Father copying the Constitution by hand or a medieval monk looking to

Used in Context
"The Supreme Court has repeatedly held that the right to marry the person you love is so fundamental that states cannot **abridge** it."—"Gay Marriage and the Constitution," David Boies

"No state shall make or enforce any law, which shall **abridge** the privileges or immunities of citizens of the United States." —*Thurgood*

"I don't venerate drug dealers. To the contrary. What we're attempting to do here is check the government's attempt to **abridge** our civil liberties through informants, eavesdropping, unreasonable searches and seizure."—*True Believer*

save time and effort. You can sometimes be accused of bad writing if you use too many, or inappropriate, abbreviations, but you can never be accused of that if you spell out everything.

"Do not, please, madam, hasten your business or **abridge** it. I don't need no receipt."—*Deadwood*, "Amateur Night"

Synonyms: abbreviate, blue pencil, compress, concentrate, condense, contract, curtail, decrease, diminish, downsize, lessen, limit, reduce, restrict, summarize, truncate

6. Abrogate
verb (*ab•row•gate*)

To formally revoke, to nullify

Used in Context
"What must God think about this anthropoid, this overgrown monkey that dares to be intelligent enough to invent things that **abrogate** his eternal laws, his unchangeable laws, eternal and irresistible as God himself?"—"The Child That Never Was," Maria Virginia Estenssoro

"Nevertheless, you are going to have to **abrogate** and egress from the premises."—*Skins*, "Cook"

Article 13 of the Constitution *abrogated* slavery: "Neither slavery nor involuntary servitude...shall exist within the United States, or any place subject to their jurisdiction."

The 21st Amendment *abrogated* Prohibition, which had been put in place by the 18th Amendment.

Many Biblical adherents
and scholars believe that
the Old Testament's Mosaic
Laws were *abrogated* by
the New Testament's "New
Covenant."

"Banning Muslim entry or creating a registry would violate First Amendment freedom of religion. Legislatively targeting news outlets based on their views would **abrogate** freedom of press. Promising to lock up political opponents upends long-held notions of fairness and due process."—"Donald Trump Is the Next Richard Nixon," Rep. John Conyers

"I have come to breathe new life into this community, to aid those who seek betterment, to **abrogate** those who would hold us back."—*Boardwalk Empire,* "William Wilson"

"We're starting a counteragent protocol that should **abrogate** the drug's effects."—*Cult,* "The Good Fight"

Synonyms: abate, abolish, annul, cancel, destroy, dissolve, invalidate, nullify, quash, reject, repeal, retract, revoke, scrub, torpedo, undo, vacate, vitiate, void

7. Abstemious
adjective (ab•*steem*•ee•us)

Describes someone who does not overindulge in drink or food

Used in Context
"My father was **abstemious** and he abhorred the salacious bon mot."
—*Home Improvement,* "Something Old, Something Blue"

"The Russian president is known to be **abstemious**, however, and rushes through meals, in addition to being a bit of a health nut."—"With

Obama and Putin in France for Dinner, Hollande Leaves Room for Seconds," Scott Sayare

"Today, the pendulum seems to have swung again. [Susan] Cheever says that most of our leading literary figures are fairly **abstemious**."—"America: Land of Lushes," Christopher Buckley

"I am an **abstemious** man. I find liquor and business do not mix."—*Sugarfoot*

Synonyms: abstinent, ascetic, austere, disciplined, moderate, restrained, self-sober, sparing, temperate

8. Abstract
adjective (*ab•strakt*)

A term that describes understanding something intellectually and conceptually rather than on specific objects and/or instances

Used in Context
"This was my first conscious perception of an **abstract** idea."—*The Story of My Life*, Helen Keller

"I figured it should be the one with the capacity for **abstract** thought, but if that ain't the consensus, then hell, let's vote."—*O Brother, Where Art Thou?*

"I've always particularly liked that poem. In the **abstract**. Now I find the image of my minute's last point a little too, shall we say, pointed."—*Wit*

"The nature of what we call democracy is sadly no longer an **abstract** discussion beloved of political science professors."—"American Democracy is Being Derailed. Can Faith Be Restored?," Richard Wolffe

Synonyms: abstruse, complex, deep, hypothetical, intangible, nonconcrete, nonrepresentational, philosophical, theoretical, transcendent, unreal

9. Abstruse
adjective (ab•*stroos*)

Describes something that is obscure, confusing, and puzzling

Used in Context
"My mind rebels at stagnation. Give me problems; give me work. Give me the most **abstruse** cryptogram, the most intricate analysis, and I'm in my proper atmosphere." *The Adventures of Sherlock Holmes,* "A Scandal in Bohemia"

"But she is known for her more **abstruse** constructions, and those will be showcased at the Met."—"What the Comme des Garçons Show Means for the Met—and Fashion," Vanessa Friedman

"Admiral, I must register my protest at this interruption. Your summons intruded just as I was digesting an **abstruse** manuscript for Dr. Goodfellow."—*Buck Rogers in the 25th Century,* "The Golden Man"

"I like it, but perhaps it's too **abstruse**. What do you think?"—*Kingdom Hospital,* "Shoulda Stood in Bed"

Synonyms: abstract, Byzantine, complex, complicated, convoluted, deep, enigmatic, esoteric, Greek to me, heavy, hidden, incomprehensible, intricate, involved, muddy, obscure, perplexing, profound, puzzling, recondite, unfathomable, vague

10. Accede
verb (uh•*seed*)

To agree to something

Used in Context
"I don't **accede** to blackmail."—*Striptease*

"Your Honor, I believe, in this trial, we have done everything humanly possible to **accede** to the requests of the defense."—*The Onion Field*

"And, Carole, as I realize you have the best interests of this organization at heart, I want you to **accede** to a somewhat unusual request."—*The Love Bug*

"The Western aim in supporting such groups, Assad said, is to destroy his regime, because he has refused to **accede** to American demands."—"Assad Speaks," Dexter Filkins

"If K12 doesn't **accede** to the union's demands, the state Board of Education could use the audit as a pretext to shut the schools down. Thuggish government marches on."—"California's Charter School Mugging,"—*The Wall Street Journal*

Synonyms: accept, acquiesce, allow, assent, cave in, commit, comply, concede, concur, consent, cooperate, endorse, give the green light, grant, let, okay, permit, play ball, subscribe, yield

11. Accretion
noun (uh•*kree*•shun)

A gradual buildup of something as a result of things being added

> Accretion can be used in the abstract, as in, "a gradual accretion of power."

Used in Context

"We are things that labor under the illusion of having a self, this **accretion** of sensory experience and feeling, programmed with total assurance that we are each somebody when, in fact, everybody's nobody."—*True Detective*, "The Long Bright Dark"

"The **accretion** of detail is a windup for a piercing moral observation."—"The Unclassifiable Essays of Eliot Weinberger," Christopher Byrd

"The shaggy-dog **accretion** of material—phone numbers, long-ago concert dates, coded references to secret loves—all seemed to belong to somebody else."—"Letter From the Other Side—Return from a Traumatic Brain Injury," Tim Power

"The actual particulars of the event are unclear, obscured by the **accretion** of the myth."—*Into Thin Air*, Jon Krakauer

"An unnatural arrangement which forces its participants into an unhealthy monogamy. An **accretion** of petty fights and resentful compromises which, like Chinese water torture, slowly transforms both parties,"—*Elementary*, "An Unnatural Arrangement"

Synonyms: accession, accrual, accumulation, addition, amplification, augmentation, buildup, enlargement, expansion, growth, increase, increment, raise, rise, swelling

12. Acerbic
adjective (uh•*sur*•bik)

Sharp or bitter in tone or attitude

Used in Context

"There is no warmer, kinder me waiting to be coaxed out into the light. I am **acerbic**. I can be cruel. It's who I am."—*Elementary*, "On the Line"

"She was **acerbic**, flamboyant, she kicked against tradition and sometimes won. Like many women of her generation she understood that femininity is always a performance, and she performed it to the hilt. She was always winning, never a victim."—"Zsa Zsa Gabor Knew Femininity Was a Performance. She Played It Perfectly," Suzanne Moore

Examples:

• "After David heard his teacher's acerbic comments, he was not motivated to complete his project."

• "Martin tried to ignore his wife's acerbic statements about his career path."

"David Thomson's new book *Television: A Biography* is an ambitious survey of television's history by an astute and **acerbic** critic."—"*Television*: The Life Story of Our Constant Video Companion," Neal Justin

"While Doctor Strange has his own solid fan base, he's not forced to carry the beloved childhood memories of several million grown men on his shoulders. That's the last thing Doctor Strange—cynical, **acerbic**, supremely confident of his role in the universe—would want, anyway."—"Benedict Cumberbatch Is the Alchemist with the Mostest in *Doctor Strange*," Stephanie Zacharek

"I'm begging you, please. I'm like a man without water. An **acerbic** comment, would it kill you?"—*Man of the Year*

Synonyms: acid, acidic, acrid, astringent, biting, bitter, caustic, cutting, harsh, sharp, tart, unpleasant

13. Acquiesce
verb (*ak•wee•ess*)

To agree to something reluctantly; to give in but without actually supporting what you're agreeing to

Used in Context
"I am disinclined to **acquiesce** your request…Means no."—*Pirates of the Caribbean: Curse of the Black Pearl*

"The contribution made by supply-side innovation—that is, inventing new materials, devices or structures, or probing the complexity of nature—is undoubtedly a good thing. It is often touted by politicians as the main way in which research adds value in civil society. As scientists, we often **acquiesce** to this linear view because it is the route through which money tends to flow."—"Take the Long View," Ian L. Boyd

"Apple should be no more responsible if someone uses a gun image in the abstract than if someone happens to type the word 'gun.' As free citizens, we **acquiesce** to infantilizing digital infrastructure at our peril."—"Apple's Emoji Gun Control," Jonathan Zittrain

"It's the wood that should fear your hand, not the other way around. No wonder you can't do it. You **acquiesce** to defeat before you even begin."—*Kill Bill, Vol. 2*

Synonyms: accede, accommodate, adapt, adjust, agree, allow, approve, bow to, cave in, come around, comply, concede, conform, consent, cry uncle, give in, go along with, okay, shake on, submit, yield

14. Acrimony
noun (*aah*•kri•moan•ee)

Bitterness and animosity in speech and/or attitude

Used in Context

"One of us suffers a personal tragedy, falls ill and whatnot, we all feel it deeply, no matter what kind of **acrimony** is in the air."—*The Sopranos*, "Whitecaps"

An acrimonious statement is like an acerbic statement, except there's a dark thread of bitterness in the context. For example: "During the campaign, the politicians engaged in acrimonious debate, accusing each other of gross malfeasance and misdeeds."

"Befitting an election filled with **acrimony**, thousands of protesters converged on state capitols across the country Monday, urging Republican electors to abandon their party's winning candidate."—"Trump Cruises to Electoral College Victory Despite Protests," Stephen Ohlemacher

"I thought the English liked **acrimony**. You see them all screaming at each other in Parliament. I watch it on cable. It's ridiculous."—*Ally McBeal,* "Ally McBeal: The Musical, Almost"

"The run-up to the Anthem-Cigna trial was marked by **acrimony** between the companies, with each accusing the other of breaching terms of their deal. Cigna stands to collect a $1.85 billion breakup fee if the merger is blocked."—"Anthem, Cigna Face Off Against U.S. to Save $48 Billion Deal," Andrew M Harris, David McLaughlin

Synonyms: acerbity, animosity, antipathy, belligerence, bitterness, churlishness, crankiness, harshness, hostility, ill will, irascibility, malevolence, malice, rancor, rudeness, spite, unkindness, virulence

Sharpness of intellect; also used to describe a keenness of sight or hearing

Used in Context

"You get your first look at this six-foot turkey, as you enter a clearing. He moves like a bird, lightly bobbing his head. And you keep still because you think that maybe his visual **acuity** is based on movement, like T-Rex, and he'll lose you if you don't move. But no, not Velociraptor."—*Jurassic Park*

"After reading one of your columns this year we connected the dots, and she abandoned the sleep aid. It is about six months later, and she feels that she has nearly entirely recovered her mental **acuity**."—"Did Popular PM Pain Reliever Trigger Memory Loss?," Joe Graedon

"As we peer deeper and with greater **acuity** into the universe, we are simultaneously forced to appreciate the complexity of all worlds, including our own."—"What's So Special About Another Earth?," Lisa Messeri

"So, it's fake? According to your impeccable sense of taste and your oenological olfactory **acuity**?"—*CSI*, "In Vino Veritas"

Synonyms: acuteness, astuteness, awareness, brains, brilliance, cleverness, comprehension, cunning, discernment, discrimination, farsightedness, grasp, guile, ingenuity, insight, intellect, intelligence, intuition, judgment, keenness, perception, perspicacity, sagacity, sensitivity, sharpness, shrewdness, smartness, understanding, vision, wisdom, wit

16. Acumen
noun (*ak*•yoo•men)

Quickness of perception or discernment and understanding, intelligence, sharpness

Used in Context

"Why do you think he removes their skins, Agent Starling? Thrill me with your **acumen.**"—*The Silence of the Lambs*

"The energy business is not a get-rich-quick scheme. It entails complex operations, often in environments that pose political challenges, with time horizons that stretch over decades and billions of dollars at stake. To succeed requires integrating technical, financial and political **acumen** over a long period."—"So You Want to Be a Diplomat? CEOs Need Not Apply," Suzanne Maloney

One of the keys to understanding this word is the word "quickness." A person who gets the big picture and understands trends well enough to make a smart decision manifests acumen.

Big-Picture thinking and the ability to use foresight to make good decisions.

"I had no idea that my business **acumen** was giving you such spasms."—*Dark Shadows*

"Budgets? Investing? Interest rates? I think the Fed does something important? Totally lost on me. I am aware that these things exist, but that is the extent of my financial **acumen.**"—"I'm 29 and I Never Learned How Money Works. It's Time To Fix That," Tim Herrera

Synonyms: acuity, astuteness, awareness, brains, brilliance, cleverness, comprehension, cunning, discernment, discrimination, expertise, good judgment, grasp, guile, ingenuity, insight, intellect, perception, sagacity, sensitivity, sharpness, shrewdness, vision, wisdom, wit

17. Addled
adjective (*add*•uld)

Confused or muddled in thought and resultant actions

Used in Context

"Her senses **addled**, Deidre was forced to retreat."—*Darkyn's Mate*, Lizzy Ford

"The Hulk's fists have **addled** your mind, thunderer."—*Hulk Vs.*

"But it sounded like gibberish, and everyone thought she was **addled** except for Mom, who understood her perfectly and said she had an excellent vocabulary."—*The Glass Castle: A Memoir*, Jeanette Walls

"I'll tell you what's wrong with you. Your head's **addled** with novels and poems."—*Monty Python's Flying Circus*, "Sex and Violence"

Synonyms: befuddled, bewildered, gone, punchy, puzzled, rattled, senile, shaken, shook, shook up, thrown, out of it, unglued, woozy

18. Adduce
verb (uh•*doos*)

To present something as evidence

Used in Context

"He then proceeds to **adduce** elaborate and sometimes slightly grotesque reasons tending to prove that mathematical knowledge is essential in theology, and closes this section of his work with two comprehensive sketches of geography and astronomy."—*Encyclopedia Britannica*, "Roger Bacon"

"No matter what excuse I **adduce**—I am very busy, you are many pages, there are a lot of books—it continues to reproach me."—"How to Overcome Constant FOMO," Rabbi David Wolpe*

"Let the teacher **adduce** some of the many striking instances in which men in apparently desperate straits have been saved by presence of mind."—*The Moral Instruction of Children*, Felix Adler

"But if you have no further arguments to **adduce**, I'll take him along now."—*The Devil and Daniel Johnston*

* FOMO, which stands for "fear of missing out," is defined by Wikipedia as "a pervasive apprehension that others might be having rewarding experiences from which one is absent."

Synonyms: cite, display, illustrate, offer, point out, proffer, prove, show

19. Adroit
adjective (uh•*droit*)

Describes someone with physical or intellectual skills and abilities

Used in Context
"Let me tell you something. Soprano is very **adroit** at keeping his family out of the frying pan."—*The Sopranos*, "All Due Respect"

"The brothers' **adroit**, inexhaustible crosstalk was at an end."—*The Falls*

"The conductor Fabio Luisi brought insight and **adroit** technique to Rossini's ambitious score, drawing fleetness, breadth and refinement from the excellent Met orchestra."—"Review: A New, Abstract *Guillaume Tell* at the Met Opera," Anthony Tommasini

"He's particularly **adroit** at disguising any tendency towards the middle-age spread."—*Prime Suspect 2*

Synonyms: able, adept, artful, clever, deft, dexterous, expert, masterful, nimble, practiced, quick-witted, savvy, sharp, skilled, skillful, up to speed

20. Adulation
noun (add•yu•*lay*•shun)

Excessive praise

Used in Context
"These are people everyone falls down around, defers to. **Adulation** is the norm."—*Criminal Minds*, "The Performer"

"He is, by consensus, a genius, and he seems to be protecting his own sincerity against the force of popular **adulation**."—"Swooning to the Strangeness of Bon Iver," Jia Tolentino

"That's when I learned a very hard lesson. Good receives all the praise, **adulation**. While evil is sent to quiet time in the corner."—*Megamind*

"He likes the instant gratification and **adulation** that the cheering crowds provide, and his aides are discussing how they might accommodate his demand."—"Donald Trump Prepares for White House Move, but His Tower May Still Beckon," Maggie Haberman, Ashley Parker

Synonyms: admiration, applause, audation, blandishment, bootlicking, commendation, esteem, exaltation, fawning, flattery, high regard, sycophancy, veneration, worship

21. Adumbrate
verb (uh•*dum*•brate)

To sketch, to outline in a shadowy way

Used in Context

"Inquisitor, I am not proposing to waste the time of the court by dwelling in detail on the activities of the accused...Instead, I intend to **adumbrate** two typical instances separate epistopic interfaces of the spectrum."—*Doctor Who*, "The Trial of a Time Lord"

This word can be used in both an artistic context—to describe a shadowy, sketchy outline of a scene or a person—as well as in a literary context in which the writer "sketches out" a potential possibility or only hints at or foreshadows a character's personality traits.

"She marked the colour—lilac—as if faintly to **adumbrate** the imperial purple of Rome."—*The Passionate Elopement*, Sir Compton Mackenzie

"Mr. Blood has made several attempts to **adumbrate** the anaesthetic revelation, in pamphlets of rare literary distinction, privately printed and distributed by himself at Amsterdam."—*The Varieties of Religious Experience*, William James

"**Adumbrate** the move for me a bit, if you would, or for us. Perhaps only for me. Say what you think that move is."—*Discussions with Richard Dawkins*, "The Four Horsemen"

Synonyms: draft, draw, give a rough idea, hint at, intimate, outline, sketch, suggest

22. Advocate
verb (*add*•vo•kate)

To support something or someone

The verb "advocate" can also be used as a noun, its definition being, "one who advocates."

Used in Context

"When you have visited a place, you will find it harder to **advocate** its destruction."—*Infinite Progress: How the Internet and Technology Will End Ignorance, Disease, Poverty, Hunger, and War*, Byron Reese

"Some experts **advocate** cutting the amount of black, unburnt carbon—soot—as a matter of urgency."—"*The Guardian* View On Climate Change Action: Don't Delay," The Guardian

"If students want a school dance, for example, it is his job to **advocate** for it with the school's administrators."—"Alternative High Schools Are Giving D.C. Students Another Shot At Graduation," Alejandra Matos

"It remains a difficult landscape for female composers, but there are institutions that **advocate** for them."—"To Help Women in Opera, Several Institutions Arise," William Robin

Synonyms: approve, back, campaign, champion, counsel, defend, endorse, exhort, plead, promote, sanction, uphold, urge, vouch for

23. Aesthetic
adjective (es•*thet*•ik)

Describes the philosophical principles of art and beauty

Used in Context
"I no longer make instruments of death. What I have here I keep for their **aesthetic** and sentimental value. Yet proud as I am of my life's work, I have retired."—*Kill Bill*

"The inclusion of Baez represents a welcome disruption of that last idea. For while it's certainly rooted in guitar, Baez's delicate folk style is another sound, like Shakur's, that falls outside the Rock Hall's established **aesthetic** core."—"The Rock and Roll Hall of Fame is Evolving—Very, Very Slowly," Mikael Wood

"Some people hang pictures themselves and place elegant objects where it suits their visual **aesthetic**. Others hire a professional to take the curatorial reins."—"Home Designs That Came From The Art," Audrey Hoffer

"In my own work, I try to create an **aesthetic** and style evocative of the past but very much grounded in the now."—"Afrofuturism: The Next Generation," Ruth La Ferla

"The comment was ambiguous: Did he mean that the former model just didn't jibe with his **aesthetic**, or something more?"—"Designer Tom Ford Says He Won't Dress Melania Trump," Emily Heil

Synonyms: artful, artistic, arty, creative, esthetic, gorgeous, imaginative, inventive, visual

24. Affectation
noun (aff•ek•*tay*•shun)

Behavior that is artificial and intended to impress others; e.g., using a cigarette holder

Used in Context

"Conversation should be pleasant without scurrility, witty without **affectation**, free without indecency, learned without conceitedness, novel without falsehood."—William Shakespeare

"I am not naturally magnetic. I feel I walk a line between awkwardness and arrogance. One, I suspect, is an **affectation** designed to disguise the other, but I am 33 and no longer sure which is which."—"'I Am Not Naturally Magnetic': Can You Learn How To Be Charismatic?," Colin Drury

"It's true: in conversation, Adams is gracious, candid and free of movie-star **affectations**."—"In *Arrival*, Amy Adams Takes a Listening Tour of the Universe," Sam Lansky

"The Zetas originated from a team of elite commandos who defected from Mexico's armed forces, so the cartel was prone to paramilitary **affectation**."—"The Teen Killers of the Drug War," Patrick Radden Keefe

Synonyms: air, airs, appearance, artificiality, exaggeration, façade, false front, insincerity, mannerism, pose, pretense, pretension, pretentiousness, put-on, putting on airs, quirk, sham, show, showing off

25. Affinity
noun (uh-fin-ih-tee)

A feeling of connection with someone or something; i.e., a sense of identification

Used in Context

"[T]he reason most of us are here is because of our **affinity** for disobedience."—*The Matrix Reloaded*

"Although her studio is inside the Beltway, Smith shows no **affinity** for urban subjects. Her paintings in this show depict only horses, the sky or flowers."—"A Painter's Unbridled Hand Matches a Sculptor's Experiment with Twisting Steel," Mark Jenkins

"If you consider people that were born here, worked here and have relatives here, then one out of 10 people have some **affinity** for Brooklyn!"—"Sebastian Leone, Borough President Who Championed Brooklyn, Dies at 91," Eli Rosenberg

"Empathy, after all, is not sympathy. Sympathy encourages a close **affinity** with other people: You feel their pain. Empathy suggests something more technical—a dispassionate approach to understanding the emotions of others."—"Is 'Empathy' Really What the Nation Needs?," Amanda Hess

Synonyms: affection, closeness, compatibility, cup of tea, empathy, fondness, leaning, partiality, rapport, same wavelength, simpatico, sympathy, understanding

26. Aggrandize
verb (uh•*gran*•dize)

To make more powerful; to increase wealth or influence

Used in Context

"I have a penchant for hyperbole to **aggrandize** myself. I've been working it out with my shrink."—*Everybody Hates Chris*, "Everybody Hates Bomb Threats"

"Lights, camera, a platform to **aggrandize** and the world's breathless anticipation? These are his four main food groups."—"Pre-Debate Guessing Game: Will the First Also Be the Last?," Sam Hodgson

"Mr. Cruz's detractors see a man who engineers moments to **aggrandize** himself at the expense of fellow conservatives."—"Ted Cruz's Security Misstep," Kimberley A. Strassel

"Our memories are not very reliable, especially in life-and-death situations. Part of it is, yes, our need to **aggrandize** the risks we take; part of it is our minds' reaction to fear."—"Accept Brian Williams's Apology," Joe Klein

Synonyms: acclaim, applaud, augment, boost, commend, dignify, distinguish, enhance, enlarge, ennoble, exaggerate, expand, extend, glorify, honor, hype, increase, magnify, overdo, praise

27. Aggregate
noun (*ag*•reh•gate)

The total of a combination of varying elements

Used in Context

"Uh, no. You don't understand. It's, uh, very complicated. It's uh, it's **aggregate**, so I'm talking about fractions of a penny, and uh, over time, they add up to a lot."—*Office Space*

"To slow global climate change, we need to reduce **aggregate** global emissions."—"For China, Climate Change Is No Hoax – It's a Business and Political Opportunity," Matthew Kahn

"'Amazon's ability to **aggregate** information about individual consumers is without peer,' said Alexander Brown, chief executive of TV network ONE World Sports."—"Amazon Explores Possible Premium Sports Package With Prime Membership," Shalini Ramachandran

"In the **aggregate**, the data suggests more people are getting killed as a result of these laws."—"Florida's 'Stand Your Ground' Law Linked to Homicide Increase," Josh Sanburn

Synonyms: accumulated, accumulation, collected, collective, combined, composite, cumulative, entirety, sum, total, whole

28. Agnostic
noun (ag•*nos*•tik)

Someone whose position on God is that it is impossible for humans to know with certainty whether or not God exists

Used in Context

"The leader in speculative philosophy is Immanuel Kant, though he includes many **agnostic** elements, and draws the inference

"Agnostic" can also serve as an adjective.

> Agnosticism is often confused with atheism. The atheist position is that there is no God. As the definition states, the agnostic position is that we cannot know.

(which some things in the letter of Butler might seem to warrant) that the essence of Christianity is an ethical theism."—*Encyclopedia Britannica*, 11th edition.

"He's in the middle of another major growth spurt, and as an **agnostic** observer of the quarterback, my mental seesaw tilts toward optimism once again."—"The Only Question Left for Kirk Cousins: 'How much?,'" Jerry Brewer

"There has been only one president who wasn't married, and none who was openly atheist or **agnostic**. Add this up, and we've been selecting our top leadership from 10% of our talent at most."—"After the Election of Donald Trump, We Will Not Mourn. We Will Organize," Gloria Steinem

"But while Lisa is a practicing Christian for whom religion is deeply meaningful, Tom is an **agnostic** whose faith was shattered after a personal loss."—"*God Game* Considers the Unholy Mix of Politics and Religion," Misha Berson

Synonyms: doubter, freethinker, materialist, questioner, skeptic, unbeliever

29. Alacrity
noun (uh•*lak*•rit•ee)

Quickness, speediness

Used in Context
"Every member is busy in his place, performing his duty with **alacrity**;

nor is sober mirth wanting."—*Dictionary of National Biography*, "Sir Thomas More"

"The TV channels feasted on tweeted Trumpisms with an **alacrity** that many observers found disturbing."—"Trump v the Media: Did His Tactics Mortally Wound the Fourth Estate?," Ed Pilkington

"As she ran off to play, I was relieved, and grateful for the **alacrity** with which children laugh at their elders."—"How I Explained the Election to My Six-Year-Old Daughter," Andy Borowitz

"The Englishman was brave, he just didn't have the power which was coming his way with **alacrity** and brute force."—"Canelo Álvarez Out-Punches Brave Liam Smith as Golovkin Showdown Looms," Steve Brenner

Synonyms: briskness, enthusiasm, fervor, keenness, passion, promptness, rapidity, sharpness, speed, swiftness, velocity, zeal

30. Alienate
verb (ay•lee•en•ate)

To distance yourself from someone, commonly through an unfriendly and sometimes hostile interaction

Used in Context
"You know, he loved you like a son. Took a hell of a lot for you to **alienate** him."—*Raiders of the Lost Ark*

"This is fun and it has a different look that doesn't **alienate** the average cookbook reader."—"The 31 Best Cookbooks of 2016," Bonnie S. Benwick

"One of the central tragedies of *Rectify* is that no one can distrust, **alienate** and punish Daniel as harshly as he does to himself."—"An 'Acute Observation of the Absurdity Of Being Alive': The Star And Creator Of *Rectify* Discuss Ambiguity and the Series' End," Melanie McFarland

"But bear in mind that, in order to achieve gains with a group, you may have to take positions that will **alienate** others."—"How to Save the Democratic Party," Nicholas Lemann

Synonyms: break off, come between, disaffect, disunite, divide, divorce, drift apart, drift away, estrange, isolate, part, push away, separate, turn away, wean, write off

31. Allegory
noun (*al•uh•gor•ee*)

The representation of abstract ideas by characters, figures, or events; hidden subtext open to interpretation by close reading or watching

Some claim *The Lord of the Rings* is a Christian allegory with Frodo as the sacrificial Christ figure. (Tolkien denied this.)

The Lord of the Rings has also been interpreted as an allegory for World War II with Sauron being an allegory for Hitler. (Tolkien also denied this.)

Used in Context
"Superman was now seen in pop culture and in the comics not just as a superhero, but as a secular messiah. There's definitely an **allegory**, a Judeo-Christian allegory that's happening in the mythology of Superman, right up to the fact that he descends from the heavens."—*Look Up in the Sky! The Amazing Story of Superman*

"**Allegory** hides more gracefully in animation than in any other medium, allowing us to bury deeper themes within a big, fun world of anthropomorphic animals."—"Lessons on Bias and Prejudice Dwell Within the World of *Zootopia*, According to Its Writers," Jared Bush, Phil Johnston

The Stephen King novel *The Shining* is about the perils of alcoholism (which King was going through at the time); in the movie, Stanley Kubrick morphed the meaning into an allegory about the annihilation of Native Americans.

"Coming on the heels of a fractious election season, *Arrival* could reflexively be interpreted as an **allegory** about immigration, communication and belligerence."—"Sleek, Sophisticated and Thoughtful *Arrival* Joins a Mini Golden Age of Sci-Fi Films," Ann Hornaday

"To walk through Fidel Castro's Cuba was to walk through a breathing **allegory.** The streets were called Virtues and Hope and Good Works and they ran around a Capitol that was a perfect replica of the one in Washington, but inches taller."—"Inside Fidel Castro's Cuba—and His Legacy," Pico Iyer

Synonyms: apologue, emblem, fable, figuration, metaphor, moral, myth, story, symbol, symbolism, tale, typification

32. Alleviate
verb (uh•*lee*•vee•ate)

To reduce the severity of pain or hardship and make it easier to endure

Used in Context

"[The] *Truce of God* [was] an attempt of the Church in the Middle Ages to **alleviate** the evils of private warfare."—*Encyclopedia Britannica*, 11th edition.

"The State Department is negotiating with the leaders of those committees behind the scenes to **alleviate** concerns about the sale."— "Obama Administration Pushes for Apache Helicopter Sale to Iraq," Josh Rogin, Eli Lake

"Acts of Congress, in the form of Medicaid, Medicare, and Social Security, did an enormous amount to **alleviate** systemic poverty."—"Daniel Ellsberg, Edward Snowden, and the Modern Whistle-Blower," Malcolm Gladwell

"Intuition might tell you that, to **alleviate** that sensation, a designer should open up the area as much as possible."—"The Psychology of the New Times Square," *The New Yorker*

Synonyms: abate, allay, assuage, diminish, ease, improve, lighten, mitigate, mollify, pacify, relieve, take the sting out

33. Allusion
noun (uh•*looj*•un)

An indirect or subtle mention of something, or reference to something, oftentimes literary

Used in Context
"This penchant for classical **allusion** in Irish lyrics is not peculiar to the repertoire of the hedge schoolmaster."—*Ulster Folklife*, "For Want of Education," Julie Henigan

"The **allusion** to *Prime Suspect*, a massive hit on both sides of the Atlantic, is well founded."—"The Haunting New Serial-Killer Thriller Heading to Netflix," Jace Lacob

"I had to rely on the Alice books for evidence of **allusion** and parodies."—"History: Untangling Alice," Gillian Beer

"But wait—that was not necessarily an **allusion** to her romantic life."—"Is Prince Harry Dating Actress Meghan Markle? Here's What We Know," Raisa Bruner

Synonyms: citation, connotation, hint, implication, imputation, inference, insinuation, intimation, mention, quotation, suggestion

34. Altruism
noun (al•troo•izm)

A spirit of unselfish helpfulness; acting on behalf of the greater good

Used in Context
"Your **altruism** is inspiring, Dad."—*Smallville*, "Lineage"

"But what happens when those extremists who advocate a bizarre morality that elevates selfishness and deplores **altruism** commandeer one of our two major political parties?"—"Media, Morality and the Neighbor's Cow: When did Ayn Rand Become the Republican Party's Bible?," Neal Gabler

"Encouraged by the corporate media, the Republicans have been waging a full-spectrum assault on empathy, **altruism** and the decencies we owe to other people."—"Donald Trump is No Outsider: He Mirrors our Political Culture," George Monbiot

"Stop using teachers' **altruism** to justify rock-bottom salaries."—"The Ubiquitous Nature of Implicit Bias," Lisette Partelow

"Donors are lauded for their **altruism** and bravery for what is promoted as a benign procedure with low long-term risk."—"At 18 Years Old, He Donated a Kidney. Now, He Regrets It," Michael Poulson

Synonyms: benevolence, charity, generosity, humanitarianism, humanity, kindness, magnanimity, philanthropy, public spirit, selflessness, self-sacrifice, social conscience, unselfishness

35. Ameliorate
verb (uh•*mee*•lee•or•ate)

To make something better, to improve a situation

Ameliorate is often used in the context of reducing pain. Medical reports will often describe a medication or modality that was specifically described "to ameliorate some of the patient's pain."

Used in Context

"And Gus Fring? Just winging that guy is not going to **ameliorate** your situation, not by a damn sight."—*Breaking Bad*, "Problem Dog"

"What he most wanted to argue about was strip mining. He was the first West Virginia official to demand total abolition and was increasingly angry when his proposals got nowhere on Capitol Hill. Twice, Congress passed bills intended to regulate the practice and **ameliorate** its effects."—"Ken Hechler, W.Va. Congressman and Author of *Bridge at Remagen*, Dies at 102," Laurence I. Barrett

"Can you think of specific actions that you could take to **ameliorate** what you fear?"—"What Do We Do Now?," Emily Bazelon, David Plotz, and Jacob Weisberg

"I asked the museum's press representatives what steps are being undertaken to improve traffic flow and **ameliorate** the crowds, but they didn't respond."—"Beautiful, Stirring, and Overcrowded," Dan Kais

Synonyms: alleviate, amend, assist, get better, help, improve, lighten, meliorate, mitigate, relieve, step up, upgrade

36. Amenable
adjective (uh•*meen*•uh•bull)

Describes someone who is open to suggestions and who will probably cooperate

Used in Context
"The system is not really particularly **amenable** to filmmakers who write and direct their own work. It's much more about the studio already having a property that has a marketable concept and then hiring the director on board."—"Interview: *We Own The Night* Director James Grey," Katey Rich

"If the country were cleared of the allegations raised by the U.N., the international community would be more **amenable** to helping resolve the border issue."—"The Soccer-Star Refugees of Eritrea," Alexis Okeowo

"But proponents of legalization say California represented the biggest victory because of its huge economy and population and also its fertile soil and **amenable** climate."—"Californians Legalize Marijuana in Vote That Could Echo Nationally," Thomas Fuller

"I'm **amenable**. Who do you have in mind?"—*Shooter*

Synonyms: acceptable, acquiescent, agreeable, biddable, cooperative, docile, easy to get along with, influenceable, manageable, obedient, persuadable, pliable, responsive, susceptible, tractable

37. Anachronism
noun (un•*ak*•row•nism)

Something from the wrong chronological time period; e.g., a wristwatch appearing in a drama about the fall of the Roman Empire

Used in Context
"You'll have to begin living it all over again as a stranger, as a…well, as an **anachronism**."—*The Twilight Zone*, "The Long Morrow"

"It is an **anachronism**, a deeply undemocratic product of a compromise with slave states that serves no real purpose today."—"How Liberals Got the Electoral College Wrong," Mark Joseph Stern

"This stark absence underscores both a shift in consumer patterns and the precious **anachronism** of what few holiday windows remain."—"We Need a Miracle on 34th Street," Guy Trebay

"In the 1970s, feminism seemed unstoppable; after Ronald Reagan's election, it was treated as an embarrassing **anachronism**."—"Democratic Politics Have to Be 'Identity Politics'," Michelle Goldberg

Synonyms: chronological error, holdover, misplacement, narrative blunder, relic, solecism

38. Analogy
noun (uh•*nal*•o•gee)

A comparison between two things; e.g., Washington, DC, is like a swamp.

Used in Context

"The closest **analogy**, the one her brain reached for and rejected and reached for again, was splashing into a lake. It was cold, but not cold. There was a smell, rich and loamy. The smell of growth and decay."— *Cibola Burn*, James S. A. Corey

"But the whack-a-mole **analogy** fails to capture the scale of the problem."—Stop Playing Whack-a-Mole with Hazardous Chemicals," *The Washington Post*

"The **analogy** I favor is introspection as a personal narrative, whereby people construct stories about their lives, much as a biographer would."—*Strangers to Ourselves: Discovering the Adaptive Unconscious*, Timothy D. Wilson

"I called Jim Dale, senior meteorologist at British Weather Services, to see if it was ever an effective **analogy** in the first place."—"'Poor Little Snowflake'—The Defining Insult of 2016," Rebecca Nicholson

Synonyms: affinity, alikeness, comparison, correlation, correspondence, equivalence, homology, likeness, metaphor, parallel, relation, relationship, resemblance, semblance, similarity, simile, similitude

39. Anathema
noun (ann•*ath*•uh•muh)

Something or someone who is despised; something abominable

Used in Context

"Both *Hard Times* and *Bleak House* open with passages that are justly famous: frequently anthologised as examples of fine writing, and much used in the classroom to teach critical analysis. Each opening is a Dickensian tour de force, and each declares war upon a target that is **anathema** to the author."—*Charles Dickens: Hard Times/Bleak House*, Nicholas Marsh

"That college is seen as a training ground for a job is perceived by professors as **anathema** to their mission of broadly educating students."—"Why Are So Many Students Failing to Find Good Jobs After College?," Jeffrey J. Selingo

"'Complete transparency is **anathema** to the very nature of a grand jury, which depends upon secrecy and anonymity for its proper functioning,' Ribaudo wrote."—"Judge Upholds Secrecy in Ferguson Grand Juror Lawsuit," Jim Salter

"Now what we're working with is more of a socialist plan for space exploration, which is just **anathema** to what this country should be doing."—"Catching Dust," Anthony Lydgate

Synonyms: abhorrence, abomination, atrocity, bane, detestation, enemy, hate, pariah

40. Annul
verb (uh•*nul*)

To make a legal document invalid; to abrogate or void an agreement

Used in Context

"[T]he sensitive are always with us, and sometimes a curious streak of fancy invades an obscure corner of the very hardest head; so that no amount of rationalisation, reform, or Freudian analysis can quite **annul** the thrill of the chimney-corner whisper or the lonely wood."—"Supernatural Horror in Literature," H. P. Lovecraft

"Voters were told that he would **annul** Protestant marriages."—"Read the Transcript of Hillary Clinton's Speech at the Al Smith Dinner," Hillary Clinton

"Should Britain **annul** all treaties and start again?"—"Britain has No Idea What To Do Next, and That's Dangerous," Anne Applebaum

"But she asked the judge to **annul** the case, saying the government was using the case to cover up its failures."—"Argentina Ex-leader Cristina Fernandez Appears in Court," *BBC News*

Synonyms: abate, abolish, abrogate, annihilate, blot out, call off, cancel, countermand, declare, delete, discharge, dissolve, efface, erase, expunge, get off the hook, invalidate, kill, negate, neutralize, nix, nullify, obliterate, quash, recall, render null and void, repeal, rescind, retract, reverse, revoke, scrub, undo, vacate, vitiate, wipe out

41. Anomaly
noun (uh•*nom*•uh•lee)

Something abnormal; something that differs from what was expected

Used in Context
"NASA's EOS satellites pinged the anomaly first."—*Man of Steel*

"While the numbers may appear an **anomaly** in America, elections are hardly beyond reproach in much of the world."—"Election Questions leave US Distrustful, Like Other Nations," Bradley Klapper

"AWS Shield Standard monitors incoming web traffic for customers and uses **anomaly** algorithms and other analysis techniques to detect malicious traffic in real-time."—"Amazon Cloud Computing Division Unveils New Cyber Security Service," Jay Greene, Laura Stevens

"The win also comes after 2016's Academy Awards ceremony had an all-white crop of acting nominees, which qualified more as trend than **anomaly**."—"This Movie Just Won the Award That Predicted the Last Two Best Picture Winners," Eliza Berman

Synonyms: aberration, abnormality, departure, deviation, difference, incongruity, inconsistency, irregularity, peculiarity, unconformity, variance

42. Antagonist
noun (ann•*tag*•oh•nist)

A person or thing in direct conflict with another person or thing

Used in Context

"Ivan was also unfortunate in having for his chief **antagonist** Stephen Bathory, one of the greatest captains of the age."—*Encyclopedia Britannica*, 11th edition, "Ivan the Terrible"

"There's generally no path forward in academe for the woman who has a powerful **antagonist** angry at her."—"C. Megan Urry, Peering Into Universe, Spots Bias on the Ground," Claudia Dreifus

"As for picking a fight with tobacco companies, the only safer political **antagonist** is North Korea."—"Tom Steyer's Smoke Signals," *The Wall Street Journal*

"After thanking the judge and his attorney in his usual high style, Cohen turned to his **antagonist**."—"Leonard Cohen Makes It Darker," David Remnick

The antagonist in a drama, whether it's a movie, book, or TV show, is pitted against the main character. Khan was Captain Kirk's antagonist in *The Wrath of Khan*.

A drug can also be an antagonist. For example, Narcan (naloxone) is an opioid antagonist. It nullifies the effects of a narcotics overdose.

Synonyms: adversary, bandit, competitor, contender, enemy, foe, opponent, opposer, rival

43. Antecedent
noun (ann•tuh•*see*•dent)

Something that happened prior to something else, such as an event, a circumstance, a style, a phenomenon, and so forth

Used in Context

"Even online chat rooms have an **antecedent** in the exchanges of nineteenth-century American telegraph operators."—"Social Media is So Old Even the Romans Had It," Nick Romeo

"The curious pronoun in Lewis's title, lacking an **antecedent**, may well refer to the rise of fascism in the United States."—"Getting Close to Fascism with Sinclair Lewis's *It Can't Happen Here*," Alexander Nazaryan

"The tooth has no known **antecedent** in the fossil record."—*Surface*: "Episode #1.1"

"The **antecedent** left intentionally ambiguous, the grateful author said only, 'They'd saved some money and thought it was high time they did something about me.'"—"Postscript: Harper Lee, 1926-2016," Casey N. Cep

"It was of course **antecedent** to the discovery of auscultation."—*Encyclopedia Britannica,* 11th edition, "Medicine"

Synonyms: ancestor, antecessor, anterior, earlier, forebear, foregoing, forerunner, former, past, precedent, preceding, precursor, precursory, predecessor, preliminary, previous, prior, progenitor

44. Anticlimax
noun (*ann*•tee•kli•max)

An unexciting, unimportant event that follows something dramatic and exciting

Used in Context
"Everything after the summit—that is, after the Beatles—can't help but seem like an **anticlimax**."—"Review: Paul McCartney's Yesterdays. All of Them," Dwight Garner

"Extraordinary events culminate in what might seem to be an **anticlimax**."—*Gran Torino*

"But we began at the top; and when you have seen the best there is, everything else is **anticlimax**."—*Peking Dust: China's Capital in World War I*, Ellen N. La Motte

"And if that happens, then the **anticlimax** of this long hiatus will be transformed into the most rousing development in franchise history."—"After Playing Long Waiting Game, Sounders Win Playoff Game," Larry Stone

Synonyms: bathos, comedown, decline, descent, disappointment, drop, letdown, slump

45. Antipathy
noun (ann•*tip*•uth•ee)

A repulsion, hostility, or anger toward a specific person or thing

Used in Context

"You must admit, Ms. Knope, that the merging of the towns has been fraught with **antipathy**. For example, I now have to share my studio with a fatuous twerp who shall remain nameless."—*Parks and Recreation*, "Anniversaries"

"When he undertakes a daunting project—the construction of a crude boat using ramshackle materials—the **antipathy** of the townspeople reaches a boiling point."—"Review: *The Vessel*: Learning to Forge Ahead After Wrenching Loss," Andy Webster

"There is, similar to the anger at the clothing the women dare to wear, an **antipathy** toward glamour."—"Why We Despise *Sex and the City*," Choire Sicha

"Out of my own personal **antipathy** to making plans came an ironclad rule: I don't schedule more than two in a given week."—"The Art of Making (and Not Making) Plans," Verena von Pfetten

Synonyms: abhorrence, animosity, animus, antagonism, aversion, detestation, dislike, distaste, enmity, hatred, hostility, ill will, loathing, opposition, rancor, repugnance, repulsion

46. Antithesis
noun (ann•tih•thu•sis)

The complete opposite of something

Used in Context

"The song ["Woodstock"] was popularized by Crosby, Stills & Nash, which is ironic since theirs was the more commercial version which is the **antithesis** of the spirit of the festival."—*Third Rock from the Sun*, "The Dicks They Are A Changin'"

"Scorsese, 74, may be among the most revered directors in Hollywood, but *Silence* is almost the **antithesis** of today's studio film."—"Martin Scorsese: 'Cinema is gone,'" Jake Coyle

"In a 1934 journal entry, she referred to faith as 'the worst curse of mankind' and 'the exact **antithesis** and enemy of thought.'"—"Can You Love God and Ayn Rand?," Jennifer Anju Grossman

"Our fundamental values demand that America stand with demonstrators opposing a regime that is the **antithesis** of all we believe."—"Leave Iran to the Iranians," Leslie H. Gelb

Synonyms: antipode, contradictory, contrary, converse, counter, flip side, opposite, other side, reverse

47. Aphorism
noun (*aah•*for•izm)

A tersely phrased statement of a truth or opinion

Used in Context
"Hello Seattle, this is Dr. Frasier Crane. I was reminded this morning of a jaunty **aphorism** that's credited to the great thinker Spinoza. Oh God!"—*Frasier*, "The Marriage Counselor"

"William Goldman's **aphorism** that 'in Hollywood, no one knows anything' remains as true in the digital age as it did in the analog."—"Review: *To Pixar and Beyond* Plumbs New Depth in Oft-Told Tale," Jonathan A. Knee

"Shon: This reminds me of the Zen **aphorism** 'the finger pointing to the moon is not the moon.'"—"'I'm Glad That I Don't Have to Figure Out the Meaning of Life': A Conversation with Max Ritvo," Shon Arieh-Lerer and Andrew Kahn

These are all aphorisms:
- Ignorance is bliss.
- You get what you pay for.
- You're never too old to learn.

"If this absorbing, illuminating book needs a motto, it is an **aphorism** of Marshall McLuhan's friend, John Culkin. 'We shape our tools,' he wrote, 'and thereafter our tools shape us.'"—"So Who Put the Cyber Into Cybersex?," John Naughton

Synonyms: adage, axiom, cliché, dictum, maxim, phrase, precept, proverb, rule, saw, saying, truism

48. Apocryphal
adjective (a•*pok*•ruh•ful)

Of doubtful authority or authenticity, though accepted as true

Used in Context
"It's **apocryphal**, Dad. A story for tourists. If Galileo had muttered 'It still moves' after they made him recant his work, they would've killed him on the spot."—*The West Wing*, "Eppur Si Muove"

Examples:

- A story that probably isn't true; an urban legend.

- The rumor that Mark Zuckerberg was giving away $4.5 million to each of 1,000 Facebook users who posted the story of the giveaway in honor of the birth of his daughter.

"As the story—however **apocryphal** it may be—goes, Macy's employees asked the company to put on a parade in the mid-1920s."—"Nose Your Way Past Crowds for an Unforgettable Holiday View," Louis Lucero II

"Although the story sounds **apocryphal**, it has the ring of truth for those who have experienced the overblown world of Silicon Valley."—"An Insider Lifting The Veil on Silicon Valley's Self-Importance and Greed," Margaret Sullivan

"Apparently, they've never heard of Coco Chanel's **apocryphal** style rule: 'Look in the mirror before you leave the house and remove one accessory.'"—"Review: *Warcraft* Is Ridiculous, But Paula Patton Is Not," Stephanie Zacharek

Synonyms: counterfeit, doubtful, dubious, false, fictional, fictitious, inaccurate, made-up, mythical, spurious, unsubstantiated, untrue, unverified

- Another Facebook hoax: the "privacy notice" that says if you post it on your wall, you'll retain ownership of all your pictures, status updates, etc. Totally false. The notice has no legal standing.

49. Apprise
verb (uh•*prize*)

To inform someone about something, to give notice to someone

Used in Context
"A few remarks from a Scizzors Bill, to **apprise** the membership in general that Miami Lodge No. 273 is in better shape financially and in membership than at any time in our history."—*The Railroad Trainman*, Volume 35—The Brotherhood of Railroad Trainmen

"Then he danced a few steps of a real jig, to **apprise** them of his coming."—*The Wreck of the Titan*, Morgan Robertson

"Even before they had settled on a name, Mr. Spade paid a visit to CEO Craig Leavitt to **apprise** him of their plans."—"When Is Kate Spade Not Kate Spade? When She's Frances Valentine," Suzanne Kapner

"Towson has committed to addressing the demands and **apprise** the campus of its progress in the student paper."—"The Revolution on America's Campuses," Jack Dickey

Synonyms: acquaint, advise, brief, describe, enlighten, explain, fill in, give a heads up, impart, inform, notify, pass on, tip off

50. Approbation
noun (app•row•*bay*•shun)

Approval or appreciation of a specific achievement or behavior

Used in Context
"See, in our school, we didn't have grades, so we didn't have A's, B's, C's, D's. The only As I got, and this is a little corny...I got their approval, their **approbation**, and their applause, and those are the only A's I wanted and I got them!"—George Carlin, *George Carlin: 40 Years of Comedy*

"Has this measure the misfortune not to meet with your **approbation**?"—*The Conspirators*, Alexandre Dumas

"If we are going to criminalize politics, why spare one committee from the **approbation** heaped on others?"—"Report on de Blasio Election Spending Is Full of Details and Holes," Jim Dwyer

"He added, in what is almost certainly the only known use in this context of adjectives of **approbation**: 'The orchestra onstage was unfazed. The composer was delighted.'"—"David Baker, Who Helped Bring Jazz Studies Into the Academy, Dies at 84," Margalit Fox

Synonyms: acclaim, admiration, approval, commendation, endorsement, esteem, high regards, praise, recognition, sanction, support,

51. A priori
adjective (ah•pree•*or*•ee)

Using prior knowledge or a self-evident fact to arrive at a conclusion

Used in Context
"Not demonstrable as a theoretical proposition, the immortality of the soul 'is an inseparable result of an unconditional **a priori** practical law.'"—*The Encyclopedia Britannica*, 11th edition.

"Well, in any event, one night, month 11 of my motionlessness, something obvious occurred to me. Our dreams are both **a priori** and a posteriori. Which means that our dreams contain our memories. Which means that there's a shared reservoir."—*Alias*, "Consciousness"

"Even if this happens, there is no **a priori** reason to expect this community to cause more harm when using it than anyone else."—"Governance: Learn from DIY Biologists," Todd Kuiken

"There is nothing that can be considered, **a priori**, to be part of the story, to be essential or inessential to the story."—"The Vacuum-Sealed Efficiency of *Mission: Impossible: Rogue Nation*," Richard Brody

Synonyms: deduced, deductive, inferred, presumptive, supposed

52. Apropos
adjective (ah•pruh•*po*)

Appropriate in a specific situation

Used in Context
"Craigslist—it's desperate, I know, but **apropos**. Personal ads are filled with desperation."—*Dexter*, "Shrink Wrap"

"There's a marvelous letter he wrote to Shaw about censorship that is very funny and **apropos**."—"Brian Bedford Interviewed on The Importance of Being Earnest," Kevin Sessums

"**Apropos** to this article, she herself has indicated that she's grown weary of the tune; I believe she's dropped it from her concert repertoire."—"How Pop Culture Wore Out Leonard Cohen's 'Hallelujah,'" Nick Murray

"**Apropos** of a Republican convention, one demonstrator simply dressed as Abraham Lincoln, the party's first elected president."—"A Carnival of Contrasting Views Near Cleveland's Republican Convention," Scott Malone, Daniel Trotta

Synonyms: about, befitting, by the way, concerning, correct, fitting, in connection with, incidentally, on the subject of, pertinent, regarding, relevant to

53. Arcane
adjective (ar•*kane*)

Known and understood by only a few

Used in Context

"And my father believed that the clues to the location of the philosopher's stone were encoded somehow in these **arcane** symbols."—*As Above, So Below*

"The four-day hearing on the divisive constitutional issue will be broadcast live, testing the public's appetite for intricate legal argument, **arcane** vocabulary and historical precedents."—"Senior judges Prepare To Hear Brexit Supreme Court Appeal," Owen Bowcott and Peter Walker

The key term is "a few." ComicCon is often a gathering of people boasting huge amounts of arcane info. Also, scholarship often includes people who have specialized in some arcane topic and know tons about it, like the scholar who knows the complete genealogy of some obscure Austrian royal family from the 14th century.

"But a majority of works date from 2000 and are often **arcane**, ineffective or not especially innovative."—"Diving Into Movie Palaces of the Mind at the Whitney," Roberta Smith

"The president should be directly elected by the people, not through an **arcane** intermediary called the Electoral College."—"5 Radical Solutions to Fix Our Busted Government," Parag Khanna

Synonyms: abstruse, cryptic, deep, esoteric, hidden, mysterious, obscure, secret, unfathomable, unknowable

54. Archetype
noun (*ark•eh•type*)

An original model or classic example of something; a pattern or paradigm for similar characters, events, or ideologies

Used in Context

"Stephen is far from being the **archetype** unworldly or nerdish scientist—his personality unwarped by his frustrations and handicaps."—"Stephen Hawking 70th-Birthday Salute," Martin Rees

"But in this novel, that characterization serves as a curious **archetype** for reviled idealists in modern-day Israel."—"In the Novel *Judas*, Amos Oz Wrestles with Jewish Attitudes Toward Jesus," Ron Charles

"All of these elements are rooted in **archetype** but have been subjected to a process not unlike gentrification."—"Consider the Coconut," Nate Chinen

"One program is the **archetype** for all the word processing that ever existed."—"The Civilization of Illiteracy," Mihai Nadin

Synonyms: classic, epitome, model, original, prime example, prototype, standard

55. Arrogate
verb (*ar*•oh•gate)

To take credit for something you didn't do; to claim a skill or ability you do not possess

Used in Context

"It is definitely alarming that a president can **arrogate** to himself this kind of power, whoever the president is."—"Obama and the Justice Department Memo," Michael Tomasky

"And so they try to **arrogate** my medical authority for their cause."—"Pediatrician: Don't Make Your Kid's Healthcare a Proxy in Your Divorce Battles," Russell Saunders

"She said such authority would be 'a stunning power for an agency to **arrogate** to itself.'"—"US Environment Agency Fights Back Over Mountaintop Mining," Natasha Gilbert

"The human and fallible should not **arrogate** a power with which the divine and perfect alone can be safely entrusted."—Charlotte Bronte

Synonyms: appropriate, assume, commandeer, confiscate, demand, encroach, expropriate, preempt, presume, seize, take, usurp

56. Assiduous
adjective (uh•*sid*•yoo•us)

Being unrelenting and industriously attentive to a task

Used in Context
"As an intern at *The Nation* in 1989, he was an amiable and **assiduous** fact-checker of my copy."—"Britain's New Political Dynasty," Norman Birnbaum

"During his residence here, he was known as an **assiduous** collector of historical data."—"Sixty Years in Southern California 1853–1913," Harris Newmark

"Through **assiduous** documentation, Glassner then showed that the various 'crises' striking fear in the hearts of Americans were not crises at all."—"Children's Crusade," David Masciotra

"Her document is remarkably **assiduous** in places, and filled with flagrant, or at least gaping, holes in others."—"Report on de Blasio Election Spending Is Full of Details and Holes," Jim Dwyer

Synonyms: attentive, conscientious, diligent, hardworking, industrious, painstaking, persevering, tireless, unremitting

57. Assuage
verb (uh•*swaj*)

To provide relief from pain or distress

Used in Context
"Not one man, no nor ten men, nor a hundred can **assuage** me. I will have you! And I will get back even as he gloats, even as I go for less honorable throats."—*Sweeney Todd*

"I pray that Our Heavenly Father may **assuage** the anguish of your bereavement and leave only the cherished memory of the loved lost and the solemn pride that must be yours."—*Saving Private Ryan*

"In the upcoming confirmation hearing, he's likely to try to highlight his concern for civil rights to **assuage** concerns of his Democratic colleagues."—"1980s Voting-Fraud Prosecution Likely Topic At Sessions' Hearing," Eric Tucker

"The military has a great deal to learn about these men and women and programs must be developed to **assuage** their fears."—"A Discharged Gay Vet: Let Us Back in the Army," Anthony Woods

Synonyms: allay, alleviate, ameliorate, appease, calm, conciliate, cool, ease, lessen, lighten, mitigate, mollify, pacify, palliate, placate, quench, quiet, relieve, sate, soften, temper, tranquilize

58. Atheist
noun (*ay*•thee•ist)

A person who does not believe in God, gods, or any deities

Used in Context
"An **atheist** is someone who denies altogether the existence of God."— *Donnie Darko*

"That mentality is what some **atheist** thinkers believe quietly promotes magical thinking, condoning it via liberal tolerance."—"The Atheist Recruiting Machine," Lauren Sandler

"When I was an **atheist**, I was a really enthusiastic atheist, and it enabled me to feel in control of my environment."—"Moby: 'I was disappointed to be heterosexual,'" Candice Pires

"China is officially **atheist** and the party strictly controls religious activities."—"Hong Kong Cardinal Says Any Deal Between the Vatican and China Would be 'Betraying Christ,'" Kevin Lui

Synonyms: agnostic, doubter, infidel, irreligionist, nonbeliever, pagan, skeptic

59. Atrophy
noun (*at*•row•fee)

The weakening and shrinking in size of some part of the body; also the diminution of some ability

Used in Context
"It hinders the immune system, causes insomnia, and speeds the **atrophy** of the brain, to name a few."—"How to Live Forever," Casey Schwartz

"Others of the fibers remain alive but shrink and **atrophy** as we age."—"Can You Regain Muscle Mass After Age 60?," Gretchen Reynolds

"That happens a fair amount. One option is **atrophy**."—"Will Trump Overhaul Public Education?," Dana Goldstein

"Was it politics that had caused this **atrophy** of the moral senses by disuse?"—*Democracy: An American Novel*, Henry Adams

Synonyms: decline, degenerate, deteriorate, shrivel, waste, waste away, weaken, wither

60. Attenuate
verb (uh•*ten*•yew•ate)

To reduce the size or weaken the strength of something

Used in Context
"The Venetian shutters often had to be lowered in the summer to **attenuate** the great heat."—*The Three Cities Trilogy*, Emile Zola

"It does not **attenuate** the power and originality of his themes that they are essentially of the piano."—*Unicorns*, James Huneker

"The final stages of the ascent, where the mountains **attenuate** into their crests and peaks, are always the hardest."—"Alone in the Alps," James Lasdun

"As important, their postcard beauty and rented emotions also **attenuate** some of the less palatable aspects of their conspiracy theories."—"Review: In Inferno, Breathlessly Globe-Trotting and Decoding to Save the World," Manohla Dargis

Synonyms: abate, assuage, debilitate, disable, ease, enfeeble, lessen, mitigate, soothe, undermine

61. Augur
verb (*aw•ger*)

To predict what will happen in the future

Used in Context
"Maybe it is even true, though their absence on June 24 does not **augur** well."—"Vet Snub Shocks Families," Leslie H. Gelb

"'I think those **augur** well for the deal,' he told Reuters in an interview."—"Monsanto Shareholders Back Bayer Deal, CEO Hopeful of U.S. Approval," Karl Plume

"The acts of defiance directed at Beijing, with some people calling for outright independence for Hong Kong, seemed to **augur** an especially stormy legislative term."—"At Hong Kong Swearing-In, Some Lawmakers Pepper Their Oaths with Jabs," Alan Wong

"Augur" can also be used as a noun; i.e., a "harbinger."

"This slowdown is worrying because of what it may **augur** for the long-term health of the global economy."—"Risk of Deglobalization Hangs Over World Economy," Simon Nixon

Synonyms: bode, foretell, herald, portend, predict, prognosticate, promise

62. Avarice
noun (*a•ver•iss*)

An excessive desire of gain; greediness

Used in Context
"I could hang myself with all the bad Christmas neckties I found at the dump! And the **avarice**! The **avarice** never ends! 'I want golf clubs!' 'I want diamonds!'"—*How the Grinch Stole Christmas*

"Excessive" is the key here—avarice is the accumulation of goods and wealth just for the sake of acquiring it and piling it up.

"The **avarice** of the companies results in misery for the passengers."—*A Man of Sample*s, Wm. H. Maher

"It is also a timely reminder that the forces of **avarice**, corruption, self-delusion and mendacity remain a constant in human history."—"The Best History Books of 2016," Sarah Dunant

"Yet scientists studying the sites today say these cryptic features are anything but haphazard: Instead they represent colossal monuments to human ingenuity—and **avarice**."—"Giant 'Arrows' Seen From Space Point to a Vanished World," Paul Salopek

Synonyms: acquisitiveness, avariciousness, covetousness, cupidity, greed, parsimony, stinginess

63. Aversion
noun (uh•*ver*•sjun)

A strong feeling of repulsion or dislike for someone or something

Used in Context
"You see, they have an **aversion** to water. One could almost call it a phobia."—*Dark City*

"We have basically over-calibrated in our reaction to germs—our **aversion** to them has created a new vulnerability."—"Following Tuberculosis From Death Sentence to Cure," Tessa Miller

"Darling, trying to account for this behavior, suggests that our **aversion** to abusing lifelike machines comes from 'societal values.'"—"If Animals Have Rights, Should Robots?," Nathan Heller

"For now, one popular suggestion by news-literacy educators is to tap teenagers' instinctive **aversion** to people telling them what to think."—"How to Teach High-School Students to Spot Fake News," Chris Berdik

Synonyms: antagonism, antipathy, detestation, disgust, dislike, distaste, hatred, having no use for, loathing, odium, repugnance

B

To resent someone's good fortune, or their having something

Used in Context

"Greaser Bob, the Original Greaser Bob, is hunting north of the picket wire and would not **begrudge** its use."—*True Grit*

"Yet, he added, most locals do not **begrudge** the summer people—most year-rounders rely on the tourist economy, after all."—"East Hampton Bar Is Set to Close, Taking More Than Its Stools," Sarah Maslin Nir

"If you want to reserve the word grief for the more personal kind of loss, I won't **begrudge** you that."—"In Praise of Social Media Mourning," Gabriel Roth

"Abortion-rights advocates by no means seek to detract from LGBT movement or **begrudge** it victories."—"Why Does Spain Love Gay Marriage But Hate Abortion?," Emily Shire

Synonyms: be jealous, covet, eat one's heart out, envy, grudge, pinch, resent, yearn for

65. Beguile
verb (bee•*gyle*)

To charm someone and win their attention

Used in Context
"I feel how weak and fruitless must be any words of mine that would attempt to **beguile** you from the grief of a loss so overwhelming."—*Saving Private Ryan*

"How any fox outside of the fable could **beguile** a crow is a puzzle to me."—*Everyday Adventures,* Samuel Scoville

"His plates seldom startle at first bite, instead they **beguile**."—"Copine: A Welcome Addition to Seattle's Fine-Dining Menu," Providence Cicero

"Will she **beguile** him into poor judgment, sidetracking his revenge crusade?"—"NBC's *Dracula* Sure Is Sexy, But It Isn't Scary," Kevin Fallon

Synonyms: betray, bluff, captivate, deceive, delude, double-cross, dupe, ensorcell, entice, finesse, flimflam, lure, manipulate, mislead, play for a sucker, seduce, trick, woo

66. Beleaguer
verb (bee•*lee*•ger)

To beset someone with enough assaults that they feel trapped, harassed, or under serious pressure

Used in Context

"In a late-afternoon press conference sure to have changed the face of Atlantic City's political landscape, **beleaguered** County Treasurer Enoch Thompson stepped down today, effective immediately."— *Boardwalk Empire*, "Two Boats and a Lifeguard"

"This is why I believe poor, **beleaguered** Mr. *Robot*, as much as Season 2 struggled, is still the show of the moment."—"The TV Club, 2016," Todd VanDerWerff

"In Act 2, which is consumed with the aftermath of the ship's collision with the iceberg, Smith joins the **beleaguered** captain, E. J. Smith (Christopher Bloch), and the bullying steamship line chairman, J. Bruce Ismay (Lawrence Redmond), for 'The Blame,' a well-staged round robin of melodic finger-pointing."—"Voices Raised Ebulliently, Passengers Of *Titanic* Head For The Deep," Peter Marks

"Hearing of Pearl Harbor, Winston Churchill in **beleaguered** Britain gloated: 'Hitler's fate was sealed,' while the Japanese 'would be ground to powder.'"—"Aboard the USS *Arizona*—Dec. 7, 1941," Robert R. Garnett

Synonyms: annoy, badgered, bedevil, beset, besieged, blockade, bother, bothered, fraught, nag, persecute, persecuted, plague, under attack, vex, vexed

"Beleaguered" can also be used as an adjective.

67. Bemoan
verb (bee•*moan*)

To express disappointment; to lament something

Used in Context
"I know you can drink whiskey, and snore and spit and wallow in filth and **bemoan** your station.—*True Grit*

"They **bemoan** the fact that poker games are too often delayed because people get up to take smoke breaks."—"11 Worst Songs of the Summer of All Time," Kevin Fallon

"Every year, my fellow movie reviewers and I **bemoan** the current state of cinema—Too many comic-book flicks!"—"The Best Movies of 2016: *Moonlight*, *Manchester by the Sea* and *Southside With You* Make the Top 10," Ann Hornaday

"We will not, however, **bemoan** thee as if thou wast forever lost to us, or that thy name would be buried in oblivion."—*The History of Minnesota and Tales of the Frontier*, Charles E. Flandrau

Synonyms: beat one's breast, bewail, complain, complain about, cry over spilled milk, deplore, grieve for, gripe, lament, moan over, mourn, rue, sing the blues for, weep for

68. Bemused
adjective (bee•*muzed*)

Being confused and unable to think clearly

Used in Context

"When I'm with her I'm confused, out of focus and **bemused**. And I never know exactly where I am."—*The Sound of Music*, "How Do You Solve a Problem Like Maria"

"She scarce listened, for at first she was **bemused** by two thoughts."— *The Job*, Sinclair Lewis

"A **bemused** line reading sneaks in when you are anticipating a hammy hard sell."—"It's OK to Like *The Big Bang Theory*," Kevin Fallon

Synonyms: abstracted, baffled, bewildered, distracted, inattentive, lost in thought, mystified, perplexed, preoccupied, puzzled

69. Benevolent
adjective (ben•*ev*•oh•lent)

Expressing kindness, generosity, and good will

Used in Context

"That's the day I realized that there was this entire life behind things and this incredible **benevolent** force that wanted me to know that there was no reason to be afraid."—*American Beauty*

"If you have a great person in charge then a **benevolent** dictator is wonderful."—"What Joan Rivers Said She Would Do If She Were Dictator of America," Asawin Suebsaeng

"It is understood that Col. Lawrence will commence this **benevolent** and patriotic work in the spring or early summer."—*Reminiscences of the Military Life and Sufferings of Col. Timothy Bigelow, Commander of the Fifteenth Regiment of the Massachusetts Line in the Continental Army,* *during the War of the Revolution*, Charles Hersey

Synonyms: altruistic, beneficent, benign, caring, compassionate, empathetic, giving, helpful, kind, kindhearted, magnanimous, philanthropic

70. Besmirch
verb (bee•*smurch*)

To trash someone's reputation

Used in Context
"You dare talk of dirty work when you **besmirch** so many souls with your nefarious filth."—*Xena: Warrior Princess*, "Heart of Darkness"

"Also I want to **besmirch** the rich, by designating them by a slang expression."—*Moral,* Ludwig Thoma

"I hate to **besmirch** the reputation of an innocent dog, but a lot of time her personality is like a rabid pit bull."—"Billy Sammeth, the Manager Fired by Cher and Joan Rivers, Tells His Side of the Story," Kevin Sessums

Synonyms: damage, defame, defile, dishonor, libel, slander, smear, sully, taint, tarnish

71. Bifurcate
verb (*by*•fur•kate)

To divide into two parts or branches

This means to split into two. It can be used thematically, as in: our political parties are bifurcated into two factions, Democratic and Republican. Or it can be used physiologically, as in: his finger was bifurcated in a table-saw accident.

Used in Context

"The doctor that does the procedure will use anesthesia and a laser to **bifurcate** the tongue."—*The Chain Gang Blog*, "Tongue Splitting: The Wilder Body Modifications," Miss Vicious

"From the single vessel with **bifurcate** spout we may pass to others in which there are two openings joined together by a handle."—*The Ceramic Art*, Jennie J. Young

"So words grow and **bifurcate**, diverge and dwindle, until one root has many branches."—*Style*, Walter Raleigh

Synonyms: bisect, diverge, divide, fork, separate, split

72. Bilingual
noun (by•*lin*•gwul)

A person who is able to speak, write and/or read in two languages; a two-language written work

Used in Context

"This is a **bilingual** paper. The English version should be here somewhere."—*Criminal Minds*, "True Genius"

"Almost to a person, the French who are **bilingual** credit English-language television with their success."—"Why Can't France Learn English?," David Sessions

"Blanche, **bilingual** refers to a person who speaks more than one language."—*The Golden Girls*, "The Audit"

Note: "bilingual" can also be used as an adjective.

Synonyms: bilingualist, linguist, polyglot

73. Bilious
adjective (*bill*•yus)

Unsettled, nauseous, something unpleasant to look at

Used in Context
"Don't sit there crooning like a **bilious** pigeon!"—*My Fair Lady*

"In fact, the GOP is a mummy-wrapped skeleton sitting in its own chilly mausoleum of **bilious** resentments and creepy sentimentality."—"GOP R.I.P.," John Batchelor

"It happened that this evening she was the victim of a **bilious** headache, and she lay supine on a sofa, unable to sit up for dinner."—*Mrs. Thompson*, William Babington Maxwell

One of the synonyms for bilious," the word "atrabilious," was used in the intensely literate dramatic series *Deadwood*.

Synonyms: atrabilious, cranky, dyspeptic, grouchy, ill-natured, irritable, peevish, sickly, under the weather

74. Binary
adjective (*by*•nuh•ree)

Characterized by or consisting of two parts or components

Used in Context

"Vaporators? Sir, my first job was programming **binary** load lifters, very similar to your vaporators in most respects."—*Star Wars: A New Hope*

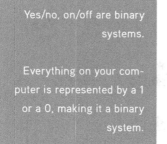
Yes/no, on/off are binary systems.

Everything on your computer is represented by a 1 or a 0, making it a binary system.

"The final act offers a **binary** choice: love or hate, forgiveness or vengeance, truth or consequences."—"*The Killing*: How AMC's Adaptation of *Forbrydelsen* Went Wrong," Jace Lacob

"Antares is probably a binary, although its **binary** character has not yet been established."—*Pleasures of the Telescope*, Garrett Serviss

Synonyms: binate, double, dual, multiple, paired, twice

75. Bipartisan
adjective (by•*par*•tis•an)

Refers to political actions involving two political parties working together

Used in Context

"Congress should establish a **bipartisan**, select committee to investigate."—"A Bipartisan Committee Should Investigate Russia's Election Hacking." *The Washington Post* Editorial Board

"We want to show the amendment has **bipartisan** support, you idiot! Early in the next congress, when I tell you to do so, you will switch parties."—*Lincoln*

"Lindsey Graham, a South Carolina Republican who oversees the Senate subcommittee that controls such assistance, said in a statement: 'If the United Nations moves forward with the ill-conceived resolution, I will work to form a **bipartisan** coalition to suspend or significantly reduce United States assistance to the United Nations.'"—"U.S. senator Threatens to Curb Aid Over U.N. Resolution on Israel," Susan Heavey, Michelle Nichols

"It was a sort of **bipartisan** mass-meeting, but there was one prevailing spirit, that born of rye and corn."—*Lincoln's Yarns and Stories*, Alexander K. McClure

Synonyms: bicameral, bilateral, bisected, dual, in concert

76. Bipolar
adjective (bi•*po*•lar)

Having two opposite or contradictory ideas

Used in Context
"That's because I'm undiagnosed **bipolar**, yeah, with mood swings and weird thinking brought on by severe stress, which rarely happens, thank God."—*Silver Linings Playbook*

"Everything in nature is **bipolar**, or has a positive and negative pole."—*Essays, Second Series*, Ralph Waldo Emerson

This is a commonly used psychiatric term, but its specific definition simply means split into two parts; thus, someone who is bipolar experiences two states of mind: manic and depressive.

"DMX has rapped and spoken about suffering from **bipolar** disorder."—"Kanye West and How Hip-Hop Tackles Mental Health," Elahe Izadi

"Dear Prudence, I am a female in my 20s living with **bipolar** disorder."—"I Don't Wanna Sex You Up," Mallory Ortberg

Synonyms: capricious, inconstant, mercurial

77. Blasphemy
noun (*blas*•fuh•mee)

Disrespect for God, holy things, or scared rituals

Used in Context
"Rule number one: no **blasphemy**. I'll not have the Lord's name taken in vain in my prison."—*The Shawshank Redemption*

Blasphemy can only exist if the blasphemer accepts a religious belief and finds it important enough that criticizing it would be a crime or violation. For example, if a member of a church suddenly started criticizing its creed, they would commit blasphemy; a nonmember is free to criticize because they do not believe or find the creed importance. Thus, blasphemy can only exist if one allows it to.

"An attempt to exclude him on charges of atheism and **blasphemy** failed."—*The Isle Of Pines*, Henry Neville

"I shall stop his recruiting, and choke his **blasphemy** with a good French sword."—*The Hour and the Man*, Harriet Martineau

Synonyms: discourtesy, heresy, impiety, impiousness, imprecation, irreverence, sacrilege

78. Blithe
adjective (blythe)

Happy, cheerful

Used in Context
"High in her tower, she sits by the hour, maintaining her hair. **Blithe** and becoming, and frequently humming, a lighthearted air…agony!"— *Into the Woods*

"Sadly, Republicans—who have repeatedly slammed Obama for this kind of **blithe** incoherence—are not immune to the same disorder."—"Lobbyist Derangement Syndrome Sweeps DC," James Poulos

"In the momentary silence that ensued the **blithe** jingling of bells was heard, accompanied by the merry sound of tabor and pipe." —*The Lancashire Witches*, William Harrison Ainsworth

Synonyms: amused, jocular, joyful, joyous, merry, pleased

79. Bombastic
adjective (bom•*bass*•tik)

Using pretentious language with overlong words, intending to impress people

Used in Context
"Look, if he wanted me dead, he would have lain in wait, not left me some **bombastic** note…He wants the game."—*Elementary*, "M"

"Outside the polling stations, men talked in **bombastic** terms about freedom and democracy."—"Polls Close in First Libyan Election in More Than 40 Years," Jamie Dettmer

"His language in those telegrams and letters was highfaluting and **bombastic**."—*England and Germany*, Emile Joseph Dillon

Synonyms: blustering, full of hot air, long-winded, loudmouthed, ostentatious, pompous, posturing, ranting, swaggering, verbose, wordy

80. Bona fide
adjective (*boh*•nuh•fyd)

Genuine, authentic, for real

Used in Context
"The first film, made in 2008, was a **bona fide** blockbuster, grossing more than $400 million worldwide."—*Carrie Bradshaw and Me*, Rebecca Dana

"So this is what love looks like, we might think, flattering ourselves that we can tell the **bona fide** from the bogus."—"Carrie Fisher and Harrison Ford: Does It Matter If Movie Romances Are Real?," Ryan Gilbey

"In reality, there were only a handful of **bona fide** voter fraud cases throughout the country."—"The GOP Created the 'Rigged Vote' Myth," Mark Joseph Stern

"They had not a **bona fide** delegation from any Southern State."—*Expansion and Conflict*, William E. Dodd

Synonyms: authenticated, honest, kosher, lawful, legitimate, real, true, valid

81. Bravado
noun (bruh•*va*•doe)

A display of boldness and courage that may or may not be authentic

Used in Context
"He was afraid of this strange young man who seemed so daring and yet had an effect of **bravado** rather than guilt."—*The Mark of Cain*, Carolyn Wells

"Men will carry off curiosity with various kinds of laughter and **bravado**, just as they will carry off drunkenness or bankruptcy."—*What I Saw in America*, G. K. Chesterton

"Then he gets rolling, and his blend of showman's **bravado** and rhetorical flair is a thing of beauty."—"What Michael Moore Understands About Hillary Clinton," Richard Brody

"We need less hubris and more humility, less **bravado** and more bravery."—"America Is Unhinged and Nobody Will Take the Blame," Tavis Smiley

Synonyms: audacity, bluster, boasting, bombast, braggadocio, bullying, daring, swaggering

82. Broach
verb (broche)

To bring up a subject for discussion or debate, oftentimes, an uncomfortable one

Used in Context

"But we have a lot of work to do before we even **broach** the subject."— *Erin Brockovich*

"Woven into the very fabric of its characters, Masters uses sex to **broach** bigger topics."—"What Porn Stars Find Sexy on TV: From *Game of Thrones* to *Deadliest Catch*," Aurora Snow

"The present was not, however, the time to **broach** the subject."— *Ralph on the Overland Express*, Allen Chapman

Synonyms: hint at, initiate, interject, introduce, mention, raise, submit, suggest, try out

83. Brusque
adjective (bruhsk)

Abrupt or blunt in speech, oftentimes coming off as rude

Used in Context

"Excuse me if I was **brusque**, but we get boo-boos in here without a dollar."—*Coming to America*

"And McCauley was surely friendlier that his **brusque** air of command indicated."—"The Strange and Mysterious Death of Mrs. Jerry Lee Lewis," Richard Ben Cramer

"He was conscious that he was **brusque**, and that Marius was cold."— *Les Miserables*, Victor Hugo

Synonyms: candid, curt, direct, gruff, impolite, offhand, rough, snippy, tart, terse

84. Bulwark
noun (*bull•*wark)

A defense and protection against assaults or dangers, whether physical or in the abstract

Used in Context
"The soul of a poet, but none of the grit and steel that acts as a **bulwark** against this, these horrors of this world."—*American Horror Story*, "Halloween, Part 2"

"Now he looks like the **bulwark** against conservative radicalism."—"How Wisconsin Helps Obama," Peter Beinart

"And he smiled at her bewilderment when he had added: 'I am your **bulwark** and your safeguard.'"—*Privy Seal*, Ford Maddox Ford

Synonyms: barricade, bastion, fortification, rampart, safeguard, security, stronghold, wall

85. Bumptious
adjective (*bum•*shus)

Describes someone who obnoxiously announces their grandiose opinions

Used in Context

"He was a rather **bumptious** type, but if anyone objected to that, it was me."—*Downton Abbey,* "Episode 5.3"

"But the roughly 50 bowls, cups, vases and pitchers in this stunning exhibition testify to a creative sensibility much different from his **bumptious** public persona."—"In *No Two Alike,* George Ohr's Pottery Plays on Convention," Ken Johnson

"Particularly effective is her clear-eyed view of the young Churchill as a **bumptious** self-promoter whose exploits in Africa were as farcical as they were courageous."—"Winston Churchill, Hungry for Recognition at Any Cost," Lynne Olson

Synonyms: arrogant, bigheaded, boastful, bragging, overbearing, self-important

86. Bureaucracy
noun (byur•*ok*•ruh•see)

A governmental system in which specific functions are carried out by individual departments

Used in Context

"That's impossible. How will the emperor maintain control without the **bureaucracy**?"—*Star Wars: A New Hope*

"The accumulation of laws and **bureaucracy** over time weighs heavily on all of us."—"Don't Destroy Government, Use It," Will Marshall

"How do we free ourselves from the choking grip of **bureaucracy**?"— *The Civilization of Illiteracy*, Mihai Nadin

Synonyms: administration, civil service, establishment, government, management, organization

87. Buttress
verb (*but•tress*)

To defend or support something, especially an argument

Used in Context
"'McConnell is doing everything he can to **buttress** his support,' Mann said."—"Ted Cruz, Rand Paul, Marco Rubio, Mike Lee: When Freshmen Attack," Patricia Murphy

"I was a mother and a home-maker and the hope and **buttress** of the future."—*The Prairie Mother*, Arthur Stringer

"Biography plays a central role in all political campaigns, with candidates deploying their life stories to **buttress** their arguments."—"The Self-Referential Presidency of Barack Obama," Carlos Lozada

Synonyms: encourage, promote, prop up, reinforce

C

Loud, jarring, unpleasant sounds in combination played for disorienting effect; a metaphor for words used for similar effect

Used in Context

"To help cut through the **cacophony** of positive and negative economic reports this month, we turned to a Nobel laureate."—Interview With Edmund Phelps, *The Daily Beast*

"It's a punishing drumbeat of constant input, this **cacophony** which follows us into our homes and into our beds."—*Elementary*, "The Marchioness"

"Then it was **cacophony**, a thousand different shouting voices."—*Little Brother*, Cory Doctorow

Synonyms: clamor, din, discord, discordance, disharmony, dissonance, noise

89. Cadence
noun (*kay•*dens)

The structured beat of sounds or words in a set rhythm

Used in Context
"I'm having a bit of a problem just trying to find my tone. They have a **cadence.**"—*Curb Your Enthusiasm*, "The Table Read"

"I feel like I can recognize the **cadence**, but I haven't been able to do it yet."—"David Gregory, Off the Air," Lloyd Grove

"At the command 'Arms,' execute port arms and continue in **cadence** to the position ordered."—*Manual for Noncommissioned Officers and Privates of Cavalry of the Army*, War Department.

Synonyms: meter, pace, pulse, rhythm, tempo, time

90. Cadre
noun (*kah•*dray)

A core of trained, qualified personnel around which an organization is formed

Used in Context
"They were not monsters. These were men, trained **cadres**. These men who fought with their hearts, who have families, who have children."—*Apocalypse Now*

A cadre of excellent heart transplant surgeons, for example, can elevate the reputation of a hospital.

A team of trained operators like Special Forces units can be considered a cadre because missions revolve around their skills and training.

"He can possibly wield control from inside through a **cadre** of loyal lieutenants in the field.—"Will El Chapo Rule From Prison?," John P. Sullivan

"This provision was in line with the concept that the peacetime Army was a **cadre** to be expanded in time of emergency."—*Integration of the Armed Forces, 1940–1965*, Morris J. MacGregor Jr.

Synonyms: infrastructure, key group, organization, personnel, staff, team

91. Cajole
verb (kuh•*jole*)

To use flattery and persistence to persuade someone to do something

Used in Context

"Then beg, entreat, **cajole**. Find the word you like best."—*Cleopatra*

"I recall mentioning that in the past to others: her using her femininity to **cajole**, to persuade."—"The Margaret Thatcher I Knew," Jamie Dettmer

"You cannot **cajole** it out of me, you cannot steal it from me."—*The Devil's Paw*, E. Phillips Oppenheim

Synonyms: beg, beguile, coax, entice, entreat, induce, inveigle, play up to, seduce

92. Callous
adjective (*kal•us*)

Not caring if someone else gets hurt, whether it's physically or emotionally

Used in Context
"The attack on the dam was a **callous** and inhuman act of destruction."—*The Hunger Games: Mockingjay, Part 1*

"We hope that, after this **callous** confession, Scotland Yard will now take action."—*Punch, or the London Charivari, May 13, 1914*

"Romney lost in part because he allowed his campaign and personality to be defined as extreme and **callous**."—"No, I'm Pretty Sure Mitt Romney 'Gets It,'" Justin Green

Synonyms: apathetic, coldhearted, heartless, indifferent, insensitive, uncaring, uncompassionate, unconcerned, unfeeling, unkind, unsympathetic

93. Canard
noun (*kuh•nard*)

An intentionally false or baseless story, rumor, or report, often derogatory

Used in Context
"It's a **canard**—cover for trying to prevent black and brown people from voting."—"Four Things Reince Priebus Could Say That Would Matter," Michael Tomasky

"The first is this **canard** that we have to balance the budget."—"The GOP's Three Fiscal Lies," Michael Tomasky

"I found here several letters from England; but, as I had presumed, that report about the sale of all my pictures was a **canard**."—*The Life, Letters and Work of Frederic Leighton*, Mrs. Russell Barrington

Synonyms: exaggeration, fabrication, fib, hoax, spoof

94. Canon
noun (*kan•un*)

A set of written or artistic works said to comprise a definitive rendering of an artist's work or a school of artistic achievement; i.e., Russian novels; 19th century poetry, greatest novels, etc.

"Canon" is also applied to pop culture achievements; e.g., *Rolling Stone* issues a list of the "50 Greatest Rock Albums of All Time," and such a list is considered a canon because of its credibility and informed opinion.

Used in Context

"It would fit in the **canon** of raunchy teen comedies alongside *American Pie* and *Road Trip*."—"British Raunchfest *The Inbetweeners Movie* Tries to Make Its Mark in America," Kevin Fallon

"She coped with isolation by running up a three-thousand-dollar-a-month phone bill and reading everything from potboilers to the pillars of the Western **canon**."—"Marlene Dietrich's Marginalia," Megan Mayhew Bergman

"Nel believes that the course should not be seen as competing with the

more traditional English **canon**."—"America's 10 Hottest Classes,"
Kathleen Kingsbury

"I did not, and Meg, you did not, grow up with a sense of the American children's **canon**."—"R. J. Palacio and Meg Medina Talk Diversity and Children's Books," Maria Russo

Synonyms: catalog, criteria, doctrine, dogma, standard

95. Cantankerous
adjective (can•*tank*•er•us)

Refers to someone who gets angry quickly and easily
and is usually difficult to interact with or work with

Used in Context
"Paul, on the other hand, has developed a **cantankerous** reputation as an uncompromising leader of the Tea Party."—"Rand Paul and Ron Wyden, Drone Odd-Couple," Eli Lake

It seems that everyone has a surly coworker or relative who gets pissed off at the drop of a hat. Best advice? Avoidance works wonders.

"It's quite true that the people round here—your sort of people, I mean—are a **cantankerous** lot."—*The Graftons*, Archibald Marshall

"As Allen points out, Italians are in a **cantankerous** mood these days."—"The Case for Cardinal Sean O'Malley," Christopher Dickey

Synonyms: argumentative, bad-tempered, belligerent, contentious, crabby, crotchety, curmudgeonly, disagreeable, grouchy, grumpy, irascible, irritable, peevish, prickly, quarrelsome, surly, testy, unreasonable

96. Capacious
adjective (kuh•*pay*•shus)

Large enough to hold a big quantity of something; can be used in the abstract; i.e., "Her heart was capacious enough to forgive them all."

Used in Context
"All right, 'capacious.' Looks like 'spacious.' What does it mean? Roomy. Oh, yeah."—*Gossip Girl*, "Desperately Seeking Serena"

"But George H. W. Bush is a man of capacious and unconditional love, so I imagine that carried him through the day."—"How Hillary's Feeling About Caroline," Christopher Buckley

"There was a very handsome cut glass water-jug, full, standing on the table in a capacious salver of hammered brass."—*The Log of the Flying Fish*, Harry Collingwood

Synonyms: commodious, expansive, huge, roomy, sizeable, spacious, vast, voluminous

97. Capricious
adjective (kuh•*pree*•shus)

Whimsical; changeable; illogical

Used in Context
"Actually, going all the way is, like, a really big decision. I can't believe I was so capricious about it. Dee, I almost had sex with him!"—*Clueless*

"A depraved and **capricious** appetite is common in horses that have a stone forming in the stomachs."—*Special Report on Diseases of the Horse*, United States Department of Agriculture

A capricious law is something that has no foundation for solid jurisprudence. For example: "Any vehicle registered in town may not affix green bumper stickers to its front bumper."

"Tennyson, I've known Colonel Taylor for a long time. This is not a **capricious** man. I warn you, he is in deadly earnest."—*The Twilight Zone*, "The Silence"

"She could be wretchedly imprecise, **capricious**, and heartless to her co-workers."—"Understanding Diana Vreeland, 'Empress of Fashion,'" Robin Givhan

Synonyms: erratic, fickle, flighty, impulsive, mercurial, quirky, unpredictable, unstable, variable, volatile

98. Caricature
noun (*kar*•uh•ka•chur)

A drawing of a person that exaggerates a particular physical feature for satirical or humorous effect; is also commonly used in the abstract; i.e., "He acted like a caricature of a soldier."

Used in Context
"Where do they come from? They look like **caricatures** of used-car dealers from Dallas. And sweet Jesus, there are a lot of them at 4:30 on a Sunday morning."—*Fear and Loathing in Las Vegas*

"A satire, an epigram, or a **caricature** may suffice to produce such a conviction."—*Folkways*, William Graham Sumner

"Do voters see an entirely different candidate than the **caricature** of himself Romney created during the primaries?"—"Shaking the Etch-A-Mitt, Ctd.," Justin Green

Synonyms: burlesque, cartoon, distortion, misrepresentation, mockery, parody, picture, rendering, satire, send-up, sketch

99. Carpe diem
noun (*kar•*pay*•dee•*em)

Seize the day

"Carpe Diem" was my class motto when I taught at the University of New Haven. My hope was that my students would take it to heart at a time when they had decades ahead of them, and truly work to achieve their goals.

Used in Context

"**Carpe diem**. Seize the day, boys. Make your lives extraordinary."—*Dead Poets' Society*

"A great deal of his best poetry is merely a variation on **carpe diem**."—*Old and New Masters,* Robert Lynd

"Your sentiment on the wisdom of **carpe diem** does not impress me today."—*Return of the Native,* Thomas Hardy

Synonyms: enjoy the present, grab the chance, live for the day, live for today, make hay while the sun shines, make the most of it, smell the roses, take the opportunity

100. Castigate
verb (*kas•*tih*•*gate)

To harshly rebuke or criticize someone

Used in Context

"If only I were not a woman, I might **castigate** you as you deserve!"—
Juliette Drouet's Love-Letters to Victor Hugo, Louis Guimbaud

"Cam Newton owes you nothing, so do not **castigate** him."—"Are You Ready for Some Football…and Riot Gear and Pepper Spray?," Juliet Macur

"And though conservatives regularly **castigate** public-sector unions as parasites, they typically exempt the police."—"Why Are Police Unions Blocking Reform?," James Surowiecki

"The company, or companies, of soldiers will be first detailed for the arduous duties of the field to **castigate** the Indians."—*The Life and Adventures of Kit Carson, the Nestor of the Rocky Mountains, from Facts Narrated by Himself*, De Witt C. Peters

Synonyms: berate, censure, chasten, chastise, excoriate, harangue, lambaste, rebuke, reprimand, reprove, scold, tell off, upbraid

101. Catalyst
noun (*kat•uh•list*)

Something that precipitates a change or causes an event

Used in Context

"Well, the **catalyst** for the recent dramatic events of the show has been Truman's father, Kirk, and his attempts to infiltrate the show."—*The Truman Show*

"The **catalyst** for a new plan should be the immediate reform and recapitalization of the banking system—with a clear time-frame."—"Stop the Bailout: Four Better Alternatives," Alan Quasha

"Margaret Thatcher's death has been the **catalyst**, in Britain, for a wide-ranging debate over her legacy."—"How Thatcher's Ideology Threatens To Kill Zionism," Samuel Lebens

Synonyms: agitator, cause, impetus, incitation, means, medium, spur

102. Catatonia
noun (cat•uh•*tone*•ee•uh)

A state of mental stupor and/or muscular paralysis, often found in schizophrenic patients

Used in Context
"He seems to be re-experiencing **catatonia**. So he could snap out of it in an hour. There's no way to be sure."—*The Fisher King*

"Fortunately Kahlbaum prevented serious error by leaving the prognosis of his **catatonia** open."—*Benign Stupors*, August Hoch

"Then you can check your notes and decide if it's schizophrenia, or **catatonia**, or psychasthenia, or what not."—*A Thought For Tomorrow*, Robert E. Gilbert

The adjective to describe this state is "catatonic."

Synonyms: catalepsy, coma, daze, insensibility, petrifaction, trance, transfixion

103. Catharsis
noun (kuh•*thar*•sis)

A feeling of emotional release usually brought about by an intense emotional experience

Used in Context

"The Purge not only contains societal violence to a single evening, but the country-wide **catharsis** creates psychological stability by letting us release the aggression we all have inside of us."—*The Purge*

"He suggests that the appeal to teenagers also goes beyond thrill-seeking and **catharsis**."—"Why Our Brains Love Horror Movies," Sharon Begley

"He had no sympathy with the poetry that had a social message and he did not understand its effect as a **catharsis**."—*The Literature of Ecstasy*, Albert Mordell

"Encountering such exaggerations on the page serves as a kind of **catharsis**, and provides a kind of perspective."—"Lifetime's *Flowers in the Attic* Review: The Incest Is There, The Strange Magic Is Not," Andrew Romano

Synonyms: cleansing, freeing, purgation, purification

104. Causal
adjective (*kawz*•ul)

Describes something that is a cause in a situation; i.e., something that can be identified as having an effect

Used in Context

"This is magical thinking, non-scientific **causal** reasoning. Now you're looking for 23 so you're finding it."—*The Number 23*

"It is also important to contextualize how many cases of autism could be accounted for if a **causal** link to SSRI proved true."—"Expectant Moms, Don't Ditch SSRIs Over Autism Fears Just Yet," Emily Shire

"In considering the **causal** laws of psychology, the distinction between rough generalizations and exact laws is important."—*The Analysis of Mind*, Bertrand Russell

Synonyms: causative, connecting, contributory, formative, generative, originative, seminal

105. Caveat
noun (*kah•vee•ot*)

A warning or caution

Comes from the Latin phrase *caveat emptor*, which means "let the buyer beware."

Some game manufacturers will include a caveat with their game: "Caution: This game is highly addictive."

Used in Context

"He wanted me to let you know you're welcome in Neverland for as long as you wish to stay...with one **caveat** (which is you can't grow up)"—*Once Upon a Time*, "The Heart of a Truest Believer"

"They pounded the issue in Charlotte and dropped the **caveat** that it should be 'rare.'"—"Democrats Push Envelope on Abortion, Drop Insistence That It Be Rare," Eleanor Clift

"Hulagu then gave his men licence to rape, kill and plunder with the **caveat** that Christians and Jews were to be spared."—"In Threatening Baghdad, Militants Seek to Undo 800 Years of History," Justin Marozzi

Synonyms: admonition, forewarning, heads up, injunction, limitation, qualification, stipulation

106. Censorious
adjective (sen•sor•ee•us)

Describes someone with a tendency to be extremely critical and disapproving

Used in Context
"You're too **censorious** Miss Bennet. Mr. Darcy takes care of Mr. Bingley in those points where he wants care."—*Pride and Prejudice*

"Yet jollity and gloom are still at war in our **censorious** age."—"A History of American Fun," Stefan Beck

"It was a mad world—a world in which it was not safe to be **censorious**."—"The Kingdom Round the Corner," Coningsby Dawson

Synonyms: accusatory, captious, carping, chiding, condemning, disparaging, faultfinding, reprehending, reproaching, severe, stern

107. Censure
verb (*sen*•shure)

To severely condemn someone or some action, often in an official manner

Used in Context

"I needed help, not **censure**; freedom, not captivity for being a madman."—*Star Trek*, "The City on the Edge of Forever"

"The article states that the agency could have voted sanctions against Maco ranging from **censure** to disbarment."—"The Woody Allen Allegations: Not So Fast," Robert B. Weide

"I was told there was a **censure** from the Sorbonne, but this I could not believe."—*The Confessions of J. J. Rousseau*, Jean Jacques Rousseau

Synonyms: admonish, blame, castigate, criticize, denounce, disapprove of, dress down, lambaste, reprimand, reproach, scorn

108. Chagrin
noun (shuh•*grin*)

A feeling of embarrassment or humiliation due to something you did, or something that happened

Used in Context

"A bore? Not at all. It's pride. Just imagine your **chagrin** when she sees you wander in and you find her with that slippery senor."—*Gigi*

"He has burrowed so deeply into his work that he hasn't even bothered to get a tan—much to New York's **chagrin**."—"*Mad Men*'s Dramatic Déjà Vu: 'Time Zones' Feels Redundant," Andrew Romano

"To my **chagrin**, the duke laid his hand on the window and closed it."—*The Prisoner of Zenda*, Anthony Hope

Synonyms: annoyance, disappointment, discomfiture, dishonor, disquiet, frustration, ill humor, indignity, infamy, irritation, mortification, shame, sorrow, vexation

109. Chauvinism
noun (*show•ven•izm*)

An excessive and prejudiced commitment to a gender, group, or cause; i.e. male chauvinism is antifeminism

Used in Context

"As you have just witnessed, **chauvinism** and religious quackery are alive and well right here in Al Bundy's garage, calling themselves The Church of No Ma'am."—*Married With Children*, "Reverend Al"

"But the proper corrective to **chauvinism** is not to reverse it and practice it against males, but rather basic fairness."—"And What About the Boys?," Ilana Glazer

"'Their patriarchy and **chauvinism**,' she says, 'was harder on Iraqi culture than Iraqis themselves.'"—"Hillary Clinton's War for Women's Rights," Gayle Tzemach Lemmon

"There is, however, always a great danger that patriotism may degenerate into **chauvinism**."—*The Moral Instruction of Children*, Felix Adler

Synonyms: bias, bigotry, discrimination, ethnocentricity, fanatical patriotism, fanaticism, intolerance, jingoism, narrowness, nationalism, prejudice, racism, sexism, xenophobia

110. Chicanery
noun (chik•*ain*•er•ee)

The use of trickery and lies to deceive, and often profit

Used in Context
"Fans of today adore the cheaters of the past, precisely because of their **chicanery**."—"Alex Rodriguez Suspension Is a Sad Moment for Baseball," Michael Brendan Dougherty

> Some examples of chicanery have been appearing on Facebook with unfortunate frequency of late. The most common scams include posting requests for money to help a child dying of cancer. Not only is there no cancer, there's no child.

"Why would I wanna pay some old hag good money for some supernatural **chicanery** coupled with sagging, wrinkled, weathered boobs?"—*Mallrats*

"A delicate webwork of forgery, bribery, **chicanery** and falsehood."—*The Misplaced Battleship*, Harry Harrison

Synonyms: deceit, deception, deviousness, dishonesty, double-crossing, duplicity, fraud, gambit, hanky-panky, maneuver, ruse, scam, subterfuge, underhandedness

111. Chide
verb (chide)

To scold someone, but with a gentle rather than a harsh tone

Used in Context
"It is not friendly, 'tis not maidenly. Our sex, as well as I, may **chide**

you for it, though I alone do feel the injury."—*A Midsummer Night's Dream*, William Shakespeare

"Our cars will **chide** us if we tailgate and watch us as we drive and jolt us awake if are distracted or drifting off to sleep."—"Secrets of Google's Robo-Car," Paul Saffo

"Though I was a few minutes late for dinner, Miss Herbert did not **chide** me for delay."—*A Day's Ride*, Charles James Lever

Synonyms: admonish, berate, blame, castigate, censure, nag, rebuke, reprimand, reprove, tell off, upbraid

112. Chimera
noun (ky•*meer*•uh)

An idle fantasy of the imagination; a ridiculously unrealistic notion; a far-fetched, essentially impossible plan

Used in Context
"Far away appeared a cloud, but as it drew nearer it became a horse: it was the **chimera**."—*Psyche*, Louis Couperus

"Do not delude me with a **chimera**, and above all do not tempt me to sacrifice my honour to it."—*Samuel Brohl & Company*, Victor Cherbuliez

"Sex is a **chimera**. I saw a crack whore eat her own arm. I saw a baby drowned like a cat."—*The Good Wife*, "The Deep Web"

Synonyms: daydream, delusion, fantasy, hallucination, illusion, mirage, pipe dream

113. Circuitous
adjective (sir•*qu*•uh•tus)

Describes a route or an explanation or argument that is overlong due to indirectness

Used in Context
"The army provided a truckload of soldiers as escorts, and we took a **circuitous** route to avoid areas not considered secure."—"Into Taliban Country," Steve Inskeep

"That hubris led to a **circuitous** career that landed Moore in some memorable places."—"What Happened to Demi?," Gina Piccalo

"We managed, however, by rapid marching over a **circuitous** route to reach the north side of Bull Run in safety."—*A Narrative of Service with the Third Wisconsin Infantry*, Julian Wisner Hinkley

Synonyms: complicated, indirect, labyrinthine, meandering, oblique, rambling, roundabout, tortuous, twisty

114. Circumspect
adjective (*sir*•kum•spekt)

Exhibiting cautious behavior before taking action or making a decision; weighing consequences and risks

Used in Context
"Mandela did not want messy personal details in his Long Walk to Freedom, and here his handlers have been just as **circumspect**."—"Nelson Mandela's Revelatory Diaries," James Zug

"But you must follow me, obey me, be **circumspect**, make no disruption, quietly do whatever work is given you"—*Zardoz*

"After that the generals began to disperse with the solemnity and **circumspect** silence of people who are leaving, after a funeral."—*War and Peace*, Leo Tolstoy

Synonyms: attentive, careful, guarded, prudent, scrupulous, vigilant, wary

115. Codicil
noun (*kod*•uh•sill)

An amendment to an existing will

Used in Context
"However, an additional **codicil**, delivered into my possession by post only this morning, and, by all indications, sent by Madam D."—*The Grand Budapest Hotel*

"Unfortunately, Whitaker never got to discuss the third **codicil** with Mrs. Astor or see her sign it."—"Brooke Astor's $60 Million Signature," Ralph Gardner Jr.

If someone has a will drafted, and then a year later decides to leave her ceramic frog collection to her inadvertently overlooked cousin, she doesn't have to have a whole new will written: she has her lawyer write and add a codicil detailing the addition.

"In his heart of hearts, he did believe that that **codicil** had been fraudulently manufactured by his friend and client, Lady Mason."—*Orley Farm*, Anthony Trollope

Synonyms: addendum, addition, add-on, appendix, postscript, rider, supplement

116. Collegial
adjective (kuh-lee-jul)

Characterized by or having authority vested equally among colleagues

Used in Context

Its primary meaning is *equal authority* among colleagues, but its secondary meaning is *camaraderie* among colleagues.

"Supposedly Supreme Court justices are **collegial** even when they disagree on points of law. Supremes' Spat Over Affirmative Action."—*Adam Winkler*

These days the more common usage is to use "collegial" to describe cordial, mutually respectful relationships between friends and colleagues.

"The seating was bipartisan, the tone was **collegial**, the president struck some centrist, even conservative notes."—"Ducking the Tough Issues," Mark McKinnon

"Paul and Robert Redford had a **collegial** but prickly relationship as illustrated by their exchange of practical jokes."—"My Pal Paul Newman," A. E. Hotchner

Synonyms: coordinated, harmonious, respectful, symbiotic, united

117. Colloquy
noun (*kole•a•quiy*)

A formal discussion or conversation

Used in Context

"We never had time to have the type of **colloquy** that is normal to have, as we are having now, here seated. I do not remember having to argue to consequences of war."—*The World at War*, "Remember"

"I was bored by the length of the **colloquy**, and sat down on the table swinging my legs."—*My Double Life*, Sarah Bernhardt

"They could scarcely have spoken a hundred words before their **colloquy** was at an end."—*Mr. Marx's Secret*, E. Phillips Oppenheim

Synonyms: conference, dialogue, discourse, huddle, palaver, seminar, symposium

118. Comity
noun (*kom•ih•tee*)

Mutual courtesy, civility, respect among people, nations, groups, etc.

Used in Context
"**Comity**. It means getting along with the other side."—*Showgirls*, "Comity Lines"

"While not an enormous policy step, it was a powerful symbol of civility and **comity**."—"No Labels, a Nonpartisan Group, Unveils Its Plan to Fix Congress," Mark McKinnon

"Republicans have pushed every procedural edge as a minority, undermining the basic trust and **comity** of the institution."—"John McCain to the Rescue as Senate Deal Breaks Nominee Logjam," Eleanor Clift

"It does not satisfy the required conditions upon which alone the **comity** of nations would respect it."—*The Oregon Territory*, Travers Twiss

Synonyms: accord, benevolence, concord, cordiality, friendship, goodwill, harmony, unity

119. Commensurate
adjective (kum•*en*•shur•ate)

Appropriately proportionate in size or extent; having the same measure

Used in Context

"His death is not **commensurate** with the tonnage of human suffering he caused."—"The Relief of 9/11 Heroes," John Avlon

"Justice demands that punishment be **commensurate** with reward."—*A History of Mediaeval Jewish Philosophy*, Isaac Husik

"[To] march along the highway in a peaceful manner ought to be **commensurate** with the enormity of wrongs that are being protested and petitioned against."—*Selma*

Synonyms: adequate, appropriate, comparable, corresponding, equal, equivalent, in accord, matching, symmetrical

120. Comport
verb (kum•*port*)

To conduct oneself in a manner intended to suggest agreement or compliance

Used in Context

"**Comport** yourself Mr. Conrad! When we're in space, the captain's word is law!"—*Futurama*, "Mobius Dick"

"He was a memorable teacher nonetheless, simply by providing himself as an example in how to **comport** yourself."—"Frank Hall, Coach Who

Chased the Chardon High School Gunman, Is a Hero," Michael Daly

"Nor did he fail to **comport** himself as not only that intimation, but the whole tenor of his character, gave reason to anticipate."—*Sketches and Studies*, Nathaniel Hawthorne

Synonyms: cohere, complement, conform, correspond, fit, harmonize, match

121. Concatenation
noun (*kon*•kat•eh•nay•shun)

A chain; a succession; a series; interdependent connections

Used in Context
"From there, the **concatenation** of escalation led to Israel's preemptive attack."—"Please Shut Up," Gershom Gorenberg

"And then I want to thank you ladies for keeping me, despite all the **concatenations** of this game that allowed my wife to actually set foot on this island. Had you not done that, it wouldn't have happened."—*Survivor*, "Perception Is Not Always Reality"

For example: "With him polling at 2%, it would take a miraculous concatenation of improbable events to make him president."

"There was a **concatenation** accordingly, every link in which had helped to make Ambrose Meyrick's position hopeless."—*The Secret Glory*, Arthur Machen

"Experience shows that one fault, in one distinct detail, is constantly the primary cause of a **concatenation** of other faults."—*Boating*, W. B. Woodgate

Synonyms: association, connection, continuity, link, linkage, nexus, relation

122. Conciliate
verb (kon•*sil*•ee•ate)

To work to bring two sides in a conflict or negotiation together

Used in Context
"Madam, please. I am sure if you found some small means to **conciliate** the queen, then the maids would probably be allowed to remain."—*The Tudors*, "Sister"

"He changed his tone, and attempted to soothe and **conciliate** the minds of his men."—*Pyrrhus*, Jacob Abbott

To say someone is acting in a conciliatory manner is by and large a compliment; i.e., an acknowledgment of reasonability. Usually, there is no tone of rancor associated with this word.

"As stated above, we took pains to **conciliate** him and soothe his hurt feelings."—*Travels in Alaska*, John Muir

Synonyms: appease, calm, calm down, mollify, pacify, placate, please, resolve differences, satisfy, soothe, win over

123. Condescending
adjective (kon•dih•*sen*•ding)

Speaking to someone with an air of superiority, using a tone suggesting you're smarter than them and know more than they do

Used in Context

"That's why I don't come to the goddamn reunions. 'Cause I can't stand that look in your eye. You know, that **condescending**, embarrassed look?"—*Good Will Hunting*

"Oh you're so **condescending**. Your gall is never-ending. We don't want nothing, not a thing from you!"—Twisted Sister, "We're Not Gonna Take It"

Condescension, and being spoken to in a condescending manner, is never well received. People take it as an insult, and commonly remember it. If you find yourself thinking, "I know better than this person and I am now going to put them in their place," can it.

"Cruz is more arrogant, having alienated even some Republican senators with his **condescending** put-downs."—"Marco Rubio, the Real Threat in 2016, Has Been Eclipsed by Ted Cruz," Peter Beinart

"And turn by turn he addressed them all, with a kindly, **condescending** dignity, in French and Italian."—*The Law Inevitable*, Louis Couperus

Synonyms: arrogant, disdainful, egotistic, haughty, patronizing, snobbish, snooty, snotty, supercilious, uppity

124. Conflate
verb (kon•*flait*)

To merge two things together, as in conflating statistics about pornography and sexual assault in a manner to suggest a connection

Used in Context

"And that's why you **conflate** sex and aggression. It's textbook misogyny."—*Two and a Half Men*, "We Called it Mr. Pinky"

"These days, the U.S. stresses level playing fields in foreign elections, a message that less-than-free governments often **conflate** with interference."—"Election Questions Leave US Distrustful, Like Other Nations," Bradley Klapper

"With *Entourage* and Vincent Chase, do you feel like audiences and producers tend to **conflate** you with the character?"—"Adrian Grenier Talks the Economy, the *Entourage* Movie, and the HBO Series' Alleged 'Misogyny,'" Marlow Stern

"Christie will need to assure the party about his own integrity, and his tendency to **conflate** government with his own self."—"Election Night 2013: The Center Speaks," Lloyd Green

Synonyms: amalgamate, blend, combine, commingle, consolidate, fuse, meld, merge, mingle, mix, unify, unite

125. Conformist
noun (kon•*form*•ist)

Someone who conforms—literally; someone who behaves and thinks in what he or she would call a socially acceptable manner; the opposite of being an iconoclast

Used in Context
"An escapist from a **conformist** world, destined to find happiness only in that which cannot be explained."—*House of 1000 Corpses*

"I find myself and my peers thinking, 'This current generation is so corporate, so **conformist**, so apolitical,' Wolf says."—"Who Invented the 'Teenager?,'" Nina Strochlic

"Due to the **conformist** spirit of the dominant crowd, native-born Americans are losing their intellectual leadership."—"The Behavior of Crowds," Everett Dean Martin

Synonyms: adherent, emulator, follower, one of the herd, rubber stamp, sheep, traditionalist, yes-man

126. Consanguineous
adjective (kon•*san*•gwin•us)

Related by blood, descended from the same ancestor

Used in Context
"Oh, eternal powers of the spirit world, oh, well-loved and well-remembered absent friend and **consanguineous** kin, dear Uncle Thaddeus, give us a

You and your parents are consanguineous relatives. The word's source is "sanguine," which means relating to blood.

sign that we may know you are near."—*Lost in Space*, "Ghost in Space"

"Like Vishnu looking after the celestials, thou shouldst always look after all **consanguineous** relatives."—*The Mahabharata of Krishna-Dwaipayana Vyasa*, Translated by Kisari Mohan Ganguli

"The popular idea is that **consanguineous** marriages are bad per se."—*Woman*, William J. Robinson

Synonyms: akin, analogous, associated, connected, interrelated, kin, kindred

127. Consensus
noun (kon•*sen*•sus)

The generally accepted opinion or view about something

Usage Note: "The phrase 'consensus of opinion,' which is not actually redundant . . . has been so often claimed to be a redundancy that many writers avoid it. You are safe in using consensus alone when it is clear you mean consensus of opinion, and most writers in fact do so."—www.merriam-webster.com

Used in Context
"Because there's no national **consensus** against such punishment. So we have to demonstrate, in court now that there is a consensus, that even Americans who believe in the death penalty find these particular executions to be cruel and unusual punishment."—*Oz*, "Good Intentions"

"Testimony from industry executives gave no sense of a **consensus** that they were."—"Boeing Won't Budge as Industry Abandons Lithium-Ion Battery," Clive Irving

"Stride had been having a little too much whisky, was the **consensus** of opinion."—*Forging the Blades*, Bertram Mitford

Synonyms: accord, agreement, concord, concurrence, consent, unanimity, unison, unity

128. Contemporaneous
adjective (kun•tem•por•*ayn*•ee•us)

Happening at the same time as something else

Used in Context
"In the end, any good reporting requires access to the most **contemporaneous** statements."—"The Lost JFK Tapes and What We Now Know," Gerald Posner

"The mobile communication device indicates non-**contemporaneous** life form...She's not from around here, no."—*Doctor Who*, "The Empty Child"

"Her flowering and expansion were **contemporaneous** with the most splendid period of Gothic art."—*Cathedrals of Spain*, John A. Gade

Synonyms: coexistent, coexisting, concomitant, contemporary, simultaneous, synchronous

129. Contentious
adjective (kun•*ten*•shus)

Refers to something that will probably cause problems and arguments between people, commonly over some ideological difference of opinion

Used in Context

"I want a divorce or whatever. It will be **contentious** and last all through next season."—*30 Rock*, "Queen of Jordan 2: The Mystery of the Phantom Pooper"

"India's relationship with its neighbors remains a **contentious** one."— *Two Nations With Different Interests*, Elliot Hannon

"Of the **contentious** scribes He asked: 'What question ye with them?'"—*Jesus the Christ*, James Edward Talmage

Synonyms: antagonistic, arguable, belligerent, combative, controversial, debatable, disagreeable, factious, litigious, petulant, quarrelsome

130. Contiguous
adjective (kun•*tig*•yoo•us)

Refers to countries, states, cities, or properties that share a common border; the word is used to describe something that is situated next to something else

Used in Context

"An alternate world separated by time and space, and yet somehow joined and **contiguous** with our own."—*Super Mario Bros.*

"There are only 22 million people in an area about the size of the **contiguous** 48 States of the United States."—"Deadly Boat Disaster Rattles Australia's Conscience," Raymond Bonner

"Their destination was a large table plain, **contiguous** to that on which we had encamped."—*The Hunters' Feast*, Mayne Reid

Synonyms: abutting, adjacent, adjoining, bordering, juxtaposed, nearby, neighboring, next door to, touching

131. Convergence
noun (kun•*ver*•jents)

The situation when things come together from different directions, either physically, like trains, traffic, or runways; or ideologically, as in minds converging on a single idea

Used in Context
"Cauchy was the first to make a rigorous study of the conditions for **convergence** of an infinite series. And was concerned with developing the basic theorems of the calculus as rigorously as possible."—*21*

"But all we've discovered is that the blaze was started from a great distance through the refraction and **convergence** of light." – *A Series of Unfortunate Events*

"However frightful Nader found it, the concept intrigued him that '**convergence**' could be found among disparate groups."—"Ralph Nader and Grover Norquist: Washington's Most Unlikely Bromance," Eleanor Clift

"At the point of **convergence** there seemed to be a narrow passage."—
Legacy, James H. Schmitz

Synonyms: coming together, confluence, crossroads, intersection, junction, meeting, merging, union

132. Convivial
adjective (kun•*viv*•ee•ul)

Friendly, agreeable, enjoyable

Used in Context
"This **convivial** mask he wears, along with his omnipresent flask, is obscuring a deep hurt stemming from his father."—"*The Spectacular Now*, Starring Shailene Woodley and Miles Teller, Is One of Sundance's Best," Marlow Stern

"He said he and other winemakers produce pot wine in small quantities, to be shared in '**convivial** moments with like-minded people.'"—"Marijuana-Laced Wine Grows More Fashionable in California Wine Country," Michael Steinberger

"He could scarcely be called gay; yet few persons more tended to animate the general spirits of a **convivial** circle."—*Zanoni*, Edward Bulwer Lytton

Synonyms: companionable, cordial, festive, gay, genial, happy, hospitable, jocund, jovial, mirthful, pleasant, sociable, vivacious, warm, welcoming

Deserving blame or punishment

Used in Context

"If your husband won't leave, then you go. You are now an accessory after the fact. You are **culpable**. You, your children, you could lose everything you own."—*Breaking Bad*, "Mas"

"But in this case, police and protestors alike are **culpable** for the mayhem on the streets."—"Occupy Oakland's Violent Turn Proves the Movement Has Lost Its Way," Christopher Haugh

"It would be **culpable** to allow such a girl to enter on the world with such a stigma as being expelled from school would mean."—*A Modern Tomboy*, L. T. Meade

Synonyms: answerable, at fault, blameworthy, caught in the act, caught red-handed, censurable, dirty, guilty, impeachable, liable, responsible, to blame

D

134. Dearth
noun (durth)

A scarcity, shortage, or lack of something

Used in Context

"Meanwhile, as I'm sure you're aware, there's a **dearth** of employees in a whole host of hands-on professions."—*Madam Secretary,* "Another Benghazi"

"The **dearth** of homes for sale is frustrating buyers."—"More Homes Sold in the D.C. Area Last Month Than Any November in the Past Seven Years," Kathy Orton

"Hillary Clinton did not grant Mr. Tapper another interview after a sit-down in May, when he pressed her on her **dearth** of news conferences."—"In Trump Era, Uncompromising TV News Should Be the Norm, Not the Exception," Jim Rutenberg

"The FDA is hoping to remedy the **dearth** of knowledge with a plea aimed at influential drugmakers."—"Why Male Breast Cancer Is Back in the Limelight, "Kevin Zawacki

Synonyms: absence, deficiency, drought, famine, inadequacy, lack, need, scarcity, shortage

135. Debase
verb (dee•*base*)

To reduce the quality, value, or worth of something, particularly something abstract, like a legacy or reputation

Used in Context

"And do the cutesy stuff? The lighter side of the news? Lower and **debase** myself for the amusement of total strangers?"—*Bruce Almighty*

"Enviable because political contests—certainly this is true of the most intensely fought and consequential ones—**debase** emotions and sanctify dishonesty."—"2016 Should Make Us Rethink Our Approach to Politicians," Barton Swaim

"Our economy is predatory and works to **debase** all human life for the common wage-earning class."—"A Universal Basic Income Is a Poor Tool to Fight Poverty," Eduardo Porter

"Instead, I endeavored to strive even harder so that I would not **debase** his legacy."—"If You Grow Up Indian-American, College Graduation Isn't Enough," Anita Raghavan

Synonyms: abase, belittle, defile, degrade, demean, disgrace, dishonor, humble, humiliate, lower, make worse, shame, vitiate

136. Declaim
verb (dee•*clame*)

To make a speech, often in a forceful way

Used in Context
"About a particular word, a pejorative word, a word that's been use to **declaim** the vagina, and she needed to help me reconceive this word."—*The Vagina Monologues*

"It was demanded of psychologists that they **declaim** on all that screaming and its meaning."—"'You've Got to Be Kidding': Why Adults Dismissed The Beatles in 1964," Michael Tomasky

"Having actors **declaim** Shakespeare in between the pieces has, if anything, a prophylactic effect."—"The Playing's the Thing: NSO Shines Despite, Not Because of, Shakespeare Gimmick," Anne Midgette

"That's because, unlike the freedom we **declaim**, the French actually cherish *Liberté*."—"Patriot Act Idea Rises in France, and Is Ridiculed," Matt Apuzzo, Steven Erlanger

Synonyms: declare, hold forth, inveigh, orate, proclaim, pronounce, speak, utter

137. Decorous
adjective (*dek*•or•us)

Describes behavior that is dignified, respectful, and usually conforming with societal and cultural mores

Used in Context

"The children, already sitting in a **decorous** ring on their low chairs, seemed after the first surprise to approve of Phyllis."—*The Rose Garden Husband*, Margaret Widdemer

"A **decorous** group of nine panelists presented their positions one at a time, following distinctly un-Israeli rules of etiquette."—"Israel's New Election Discourse," Don Futterman

"It's not decent, it's not **decorous** to laugh at any incident in the lives of holy men."—*The Bramleighs Of Bishop's Folly*, Charles James Lever

Synonyms: becoming, correct, decent, proper, respectable, well-behaved, well-mannered

138. Decry
verb (dee•*kry*)

To openly and usually harshly criticize someone or a policy

Used in Context

"The device that Dr. Granger was testing could save countless lives, and the person who attempted to **decry** it was an imposter, so…how could we not?"—*Elementary*, "The Hound of the Cancer Cells"

"He accused conservatives of hypocrisy, saying they **decry** political correctness from liberals but act offended about issues such as the secularization of the Christmas holiday."—"Obama Says He's Received Taunting Letters Since Trump's Victory," Dave Boyer

"The senator is just the latest public figure to **decry** student use of so-called study drugs without a formal diagnosis."—"Study Drugs Under Fire: Can Chuck Schumer Stop 'Academic Doping?,'" Caitlin Dickson

"Diaz said protesters **decry** the 'company's trafficking on indigenous cultural heritage.'"—"With Disney's *Moana*, Hollywood Almost Gets It Right: Indigenous People Weigh In," Alli Joseph

Synonyms: belittle, condemn, criticize, deprecate, derogate, disparage, run down

139. De facto
adjective (dee•*fak*•tow)

Happening or existing in reality as a fact, whether or not it is legal or acceptable

Used in Context
"All we need is a place to meet in the city. A **de facto** safe house."—*Homeland*, "Good Night"

"After leading the initial surveys, he became the **de facto** spokesperson on the catastrophe."—"Terry Hughes: Reef Sentinel," Daniel Cressey

"On Monday, they celebrated his resignation and acted as the **de facto** victors of the referendum."—"Italy Enters a Transition Phase, Complex but Familiar, as Its Premier Quits," Jason Horowitz

"The language of this bill is a **de facto** abortion ban for most pregnant federal prisoners."—"The GOP's Hidden Ban on Prison Abortions," Harold Pollack

Synonyms: actually, beyond doubt, effectively, genuinely, indisputably, in fact, in reality, really, truly, veritably

140. Deferential
adjective (def•er•*en*•chul)

Being respectful and polite to others

Used in Context
"It's the double standard. The separate quarters, the **deferential** treatment. It's the way you practically pulled my chair out from me when we first met."—*G.I. Jane*

"At speechwriting meetings, Michel was **deferential** but quick with answers, just as the president liked."—"Bush's Ghostwriter," Bryan Curtis

"A **deferential** waiter informed the American that it had been taken with every possible care to his suite."—*The Man Upstairs*, P. G. Wodehouse

Synonyms: admiring, civil, courteous, ingratiating, obedient, obsequious, reverential, submissive

141. Deign
verb (dane)

To do something reluctantly, yet fully; to do something with an attitude that you're too important to be doing what you're doing

Used in Context

"And what's worse, you don't care. Because this place, where so many people would die to work, you only **deign** to work. And you want to know why she doesn't kiss you on the forehead and give you a gold star on your homework at the end of the day."—*The Devil Wears Prada*

"Nor does she **deign** to look at you until you are back in the city street where you met."—*Seductio Ad Absurdum*, Emily Hahn

"Should we be grateful for whatever music they **deign** to release and grade them on a curve because of it?"—"*High Hopes* Review: Bruce Springsteen Lowers the Bar," Andrew Romano

Synonyms: agree, condescend, consent, demean yourself, force yourself, patronize, stoop

142. Deleterious
adjective (dee•leh•*teer*•ee•us)

Describes something that has a harmful effect

Used in Context

"I can sue. If you tell the papers about Kathy Selden, it would be 'detrimental and **deleterious**' to my career. I could sue you for the whole studio."—*Singin' In The Rain*

"But the truth is that they have real and **deleterious** effects on conservative politics."—"D'Souza's Never-Ending Right-Wing Hustle," Jamelle Bouie

"Corporations exerted an unchecked and **deleterious** influence on the lives of workers."—"Impeach the Supreme Court Justices If They Overturn Health-Care Law," David R. Dow

"I hope the bill will pass without any **deleterious** amendments."— *Mark Twain's Speeches*, Mark Twain

Synonyms: deadly, destructive, detrimental, injurious, lethal, pernicious, poisonous, ruinous, toxic, venomous

143. Delineate
verb (dee•*lin*•ee•ate)

To explain something in detail

Used in Context
"Well, they're just a little difficult to **delineate**, but, I mean, yes, there are two sides to every story."—*Breaking Bad*, "Caballo Sin Nombre"

"Stereotypes exist to **delineate** but also in order to be defied."—"In Praise of *Awkward*: OMFG MTV, Like, Really Gets High School," Amy Zimmerman

"She has parcelled out her purgatory, as we **delineate** this upper world on a map."—*The Parables of Our Lord*, William Arnot

Synonyms: define, demarcate, depict, describe, detail, draft, limn, outline, portray, represent, sketch out, trace

144. Demagogue
noun (*dem•uh•gog*)

A leader who tries to stir up people by appeals to emotion and prejudice

Used in Context

"Especially if, like the *New York Post* or a borough president, they can score **demagogue** points by doing so."—"Stop Moping! The Marathon Is Exactly What New York Needs Right Now," Jay Michaelson

A demagogue uses polarizing propaganda that motivates members of an in-group to hate and scapegoat some out-group(s), largely by promising certainty, stability.

Political candidates often use demagoguery to appeal to their core constituents. Some use rhetoric to instill fear in people of Muslims, African-Americans, Mexicans, gays, transgenders, etc.

"Yet Castro was also a manipulative **demagogue**, an oppressor and a relentless persecutor of those who dared challenge his will."—"Fidel Castro: Guerrilla Leader, Dictator—and An Unrepentant Revolutionary," Simon Tisdall

"D'Onofrio plays the Wizard as a kind of insecure **demagogue**, saying he was interested in the character's psychological dimensions."—"NBC's *Emerald City* Gives Dorothy a Gun and Sends Her Off To a Very Different Oz," Steven Zeitchik

"This so-called V and his accomplice, Evey Hammond . . . neo-**demagogues**, spouting their message of hate. A delusional and aberrant voice delivering a terrorist's ultimatum."—*V for Vendetta*

Synonyms: agitator, fanatic, firebrand, fomenter, hothead, rabble-rouser

145. Denigrate
verb (*den*•ih•grate)

To defame someone, to sully their reputation

Used in Context
"You want to make a play for Rayna Hecht, by all means, have a meeting and make your pitch. But to **denigrate** me? To spread lies about my dedication to my firm?!"—*The Good Wife*, "The One Percent"

"I do not **denigrate** the good intentions of those who gave birth to these abject social policy failures."—"A Business Manifesto to Make Poverty History," John Blundell

"You may have noticed, not to **denigrate** anyone, but this is a transitional neighborhood. I mean, demographically speaking, you still have a lot of marginal types."—*The Sopranos*, "Johnny Cakes"

Synonyms: belittle, besmirch, disparage, impugn, insult, libel, malign, slander, vilify

146. Deplorable
adjective (dee•*plor*•uh•bull)

Worthy of severe condemnation or censure; dreadful

Used in Context
"You'll have to get used to Dr. Malcolm, he suffers from a **deplorable** excess of personality, especially for a mathematician."—*Jurassic Park*

"Deplorable" can also serve as a *noun*.

Hillary Clinton got into a bit of public relations trouble during the run-up to the 2016 Presidential election when she described Donald Trump's supporters as a "basket of deplorables."

"A landlord's worst nightmare is having a tenant who leaves the place in **deplorable** condition."—"Tips for Negotiating Cheaper Rent," Lia Sestric

"We should have no hesitation in calling **deplorable** attitudes **deplorable**—without imagining that those who hold them are **deplorable** people."—"Why Trump Is Different—and Must Be Repelled,"—Adam Gopnik

"We passed the night miserably wet and cold, and in the morning I heard heavy complaints of our **deplorable** situation."—*A Narrative Of The Mutiny, On Board His Majesty's Ship* Bounty; *And The Subsequent Voyage Of Part Of The Crew, In The Ship's Boat*, William Bligh

Synonyms: appalling, awful, despicable, ghastly, terrible, unpleasant, vile

147. Despoil
verb (deh•*spoyl*)

To strip everything of value from a place; pillage, to plunder

Used in Context
"**Despoil**? For what purpose?...By keeping us in constant turmoil, they hope to force the council to accede to their demands."—*Star Trek*, "The Cloud Miners"

"So I called Bergman and said, 'Do you mind if I **despoil** your script?'"—"Mel Brooks Is Always Funny and Often Wise in This 1975 *Playboy* Interview," Alex Belth

"Time was precious; he therefore hastened to **despoil** his victim, in whose vestments he clothed himself."—*The Guide of the Desert*, Gustave Aimard

Synonyms: damage, deface, defile, denude, desecrate, loot, plunder, ruin, sack, vandalize, wreck

148. Desultory
adjective (dee•*sul*•tor•ee)

Lacking order, fitful, disconnected

Used in Context
"I want you to be honest. I mean, if it's stilted or **desultory**, don't sugarcoat it. The critics never do."—*The Secret Life of Marilyn Monroe*, Arthur Miller

"Most of that is the **desultory** ticky-tacky kind that litters the right side of people's Facebook profiles."—"Facebook's Dilemma: Invade Privacy or Go Bust," David Frum

"In the **desultory** history of this question, two facts have been stated requiring distinct proof."—*The Felon's Track*, Michael Doheny

Synonyms: aimless, chaotic, erratic, haphazard, indiscriminate, orderless, rambling, random, unfocused, unsystematic, without focus

149. Deus ex machina
noun (*day*•us•*mak*•in•nuh)

Literally means "God of the machine," and it refers to a character or event that comes out of nowhere to solve a plot problem in a story.

Used in Context
"Then out of the mist, a whirring of helicopter blades, and, **deus ex machina**, a man descends from the chopper to winch you aboard."— "Girl Rescued by Prince William Speaks!," Tom Sykes

"By the end of each half hour, conflict has been quickly resolved, often by some **deus ex machina**."—"Happy 25th Birthday, *Golden Girls!*" Andy Dehnart

"But there was always a **deus ex machina** for us when we were in trouble."—*Our Hundred Days in Europe*, Oliver Wendell Holmes

Synonyms: contrivance, device, divine intervention, gimmick

150. Devolve
verb (dee•*volv*)

To transfer power; also, to deteriorate slowly over time

Used in Context
"Most marriages **devolve** eventually . . . that's all it is, it's a business partnership, with the added benefit of attraction."—*Arthur*

"This will, inevitably, **devolve** into the comedian freaking out and crying on the floor."—"Brett Gelman Has Dinner with Your Favorite TV Sidekicks," Rich Goldstein

"He must be shown that it is immoral for man to **devolve** back to the animal level."—*An Outline of Sexual Morality*, Kenneth Ingram

"Devolve" is essentially the opposite of "evolve."

Synonyms: delegate, transfer, pass to, weaken

151. Dialectic
noun (dye•uh•*lek*•tik)

The practice of logical discussion of ideas, principles; the totality of that process

Used in Context

"The historian Arnold Toynbee famously theorized that history proceeds by a special type of **dialectic**: challenge and response."—"Evan Bayh's Shameful Retreat," Lee Siegel

"They are the yin and the yang of the whole film and they dance the **dialectic** to perfection."—"Polanski's Brilliant Comeback," Simon Schama

"According to Hegel the **dialectic** is the self-development of the Idea."— *Feuerbach: The Roots of the Socialist Philosophy*, Frederick Engels

Synonyms: argument, controversy, debate, deliberation, dispute

152. Dichotomy
noun (dye•*kot*•uh•mee)

Separating a process or debate into two distinct sections; the tonal meaning suggests these two parts are in direct conflict with, and/or contradict each other; i.e; the dichotomy of good vs. bad

Used in Context

"The few possess much, while the masses possess little but their television sets. This **dichotomy** led to revolution in which Antoinette and her husband were beheaded. Today, leaders are impeached rather than beheaded."—*Bill & Ted's Excellent Adventure*

"No, the whole point of a superhero with a secret identity is the **dichotomy**."—"Model Minority Rage: Why the Hulk Should Be an Asian Guy," Arthur Chu

"One almost senses a **dichotomy** between Franklin the politician and Franklin the man and moralist."—*Benjamin Franklin*, Frank Luther Mott

"She came to us a stranger, but she left with another name, friend. A lot of **dichotomy** in such a small package."—*Northern Exposure*, "My Mother, My Sister"

Synonyms: difference of opinion, disagreement, dispute, disunion, separation

153. Didactic
adjective (die•*dak*•tik)

Conveying instruction; teaching some moral lesson

Used in Context

"Fascinating to hear the same arrogant quality in your own voice. You are a bit of a pendant, Jason, a bit **didactic**."—*Criminal Minds*, "Broken Mirror"

"So she has chosen the path as her literary heroes, Charles Dickens and George Orwell: the entertaining but **didactic** novel."—"Join Caitlin Moran's Riotous Feminist Revolution," Lizzie Crocker

"Resuming the main thread of the argument, it may be said that the Italians also shared the Roman partiality for **didactic** poetry."—*Renaissance in Italy: Italian Literature*, John Addington Symonds

Synonyms: donnish, edifying, educational, informative, instructive, pedagogic, pedantic, preachy, teaching

When someone is didactic, they're teaching or presenting information, oftentimes using a story, and there is commonly a moral component to the instruction.

For example: *Animal Farm* didactically speaks to the evils of Communism.

154. Diffident
adjective (*diff*•ih•dent)

Lacking self confidence, insecure, reserved, timid

Used in Context

"The quality of a young lady's breeding is indicated by her deportment when elders are present. At such times, her manner should be sedate and **diffident**."—*Heidi*

"He was charming, **diffident**, but above all very friendly, with no airs or graces."—"How John Lennon Rediscovered His Music in Bermuda," *The Telegraph*

"Serious men, quiet and **diffident**, are most terrible in their explosions of wrath."—*The Four Horsemen of the Apocalypse*, Vicente Blasco Ibanez

Synonyms: bashful, demure, embarrassed, hesitant, humble, meek, modest, quiet, reticent, self-effacing, shy, unassuming

155. Digression
noun (dye•gres•shun)

Abandoning a narrative thread when speaking or in writing to talk about something irrelevant to the main topic

Used in Context

"At least that's what I pray it is. Lighthearted and momentary **digression**. The briefest indulgement in automotive pleasure."—*Sin City*

"St. Bernard's may punish you, even for the slightest **digression**, but it'll never cast you out, even for the largest."—*Detroit Rock City*

"From this **digression** into the sphere of personal reminiscences I return now and take up again the thread of the narrative."—*Russia*, Donald Mackenzie Wallace

"From this **digression**, let us return, and resume our Journal."—*A Journal of a Young Man of Massachusetts*, Benjamin Waterhouse

Synonyms: aside, deflection, departure from the subject, detour, deviation, excursion, footnote, foray, parenthesis

156. Dilatory
adjective (*dill*•uh•tor•ee)

Inclined to put off what ought to be done at once

Used in Context

"He apologizes for running late, or as he puts it, being **dilatory**."—*Hot in Cleveland*, "Everything Goes Better With Vampires"

Dilatory means to delay, and is commonly used as a tactic.

"He had been **dilatory** but now he intended to get down to business."—*The Lady Doc*, Caroline Lockhart

Dilatory political tactics include the filibuster to delay a pending vote.

It can also be used to describe someone who is a procrastinator.

"Decision making is slow, acquisition processes are **dilatory**, and maintenance of the equipment bought is poor."—"India's Tryst with Terror," Kanwal Sibal

Synonyms: dallying, delaying, lax, lazy, negligent, putting off, slack, tardy, time-wasting, unhurried

157. Diminution
noun (dim•ih•*new*•shun)

The reduction or diminishing of something

Used in Context

"But human freedom, then, was used in such a way as to diminish goodness in the world, and that **diminution**, that lack, that missing goodness, that is what we call evil."—*The Case for Faith*

"Equally important, the **diminution** of the middle orders threatens one of the historic sources of economic vitality and innovation."—"In the Future We'll All Be Renters: America's Disappearing Middle Class," Joel Kotkin

"This **diminution** of force was not, in itself, an object of much concern."—*The Life of George Washington*, John Marshall

Synonyms: abatement, alleviation, attenuation, cutback, decay, decline, decrease, dwindling, lessening, shrinking

158. Disclaim
verb (dis•*klame*)

To deny responsibility for something

Used in Context
"Surface and identify self. Unless I receive an immediate answer, I **disclaim** responsibility for the consequences. End of message."—*The Bedford Incident*

"You **disclaim** these voices from the past, but to LGBT people, your voice sounds a lot like theirs."—"Do LGBTs Owe Christians an Olive Branch? Try The Other Way Around," Jay Michaelson

"He hastened to **disclaim** the extravagant generosity of which she accused him."—*The Black Bag*, Louis Joseph Vance

Synonyms: abjure, contradict, decline, disaffirm, disavow, disown, negate, recant, reject, renounce, repudiate, revoke, spurn, turn your back on, wash hands of

159. Disconcerting
adjective (dis•kun•*sert*•ing)

Refers to something that makes you feel uneasy, distressed, or confused

Used in Context

"I'm aware this is probably **disconcerting** news, but I'm willing to wager this man was elected sheriff sometime in the last two years."— *Django Unchained*

"The blush was **disconcerting**, but the sensation, on the whole, was pleasurable."—*Emmy Lou*, George Madden Martin

"Yes, it is **disconcerting** to see some of our best and brightest leaving the halls of Congress."—"Olympia Snowe Latest to Leave as the Senate's Center Collapses," Mark McKinnon

"It is these **disconcerting** surprises which try one's spirit more than anything else."—*Letters from Mesopotamia*, Robert Palmer

Synonyms: agitating, alarming, bewildering, demoralizing, disturbing, frustrating, perplexing, unsettling

160. Discordant
adjective (dis•*kor*•dant)

Describes the relationship when you are in disagreement with someone; also describes an unpleasant cacophony of sounds; off-key

Used in Context

"Absolutely lost…they look **discordant**. It seems like I need to start over with something."—*Project Runway*, "Larger Than Life"

"But people now had enough of a sense of Obama to know that the statement was **discordant** with his whole approach and demeanor."—"Bittergate," David Plouffe

"They're **discordant**, disconnected. Stark's already got them turning on each other."—*Avengers: Age of Ultron*

"No doubt Romney was sincere in wanting to help the homeless woman, but it sounded a **discordant** note."—"Romney's Embarrassment of Riches," Howard Kurtz

"Again that laugh—so musical in sound, yet so **discordant** to my heart."—*Curious, if True*, Elizabeth Gaskell

Synonyms: antagonistic, cacophonous, dissonant, harsh, incompatible, jarring, quarreling, strident, uncongenial

161. Discredit
verb (dis•*kred*•it)

To defame someone, to injure their credibility, to question someone's veracity

Used in Context

"Do tell. Is there a way to **discredit** the state's shrink, Dr. Rodeheaver? Unless you **discredit** the shrink, Carl Lee does not have a chance."—*A Time to Kill*

"Instead, he rushed to use the firearms issue as one more tool to bludgeon and **discredit** his Republican opposition."—"Angry Gun-Control Debate Does Damage to Both the Right and the Left," Michael Medved

"Politicians used 9/11 and the new wars that resulted as a wedge issue to win elections and **discredit** opponents."—"The Lessons of 9/11," Richard A. Clarke

"Things have taken place that may be explained in two ways; both explanations do you **discredit**."—"Pepita Ximenez," Juan Valera

"The Civil Rights Movement was running a voter's registration drive. Rumor is, Shaw was working on some arms deal to **discredit** the Civil Rights Movement. Nobody really knows what they were doing there, but hell, they stood out like cotton balls."—*JFK*

"I want you to give me every single copy of that obscenity that the two of you made to **discredit** Hank. That DVD. Every single copy. You understand me?"—*Breaking Bad*, "Ozymandias"

Synonyms: bring into disrepute, damage the reputation of, destroy, disgrace, dishonor, disparage, harm the reputation of, ruin, shame, slander, slur, smear, vilify,

162. Discursive
adjective (dis•*kur*•sihv)

Wandering from one subject to another; also, its second definition means using logic and reason to make a point or win an argument

Used in Context

"To say things in a roundabout way, your last two answers have had very little of the **discursive** quality about them."—*Monty Python's Flying Circus*, "Royal Episode 13"

"And being alone, he is not concise, but garrulous and **discursive**."—*The Poetry Of Robert Browning*, Stopford A. Brooke

"I shall establish myself as a mild eccentric. **Discursive**, withdrawn, but possessing one or two loveable habits, such as muttering to myself as I bumble along innocent pavements."—*Tinker Tailor Soldier Spy*, "Return to the Circus"

Synonyms: deviating, digressive, erratic, excursive, long-winded, prolix, rambling

163. Disenfranchise
verb (dis•en•*fran*•chize)

To deprive a person or a group of rights or privileges, especially the right to vote

Used in Context

"They teach us self-government, and they **disenfranchise** us."—*Strike!*

"He implied that the opponents who are calling for him to drop out of the race are seeking to **disenfranchise** the voters."—"Weiner's Desperate Rockaway Trip," Michael Daly

"Translation: **disenfranchise** voters who traditionally are part of the Democratic coalition, namely minorities."—"Bigotry Is Back, 60 Years

After Brown v. Board of Education," Dean Obeidallah

"Not only this, but he proposed to the provincial assembly a measure to **disenfranchise** all persons who have concubines."—*China, Japan and the USA*, John Dewey

Synonyms: circumscribe, deprive, hobble, keep under thumb, oppress, restrict, subjugate, suppress

164. Dishearten
verb (dis•*hart*•en)

To make someone lose their enthusiasm for an idea or a project; to shoot down someone's hopeful notions

Used in Context
"Meanwhile, rumor has it the LAPD has set up a not-so-welcome wagon to **dishearten** the criminal element from filling the void left by Mickey's absence."—*LA Confidential*

"Now and then a subscriber withdrew his name, which always cut him to the quick, but did not **dishearten** him."—*John James Audubon*, John Burroughs

"The incident was all that was needed to **dishearten** and disgust him."—*The Crisis, Complete*, Winston Churchill

Synonyms: bring down, crush, dampen the spirits of, deject, demoralize, depress, discourage, disincline, dispirit, humiliate, put a damper on, sadden

165. Disinclined
adjective (dis•in•*klynd*)

An unwillingness to do something; a reluctance to agree to something

Used in Context
"Once people believe something, they are **disinclined** to change their minds—even when overwhelming evidence suggests they should."—"Untruth and Consequences in Ferguson," Matt Lewis

"I felt hungry and greedy and very sad, and **disinclined** to fight."—*The Martian*, George Du Maurier

"You shoved a knife in her ear, so I think she'll be **disinclined** to chat."—*Luther*, "Episode #1.2"

Synonyms: averse, balking, hesitating, loath, not in the mood, opposed, uneager, unenthusiastic, unwilling

166. Disingenuous
adjective (dis•in•*jen*•yoo•us)

Not straightforward or candid; insincere or calculating

Used in Context
"We're happy to be back, but I would be **disingenuous** to say that things will be as they were before, at last in the short term."—*Pretty Little Liars*, "Surfing the Aftershocks"

"He would rather endorse someone with genuine doubts than someone with **disingenuous** beliefs."—"*The Good Wife's* Religion Politics: Voters Have No Faith in Alicia's Atheism," Regina Lizik

"Certain simple purposes emerged from the **disingenuous** muddle of her feelings and desires."—*Ann Veronica*, H. G. Wells

> This word is related to the word "genuine" in that a disingenuous person is not being genuine. That's why the antonyms to disingenuous are "honest" and "sincere."

Synonyms: crooked, cunning, deceitful, devious, dishonest, duplicitous, guileful, hypocritical, insincere, mendacious, shifty, underhanded, untruthful

167. Disparity
noun (dis•*par*•ih•tee)

Inequality; a notable difference between things or people

Used in Context
"The astonishing **disparity** between Adam's perception and his actual route is there for all to see."—*Mythbusters*, "Walk a Straight Line"

"The **disparity** has left some dealers convinced that maps Smiley stole now hang on the walls of private collectors around the world."—"The Million-Dollar Map Thief," Nick Romeo

"Even in the medieval era this **disparity** made Christians uncomfortable."—"Oops! Jesus' Last Steps Are in the Wrong Place," Candida Moss

"He smiled ironically as he remembered the **disparity** between his own fortunes and those of his former wife."—*Otherwise Phyllis*, Meredith Nicholson

Synonyms: discrepancy, disproportion, dissimilarity. divergence, gap, imbalance, inconsistency, unevenness

168. Dispassionate
adjective (dis•*pas*•shun•ate)

Not allowing emotions to influence a decision

Used in Context

"You know, it's my job as a photographer to maintain a distance, to be a '**dispassionate** observer.' It's easier said than done."—*Bones*, "The Survivor of the Soap"

"Precisely because of their obsession with numbers and data, they are **dispassionate** about social issues."—"The Insurance Industry's Liberal Turn," Daniel Gross

"Mrs. Francis Ogilvie bore the character of being a cold and **dispassionate** woman."—*Peter and Jane*, Sarah MacNaughtan

Synonyms: calm, composed, cool, detached, disinterested, impartial, neutral, nonpartisan, objective, unbiased, unemotional, unflustered, unruffled

169. Disputatious
adjective (dis•pyoo•*tay*•shush)

Extremely argumentative, often without justification or cause

Used in Context

"You are always in a **disputatious** mood when you choose that pipe."—
The Adventures of Sherlock Holmes: The Copper Beeches

"It's simply impossible for me to 'belong' to this quarrelsome, hostile, **disputatious**, and deservedly infamous group."—"Anne Rice's Christianity Crisis," Kirsten Powers

"The captain had just given him some instructions, but he did not seem to take kindly to them, and was inclined to be **disputatious**."—*Reminiscences of Travel in Australia, America, and Egypt*, Richard Tangye

> Another iteration of this word (but having the same meaning) is the adjective "disputative."

Synonyms: antagonistic, belligerent, cantankerous, combative, confrontational, contentious, litigious, pugnacious, quarrelsome

170. Dissemble
verb (dis•*sem*•buhl)

To pretend in order to conceal facts that you don't want someone else to know; to hide your real motives

Used in Context

"Instead of too big to fail, they embrace the unfettered right to cheat and **dissemble**."—"We Need a New Ross Perot," Joel Kotkin

"A sudden sense of shame at being compelled to **dissemble** before a subordinate had lashed him across the face."—*A Man's Woman*, Frank Norris

"To **dissemble** for a month or so would not hurt him, and might even amuse him as a new game."—*Halcyone,* Elinor Glyn

Synonyms: beat around the bush, camouflage, conceal, dither, evade, fake, falsify, feign, hedge, put on an act, stonewall

171. Dissolute
adjective (*dis•oh•loot*)

Overdoing eating, drinking, drugs, and sex until it reaches the level of being harmful and ridiculous

Used in Context
"You have turned out to be not a normal leader, but a **dissolute**, abnormal, moral imbecile. There's only one thing left to do and you know what that is. There's but one way out, and you better take it."—*J. Edgar*

"Even if they do not manage to take and hold power, they are examples of the **dissolute** lives that sons of dictators often lead."—"Dictators' Sons, From Egypt to Libya, Are Doomed," Stephen Kinzer

"The worst was, that the **dissolute** life he led grievously affected the business."—*Fruitfulness,* Emile Zola

Synonyms: debauched, degenerate, depraved, intemperate, lascivious, lecherous, self-indulgent, unconstrained, wanton

172. Divergent
adjective (dye•*ver*•gent)

Deviating from what is considered the normal path or plan

Used in Context

"Eventually, we found a new respect for our **divergent** cultures and traditions. The efforts of people like Quarren and the Doctor paved the way for our unity."—*Star Trek*, "Living Witness"

"The two even used to kid each other about their **divergent** political affiliations."—"One Woman's War on Gangs," Christine Pelisek

In 2014, the science fiction film *Divergent* was released. It was directed by Neil Burger and based on the novel of the same name by Veronica Roth.

"Burr could get no help from any of the **divergent** parties he had attempted to gain."—*A History of the United States*, Cecil Chesterton

Synonyms: conflicting, contradictory, contrary, differing, disparate, opposing, variant

173. Doppelganger
noun (*dop*•ul•gang•er)

A counterpart of another person; i.e., someone who looks exactly like another person; sometimes used to refer to a ghostly apparition of a living person

Used in Context

"So she embarked on a quest to find her Palestinian **doppelganger**."
—"Israel, Hamas, WhatsApp and Hacked Phones in the Gaza Psy-War," Itay Hod

"Mr. Westfall began to watch for Louise and to trot after her like a **doppelganger**."—*Danger! A True History of a Great City's Wiles and Temptations*, William Howe

"So, a while back, we discovered the most amazing thing: Lily had a **doppelganger** who was a Russian stripper."—*How I Met Your Mother*, "46 Minutes"

"The final part of the ritual: Klaus must drink the blood of the **doppelganger** to the point of your death."—*The Vampire Diaries*, "The Last Day"

Synonyms: alter ego, double, duplicate, mirror image, spirit, twin

174. Duplicity
noun (doo•*plis*•ih•tee)

The act of lying, being deceptive, dissembling, betraying

Used in Context

"We are here today because we find ourselves in a world where **duplicity** and theft are tested daily as replacements for innovation and perseverance."—*Duplicity*

"As the intelligence community examines bin Laden's laptop and other gear, the extent of that **duplicity** will become clearer."—"Afghanistan's Role in Osama bin Laden Raid," Bruce Riedel

"Has diplomacy been entirely stripped of fraud and **duplicity**?"—*History Of Florence And Of The Affairs Of Italy*, Niccolo Machiavelli

In 2009, the crime thriller *Duplicity* was released. It was written and directed by Tony Gilroy, and starred Clive Owen and Julia Roberts. It was both hailed and criticized for its very complex plot.

Synonyms: artifice, betrayal, chicanery, deception, dirty dealing, dirty trick, dishonesty, disloyalty, fraud, fraudulence, guile, hypocrisy, Judas kiss, perfidy, skullduggery, stab in back, treachery, two-facedness, unfaithfulness

E

175. e.g.
(adverb) (eee•gee)

For example (*exempli gratia*)

Examples:

- I can play quite a few musical instruments; e.g., the flute, the guitar, and the piano.
- She likes a lot of Italian foods; e.g. pasta, pizza, and Italian pastry.
- I'm a big fan of Stephen King books; e.g., *The Shining, The Stand, The Green Mile,* and *Misery.*

Used in Context

"Yesterday, **e.g.**, I was interviewed on leadership and global crises during the annual 'Out on Wall Street' gathering."—"Petraeus Will Appear at an Event Featuring the ACORN 'Pimp,'" Ben Jacobs

"**E.g.** means for example."—*Get Shorty*

"Well, according to the *Newville Journal of Medicine,* monkeys are easily influenced by positive reinforcement; **e.g.**, the giving of a banana."—*Jimmy Neutron, Boy Genius*

Synonyms: for the sake of example, such as

176. Ebullient
adjective (eh•*byool*•ee•ent)

Extremely happy and excited

Used in Context
"I'm **ebullient**! I'm bubbling with glee!"—*The Simpsons*, "My Fair Laddy"

"But it's the **ebullient** 'Faith,' one of two original compositions, that marks the return to movie music after 20 years for Stevie Wonder."—"Stevie Wonder, Adam Levine and Pharrell Williams Could Join the Original Song Race," Michael Ordona

"Such films as *Halloween III* and *Sorcerer* used electronics to generate moody tones and alien textures—far from the **ebullient** sounds of new-wave pop."—"Loved the Synths in *Stranger Things*? Flash Back with Survive," Aaron Leitko

"As a primary step he was obliged to suppress his **ebullient** brother-in-law."—*The President*, Alfred Henry Lewis

Synonyms: buoyant, cheerful, enthusiastic, good-natured, high-spirited, in good spirits, jolly, jovial, joyful, merry, smiling

177. Eclectic
adjective (eh•*klek*•tik)

Made up of or combining elements from varying sources

Used in Context
"An **eclectic** mix of idealistic and opportunistic politicians and NGOs

I once recorded a commercial for our university radio station WNHU in which I said that the station offered an "eclectic mojo" of music.

mobilized people against land acquisitions."—"What Happened to India?," David Frum

"But now they're home to edgy, ultracreative establishments, a new generation of dining inspired by an **eclectic** range of traditions."—"6 Standout Restaurants in Los Angeles Strip Malls," Sam Lubell

"Its **eclectic**, bohemian decor of old furniture combined with piles of wood and snaking electrical cords turned into a death trap."—"Oakland Artists Fear Crackdown After Ghost Ship Fire," Jocelyn Gecker

"His **eclectic** ear enabled Atlantic to have Aretha Franklin, Otis Redding, and Led Zeppelin on the same bill."—"Remembering Music Pioneer Ahmet Ertegun," Peter Brown

Synonyms: assorted, diverse, diversified, miscellaneous, mixed, varied, wide-ranging

178. Edify
verb (*edd*•ih•fy)

To spiritually or morally instruct

Used in Context
"Once in the year let us meet here, to compare experiences, resolve difficulties, and to comfort and **edify** one another in our work."—"One Snowy Night," Emily Sarah Holt

"Similarly, the vaudeville toughness of Ellison's letter felt designed more to make a cultural point than to **edify** students."—"The Trap-door of Trigger Words," Katy Waldman

"An author's greatness these days is measured by his or her ability to **edify** and liberate. Such interpretative agendas are more problematic when imposed on much older works....For the sake of creative freedom and intellectual honesty, authors as well as scholars deserve more autonomy from the zeitgeist."—"The 'Tragedy' of Harper Lee," Rajiv Thind*

"Historic fidelity is to him a matter of indifference; he is only anxious to **edify** the reader."—*The Apostles*, Ernest Renan

* This quotation also includes another of our 499 words, "zeitgeist."

Synonyms: educate, enlighten, inform, instruct, teach, uplift

179. Efficacy
noun (*ef*•uh•ka•see)

The ability to produce desired results; skills

Used in Context
"The horsemen left egg on the face of what they call the alphabet agencies, calling into question the **efficacy** of the FBI's task force as well as the man in charge of the investigation, Special Agent Dylan Rhodes, who was publicly ridiculed."—*Now You See Me*

"Even as opposition to the HPV vaccine gains momentum, evidence of its **efficacy** is accumulating."—"Critics Assail Paper Claiming Harm From Cancer Vaccine," Dennis Normile

"Some are opposed to capital punishment in every instance because they doubt its **efficacy** or morality."—"U.S. Seeks Death for Charleston Shooting Suspect. Victims' Families Prefer Mercy," Alan Blinder

"On average, the vaccine has an **efficacy** of about 60 percent."—"When You Get the Flu This Winter, You Can Blame Anti-Vaxxers," Kent Sepkowitz

Synonyms: competence, effectiveness, efficiency, usefulness, value, worth

180. Effrontery
noun (eh•*frunt*•er•ee)

Arrogant and insulting behavior

Used in Context
"He stumbled away to wash his hands, utterly crushed by her **effrontery**."—*Where Angels Fear to Tread*, E. M. Forster

"The conclusion of an audit earlier this month by the District of Columbia inspector general suggests the latter. In one revealing quote cited in the report, a senior district official commented on the **effrontery** and efficacy of the parking-ticket system: 'One of the beauties of parking, it's like the [Internal Revenue Service]. If you get a parking ticket, you are guilty until you have proven yourself innocent....And that's worked well for us.'"—"Cry, Your Car's on Hidden Camera," Kathleen Parker

"'Mao is dead, and so is his China,' Francis Underwood, the series' relentlessly scheming main character, lectures a Chinese billionaire in one episode that aired undisturbed. For Chinese authorities, the upside of tolerating such **effrontery** is that it buttresses a dark, skewed vision of American politics."—"A Chinese Infatuation with *House of Cards*," Ruth Marcus

"And you, Scarecrow, have the **effrontery** to ask for a brain, you billowing bale of bovine fodder!"—*The Wizard of Oz*

Synonyms: arrogance, audaciousness, audacity, balls (*vulgar*), boldness, cheek, impudence, nerve, overconfidence

181. Effusive
adjective (eh•*fyus*•iv)

Refers to dramatic and often hyperbolic praise or expression of feelings in any form

Used in Context
"Trevor has made an attempt to interact with the world, and that was the assignment. And if I were an **effusive** person given to easy praise, I would call that admirable."—*Pay it Forward*

"The Downing Street file reveals that while global leaders were loudly singing her praises her own cabinet colleagues were notably less **effusive**."—"Margaret Thatcher's Resignation Shocked Politicians in US and USSR, Files show," Alan Travis

"But ask about their dogs, and they become **effusive**."—"Islanders Moved to Brooklyn, but the Players and Their Dogs Stay on Long Island," Allan Kreda

"The praise was so **effusive** that the Cannes jury awarded Dern the Best Actor prize."—"Bruce Dern's Long, Strange Trip to Leading Man in Alexander Payne's *Nebraska*," Marlow Stern

Synonyms: chatty, demonstrative, extroverted, fulsome, garrulous, loquacious, overenthusiastic, overflowing, talkative

182. Egalitarian
adjective (ee•gal•uh•*tare*•ee•en)

Favoring social equality

Someone who is an egalitarian favors laws that make everything in society fairer for all people, including access to housing, education, loans, etc. Egalitarianism takes literally the proclamation in the Declaration of Independence that "all men are created equal."

Used in Context

"Indeed, there was something in the very crudity of his social compliment that smacked, strangely enough, of that **egalitarian** soil."—"What I Saw in America," G. K. Chesterton

"Or we would need to adopt labor laws and norms of business behavior that would force markets to distribute incomes on a more **egalitarian** basis."—"Republicans Are Finally Willing To Spend On The Economy—At The Exact Wrong Time," Steven Pearlstein

"Viewers in the Third World marveled at the **egalitarian** treatment given to Alice, the housekeeper, a mere 'servant.'"—"*The Brady Bunch* Ambassadors," Tunku Varadarajan

"We are talking about a non-exclusive, **egalitarian** brotherhood where community status and more importantly, age, have no bearing whatsoever."—*Old School*

Synonyms: classless, democratic, equal, free, unrestricted

183. Egregious
adjective (ee•*gree*•jus)

Ridiculously bad

Used in Context
"And on his website he has posted a number of archival videos of him engaging in **egregious** behavior."—"Jimmy Connors Memoir Shows He Wasn't Misunderstood, He Was Just a Jerk," James Zug

"Beam believes Wilson's most **egregious** transgression was assuming he understood the forces that shaped Nabokov, a presumption Nabokov found repellent."—"Vladimir Nabokov and Edmund Wilson: The End of a Beautiful Friendship," Elaine Margolin

"But as long as they avoid **egregious** misbehavior, senior officers charged with prosecuting America's wars are largely spared judgments of any sort."—"Donald Trump's Swamp of War: What Does He Know That Career Military Officers Don't?," Andrew J. Bacevich

"This is **egregious**, do you hear me? **Egregious**! We were cellmates together, Andy. You got payback coming!"—*Talladega Nights: The Ballad of Ricky Bobby*

Synonyms: blatant, flagrant, notorious, outrageous, shocking

184. Ellipsis
noun (ee•*lip*•sis)

Omission of parts of sentences with a series of periods (. . .)

If you want to use a paragraph from a source in a paper, and it's ten sentences long but the point you want to use is in the first and tenth sentences, you would write is as "First sentence . . . tenth sentence" and then cite the source.

Used in Context

"But I noticed that when you quoted this section on page 116, you left 'general welfare' out and put an **ellipsis** in its place."—"Rick Perry on the Record," Andrew Romano

"The three band members are pictured on their sides in foetal position, forming the **ellipsis** of the title."—"Biffy Clyro: Nude Cover Signals 'Rebirth,'" Kev Geoghegan

"But it comes with its own built-in question mark, or **ellipsis**, or both." —"*Really* Compares the Fixed Image With Life's Flux," Ben Brantley

"There must be an **ellipsis**. It doesn't say how to prevent scar tissue. Doctor, you might try wrapping the nerve endings with tantalum foil."—*M*A*S*H*, "Your Retention Please"

Synonyms: abbreviator, abridgement, deletion, omission, punctuation, stylistic device

185. Elocution
noun (ell•oh•*cue*•shun)

A person's style of verbal delivery of a speech or the spoken word

Used in Context

"And Robert De Niro's Jake LaMotta in *Raging Bull* wasn't exactly the king of **elocution**."—"Mumbling Wins Oscars!," Zachary Pincus-Roth

"Hearing culture presents us with ideals of speaking with good **elocution**, restraint and self-control."—"The Deaf Body in Public Space," Rachel Kolb

"She also sought to obliterate her native accent with five-shilling weekly **elocution** lessons."—"Jean Alexander Obituary," Stuart Jeffries

"It's true, I'm not a doctor, and yes, I acted a bit; well, I recited in pubs and taught **elocution** in schools."—*The King's Speech*

Synonyms: articulation, delivery, diction, enunciation, expression, language, pronunciation, speech

186. Elucidate
verb (ee•*loo*•si•date)

To clearly and fully explain something

Used in Context

"Just gather 'round, I'll **elucidate** of what goes on outside when it gets late. Along about midnight, the ghosts and banshees, will get together for their big jamboree."—*Ichabod and Mr. Toad (or The Legend of Sleepy Hollow)*, Washington Irving

"Earlier, I asked plaintiff's counsel to **elucidate** his opinion on this matter."—*Shūbun*

"This letter might **elucidate** it—might throw light where so much was needed."—*How It All Came Round*, L. T. Meade

"To **elucidate** his point, he turned a boot upside down and pointed to the thick, tire-like treads on its sole."—"Obama's Fashion Faux Pas," Nicole LaPorte

Synonyms: clarify, describe, explicate, expose, expound, illuminate, make clear, reveal

187. Emanate
verb (em•uh•nate)

To flow out from a source or origin, to issue

Used in Context

"How does a bird produce the melodious notes that **emanate** from his throat?"—"Our Bird Comrades," Leander S. Keyser

"Love seemed to **emanate** from a single point of light…sometimes it was red, sometimes blue."—"Three Cancer Patients Explain How A Psychedelic Drug Eased Their Fears," Laurie McGinley

"It offers a satisfyingly expressionist vision of trauma and mental derangement, in which everything onstage seems to **emanate** from the mind of the central character."—"*Anastasia*, a Grand Duchess or a Great Pretender?," Roslyn Sulcas

"Perfume too seemed to **emanate** from the glorious hair and white-clinging vestments of She herself."—*She*, H. Rider Haggard

Synonyms: come, derive, discharge, emit, exit, exude, give off, radiate, spring, stem

188. Emasculate
verb (ee•*mas*•cue•late)

To remove a male's testicles; also, to take away someone's spirit or motivation

Used in Context
"If you're gonna continue to **emasculate** me with this Barbie dress-up shit, I'm using your laptop."—*Zack and Miri Make a Porno*

"And it seemed like Nic was trying to **emasculate** and castrate this supposedly clichéd action hero."—"Ryan Gosling and Nicolas Winding Refn on Sex, Violence & More," Marlow Stern

"He begins to see Bertha as she is: her unscrupulousness in money matters, her ceaseless effort to **emasculate** him."—*The Social Significance of the Modern Drama*, Emma Goldman

Synonyms: enfeeble, reduce, render impotent, weaken

189. Emergent
adjective (ee•*mer*•jent)

Appearing, issuing, or occurring, often for the first time

Used in Context
"In his new book, *Present Shock*, the media theorist Douglas Rushkoff takes a stab at describing an **emergent** cultural phenomenon."—"Not

Much New in Douglas Rushkoff's Reading of the Future," Jacob Silverman

"There is no direct correspondence between the literacy of **emergent** writing and that of automated writing and reading."—*The Civilization of Illiteracy*, Mihai Nadin

"It is an **emergent** property. Complex systems can behave in ways that are entirely unpredictable."—*Star Trek: The Next Generation*, "Emergence"

Synonyms: budding, embryonic, emerging, evolving, nascent, sprouting

190. Empathy
noun (*em*•puh•thee)

Understanding and identifying with someone else's feelings

Used in Context
"They've begun to feel human emotion. **Empathy**, love. If they find a way to unify, they could become a real threat."—*V*, "Pound of Flesh"

"They display complex emotions such as **empathy**, use tools, construct diverse cultures."—"This Man Was Shocked When His Chimpanzee Sued Him," Jacqui Goddard

"There is a great deal of **empathy** between people who are not only of the same age, but genetically identical."—*Anything You Can Do...*, Gordon Randall Garrett

Synonyms: commiseration, compassion, pity, sympathy

191. Empirical
adjective (em•*peer*•uh•kul)

Refers to facts based on observation and experimentation rather than emotion and assumptions

Used in Context
"Cause I need some sort of proof, some kind of verifiable, **empirical** data."—*A Beautiful Mind*

"Indeed, **empirical** evidence makes hash of the myth that culture makes the athlete."—"What Makes a Great Olympian? Sometimes It's Genetics," Jon Entine

"The mechanical doctrines are used in the attempt to interpret the **empirical** knowledge."—*The Psychology of Singing*, David C. Taylor

Synonyms: experiential, observed, practical, reality-based

192. Emulate
verb (*em*•yoo•late)

To imitate someone admired in order to equal or surpass their successes

Used in Context
"Is that how it worked? They program you to be my friend? **Emulate** all the qualities I respect. Tell me jokes."—*Battlestar Galactica*, "Sometimes a Great Notion"

"We females believed that to be successful we had to 'man up' and **emulate** masculine emotional restraint."—"Why Do Women Cry More Than Men?," Anne Kreamer

"Slowly, the modern masses are learning to **emulate** their erstwhile masters in the art of eating."—*Cooking and Dining in Imperial Rome*, Apicius

Synonyms: ape, copy, imitate, impersonate, mimic, model yourself on, take off, try to be like

193. Encroach
verb (en•*kroche*)

To intrude beyond established limits, to trespass on one's property or infringe on someone's rights

Used in Context
"How does this symbolize constraints on girls and women, and **encroach** on our right to be simply as we are, at any given moment?"—"Ashley Judd Slaps Media in the Face for Speculation Over Her 'Puffy' Appearance," Ashley Judd

"In the tendency of the federal government to **encroach** upon the States lay, he thought, the danger of the federal Constitution."—*Martin Van Buren*, Edward M. Shepard

"It will be said, that this court may **encroach** on the jurisdiction of the State courts."—*The Writings of Thomas Jefferson*, Thomas Jefferson

Synonyms: impinge, invade, make inroads, overstep, usurp

194. Endemic
adjective (enn•*dem*•ik)

Describes a disease, outbreak, or sociocultural behavior localized to a specific region or place; also, natural to a particular place

Used in Context
"An outbreak in Madagascar, where the disease is **endemic**, already has involved more than 100 people and killed almost half."—"Bubonic Plague Is Back (but It Never Really Left)," Kent Sepkowitz

"In geographical position Varallo is the most western city of North Italy in which painting and sculpture were **endemic**."—"Ex Voto," Samuel Butler

"My redundant undertakings would allay mistrust of my kind, **endemic** in such camps as these."—*Deadwood*, "Amateur Night"

Synonyms: common, indigenous, local, prevalent, regional, rife

195. Enervate
verb (en-er-vayt)

To weaken, to drain the vigor, energy, or vitality of someone

Used in Context
"There is a point where the stimulating atmosphere of the salon begins to **enervate**."—"The Women of the French Salons," Amelia Gere Mason

"Shun all that may **enervate** or diminish your youthful energies."—
Beethoven's Letters 1790-1826, Lady Wallace

I've always taught my students that "enervate" was one of the most misdefined words in the English language. It means "to weaken," yet because it has the prefix "ener," many people think it's associated with "energy."

"In addition to shooting everything, I keep a meticulous logbook charting this strange plunge back in time, the key to all the memories and feelings that **enervate** me to this day."—*My Winnipeg*

Synonyms: debilitate, enfeeble, exhaust, sap, sap the strength of, wipe out

196. Enhance
verb (enn•*hants*)

To improve something; to add to something's value or beauty in some way

Used in Context
"My desires are not so provincial. There's more than one chest of value in these waters. So perhaps you may wish to **enhance** your offer."—
Pirates of the Caribbean: Dead Man's Chest

"Rules to **enhance** fertility enlarged the population and gave strength in numbers."—"The Real Reason for Christmas," Nicholas Wade

"It does not **enhance** the humour of his sketches in any special degree, but only renders him more difficult to read."—*Lancashire Humour*, Thomas Newbigging

Synonyms: add to, appreciate, augment, boost, develop, elevate, enlarge, heighten, increase, intensify, magnify, pad, strengthen, upgrade

197. Enigma
noun (enn•*ig*•muh)

Someone or a concept that is not easily understood; a puzzle, a riddle

Used in Context
"Consider your daughter. A cipher, an **enigma**, a search, a search for answers."—*The Prestige*

"But Stone, it appears, has lived most of his 45 years as something of an **enigma**."—"The Militiaman Next Door," Mary M. Chapman

"His puzzled mind went groping for some reasonable solution of the **enigma**."—*Ralph on the Overland Express*, Allen Chapman

"For centuries Oak Island has been a riddle wrapped in an **enigma**."— *The Secret of Solomon's Temple*, "The Curse of Oak Island"

Synonyms: conundrum, mystery, puzzler, mind-twister

198. Enmity
noun (*enn*•mih•tee)

Hatred between enemies

Used in Context
"Alack, there lies more peril in thine eye than twenty of their swords. Look thou but sweet, and I am proof against their **enmity**."—*Romeo and Juliet*, William Shakespeare

"Making peace with your enemies can be pragmatic and lasting; making peace by ignoring their **enmity** is foolish—and sterile."—"Open Zion Should Not Mean Open Season on Israel," Gil Troy

"If a paper prints a line about him it's his enemy, and it don't pay to have the **enmity** of a man worth nearly a hundred millions."—*Anthony Trent, Master Criminal*, Wyndham Martyn

"But in time, it is sin that will consume them. They will know **enmity**, bitterness, the wrenching agony of the one splintering into the many."—*Battlestar Galactica*, "Razor"

Synonyms: acrimony, animosity, animus, antagonism, antipathy, bad blood, bad feelings, dislike, hate, hostility, ill will, loathing, malevolence, malice, rancor, spite, unfriendliness

199. Ennui
noun (*on*•wee)

Boredom and weariness from a lack of interest; the feelings that arise from a total loss of excitement or enthusiasm

Used in Context
"He's a spoiled little shit-face, tormented by **ennui** and world-weariness, weighed down by the void of existence!"—*Funny Games*

"In a fit of generosity or **ennui** or something I pitch in and help."—*My Wonderful Visit*, Charlie Chaplin

"As often happens in hostage situations, a sense of **ennui** enveloped the participants."—"Fiscal Cliff Hostage Situation Day 28: Ennui Sets In," Daniel Gross

"Please remember why you are here. To divert the noble lords and ladies of Paris. Unless they take poison to end the **ennui** of their empty lives."—*The Hunchback of Notre Dame* (1939)

Synonyms: apathy, (the) blahs, (the) blues, depression, dissatisfaction, (the) doldrums, lack of interest, languor, lassitude, listlessness, melancholy, sadness, tedium, weariness

On Hall and Oates' fourth album—cleverly titled *Daryl Hall & John Oates*—there is a song called "Ennui On the Mountain." The lyrics express the band's desire for nothing but a mountain retreat for themselves, the roadies, and the girls, but then admit that even if all that came true, it would probably end up being ennui on the mountain.

200. Ensorcell
verb (en•*sor*•sull)

Bewitched by someone or something; entranced

Used in Context
"ACN won't be attending the Saturnalia of incestuous ingratiation that does little to instill confidence in the public that the press isn't **ensorcelled** by the powerful."—*The Newsroom*, "Contempt"

"She's got . . . I really . . . I'm bewitched. I'm **ensorcelled**."—*The West Wing*, "Bartlett for America"

"It's somewhat odd to say that there is romance in the *Titanic* story (and I'm not talking about the movie, although that certainly contributed to the obsession), and acknowledge that the world has been **ensorcelled** by the tragedy since 1912."—Foreword to *The Sinking of the Titanic and Great Sea Disasters*, Stephen Spignesi

Synonyms: enchanted by, fascinated by, obsessed with, seduced by

201. Entropy
noun (*enn•trow•pee*)

A measure of the disorder that exists in a system; i.e., the energy unavailable for work

Used in Context
"Wiggle your big toe. . . . As I lay in the back of Buck's truck, trying to will my limbs out of **entropy** . . ."—*Kill Bill: Vol 1*

"Until Tuesday, Occupy Wall Street seemed, at least from the outside, to be entering a stage of **entropy**."—"Harsh NYPD Action May Reinvigorate Occupy Wall Street Movement," Michelle Goldberg

"**Entropy** explains why, left to the mercy of the elements, mortar crumbles, glass shatters and buildings collapse."—*Wonders of the Universe*

"I've learned my lesson. It's **entropy**, Lionel, decay."—*Person of Interest*, "Aletheia"

Synonyms: ataxia, breakup, chaos, collapse, decay, decline, degeneration, destruction, falling apart, worsening

202. Equable
adjective (*ek*•wuh•bull)

Describes someone who is calm and not easily flustered or angered

Used in Context
"I should like to make one thing quite clear, once and for all. I am not out of sorts. I am in a perfectly **equable** mood. I do not require being made to feel better!"—*Mary Poppins*

"He is an **equable** man who treats people fairly and has many friends."—"Bob Rubin's House of Cards," Jeff Madrick

"They hardly knew the man, usually so **equable** and quiet as to be almost stolid."—*That Stick*, Charlotte M. Yonge

Synonyms: agreeable, composed, consistent, even tempered, imperturbable, levelheaded, orderly, placid, serene, stable, steady, unflappable

203. Equivocate
verb (ee•*quiv*•oh•kate)

To be deliberately ambiguous or unclear

Used in Context
"Are you saying you won't do it?...I am not a man to **equivocate**."—*Prison Break*

"As Brookhiser fully appreciates—he does not **equivocate** or run from the truth—Lincoln was no radical, no abolitionist."—"Lincoln Was the Founders' Heir Apparent," Harvey J. Kaye

From the field of publishing: An editor sends a writer the following note: "I have received your manuscript. I shall waste no time reading it." This is equivocating on the meaning of the phrase "waste no time."

"Faith, here's an equivocator, who committed treason enough for God's sake, yet could not **equivocate** to heaven."—*Macbeth*, William Shakespeare

"I could not **equivocate** with this woman, I could no more lie to her sorrow than to the Judgment."—*The Crossing*, Winston Churchill

Synonyms: beat around the bush, be evasive, cavil, dodge, elude, evade, falsify, fib, fudge, hedge, prevaricate, quibble, waffle

204. Errant
adjective (*air•*ant)

Deviating from the proper, acceptable course, whether physically or in the abstract; the tone of the word suggests a serious error or sin, not just a harmless mistake

Used in Context

"I thought I messed it up, so I ran it twice. No **errant** prints, all a match to one woman."—*CSI*, "Got Murder?"

"The nose—as anyone knows who ever has received a stinger from an **errant** baseball—has countless pain fibers."—"The Writhing, Miserable Reality of Force Feeding at Guantánamo Bay," Kent Sepkowitz

"Meanwhile, back at Delta Psi, our brothers play a little ping-pong of their own. An **errant** ball lands in a brother's beer, and he just drinks it."—*Neighbors*

"The Pentagon has confirmed an **errant** test missile is in fact on a direct course for the tristate area. So far, all attempts to detonate or intercept the missile have been unsuccessful."—*My Super Ex-Girlfriend*

Synonyms: aberrant, delinquent, drifting, erratic, erring, misbehaving, mischievous, naughty, offending, unorthodox, wayward

205. Erudite
adjective (*air*•uh•dyte)

Characterized by extensive reading or knowledge; well instructed; learned

Used in Context
"Last week, I was with a group of fairly **erudite** people who were discussing the novel *Moby Dick*. I was afraid to admit I hadn't read it, so I lied."—*Zelig*

"Obama was brilliant that night—great stump speech; full, frank, **erudite** answers to questions."—"If Hillary Is Worthy, Then So Is Caroline," Geraldine Brooks

"Such were the sentiments of the most **erudite**, most pious, and most eminent school of learning existing in the capital of France."—*Joan of Arc*, Ronald Sutherland Gower

"Bohr was born in Copenhagen, wealthy and **erudite**, virtually an aristocrat."—*Atom: The Clash of the Titans*

Erudition is the depth, polish, and breadth that education confers. Someone who is erudite is knowledgeable, well-spoken, and manifests intelligence, intellectual deftness, and cognitive scope and confidence.

It is good to be known as erudite.

Synonyms: academic, bookish, brainy, cultivated, educated, highbrow, knowledgeable, learned, literate, savvy, scholarly, studious, well educated, well-read, widely read, wise

206. Eschew
verb (ess•*que*)

To avoid doing something on principle, or as behavior; to abstain from something

Used in Context

"Your work, so far, has been experimental. You **eschew** conventional narrative."—*Masters of Horror*, "John Carpenter's Cigarette Burns"

"Like Americans did when they elected Barack Obama, we should **eschew** our old shibboleths and forge ahead on a revolutionary path."—"A Moderate Coalition: Include Arab Parties," Daniel Gavron

"A president might **eschew** the role of Father Figure in Chief, instead addressing schoolchildren about his constitutional duties."—"Presidents and Pupils Don't Mix," Conor Friedersdorf

"He did not **eschew** work because he was lazy, it seemed; but he saw no use in it."—*Ruth Fielding and the Gypsies*, Alice B. Emerson

"There's only a handful of religious traditions that **eschew** the notion of war altogether. Most take the position that it's inevitable and therefore must strive to be moral."—*Madam Secretary*, "Spartan Figures"

Synonyms: abandon, abjure, abstain, disdain, forego, forswear, have nothing to do with, renounce, shun, steer clear of, swear off

Difficult to comprehend; something often only understood by a few informed people

Used in Context

"The rear windows leapt up like frogs in a dynamite pond. The dashboard was full of **esoteric** lights and dials and meters, San Francisco acid wave that I would never understand."—*Fear and Loathing in Las Vegas*

"One day she asked me for the most **esoteric** information I could think of concerning pop music.—"Dave's Whipping Boy," Paul Shaffer

"Sprinkled with Paul's original theology, his letters were as often pedantic (whether Christians should eat meat or be vegetarian) as they were **esoteric**."—"The Truth About Jesus," Rev. Madison Shockley

"He was never, and never wished to be, in the least **esoteric**; his object was to be understood by all."—*Thomas Moore,* Stephen Gwynn

"It remains an intriguing but unprovable concept. This is science at its most **esoteric**. It's like philosophy, religion even, because all it has going for it is beauty. We have a mathematical description of the first few moments after creation but nothing more."—*The Big Bang Machine*

Synonyms: abstruse, arcane, cryptic, hidden, impenetrable, inscrutable, mysterious, mystical, obscure, secret

208. Espouse
verb (eh•*spows*)

To take a position on an issue or a person; to support an ideology

Used in Context
"For those either of, or aspiring to, the new vast middle class, that we **espouse** it as a matter of right, and have ceased to ask what is it good for? You see my point?"—*Oleanna*

"Espouse" is one of those words that has a secondary meaning hidden its construction. The word also means "to take a spouse" (i.e., "es-spouse").

"When it came to politics, Robbins and Sarandon tended to **espouse** and admonish rather than try to persuade."—"Hollywood's Liberal Heartbreak," Lloyd Grove

"Her wealth left her free to **espouse** the cause of womanhood at large."—*The History of Sir Richard Calmady*, Lucas Malet

"Both men **espouse** a fringe theory called panspermia. It's the belief that life originated elsewhere in this universe."—*The X Files*, "Biogenesis"

Synonyms: adopt, advocate, back, champion, defend, embrace, take up, uphold.

209. Estimable
adjective (*ess*•tih•muh•bull)

Describes something or someone deserving respect; someone or something praiseworthy

Used in Context

"...which was passed last year by the senate and which has been debated now by this **estimable** body for the past several weeks, today we vote."—*Lincoln*

"To save himself, Nixon nominated the **estimable** Elliot Richardson to be his new attorney general."—"How Kennedy Brought Down Nixon," Chris Matthews

"Why should you wish so **estimable** an individual to be locked up?"—*The Genial Idiot*, John Kendrick Bangs

> "Estimable" is sometimes confused with "inestimable." See the section on "inestimable" in the "I" section of this volume.

Synonyms: admirable, appreciable, commendable, deserving, esteemed, excellent, good, laudable, meritorious, reputable, respectable, venerable, well-thought-of

210. Ethnocentric
adjective (eth•no•*sen*•trik)

Refers to the belief in the superiority of your own race or ethnicity

Used in Context

"The very sharp opposition which you make between the concepts of liberty and equality. This is not only an **ethnocentric** way of looking at it, but a peculiarly British way of looking at it."—*The Stuart Hall Project*

"This embrace of the European style of **ethnocentric** nationalism is alien to American conservatism, even if conservatives here have often practiced a racist politics."—"It's Worse Than You Think," Franklin Foer

"They also report that this isolationist, nationalist, **ethnocentric** world-view is related to one's level of education."—"Why Voters Don't Buy It When Economists Say Global Trade Is Good," N. Gregory Mankiw

"The most intense patriots are often **ethnocentric** and chauvinistic."—*The Fair Play Settlers of the West Branch Valley, 1769-1784*, George D. Wolf

Synonyms: bigoted, fanatical, intolerant, jingoistic, misogynistic, racist, narrow-minded, nationalistic, xenophobic, zealous

211. Ethos
noun (*ee•*those)

The character and philosophy of a particular group, era, or social compact

Used in Context
"Kurt must have violated some **ethos** of the suburbs, like cheating on his wife or ripping off his neighbors. Those are all accepted derivations of the suburban ethos."—*Bones*, "The Beautiful Day in the Neighborhood"

"During World War II, the **ethos** was 'use it up, wear it out, make it do, or do without.'"—"Millennials Will Be Just Fine," Justin Green

"The history of superheroes on the screen falls into four distinct stages, each reflecting the **ethos** of their time."—"The Superhero Backlash," Richard Rushfield

"The **ethos** of a group is just a catch-all term for the ways in which the members of a group rub against each other."—*The Ethical Engineer*, Henry Maxwell Dempsey

"'Seek and ye shall find, work and ye shall prosper.' These were the watchwords, the **ethos** of my education, the values instilled in me while I was growing up in a town you've probably never heard of."— *The Hudsucker Proxy*

Synonyms: attitude, beliefs, customs, disposition, habits, ideology, mind-set, principles, spirit, traits

212. Euphemism
noun (*yoo*•feh•mizm)

A mild or vague word or phrase replacing one considered harsh or offensively direct

Used in Context
"History is likely to dispense with the **euphemism** of 'mowing the lawn' and call this what it is: perpetual war."—"What Gaza Means For Iran," Ali Gharib

"Whatever became of infidelity in the afternoon—would one Tweet it afterward with a **euphemism** or a rating?"—"The Secret Sex Lives of Chefs," Gael Greene

"'She was disarming.' That's not a **euphemism**."—*Closer*

"Is that a **euphemism**? 'A drink?' Saying 'a drink' when you actually mean something else?"—*The History Boys*

Synonyms: beating around the bush, circumlocution, indirectness, pretense, tautology

These are all common euphemisms:

- *bite the dust* = die
- *"Dear John" letter* = breakup letter
- *fell off the back of a truck* = stolen
- *letting someone go* = firing someone
- *revenue enhancement* = taxes

213. Evaluative
adjective (ee•*val*•yoo•uh•tiv)

Assigning a value to something; expressing a judgment about something based on its value

Used in Context

"Contemporary **evaluative** criticism is now inextricably linked to the aesthetic. Put very briefly, the conception of aesthetics to which I refer is that which came to fruition in 18th Century and most profoundly in Immanuel Kant's *Third Critique*."—"What is Evaluative Criticism?," Andrew Klevan

"The constant streams of **evaluative** data that teachers must generate present a similar irony."—"A Teacher Returns to the Classroom and Gets Schooled," Nick Romeo

"What is it about nostalgia that so effectively scrambles our **evaluative** faculties?"—"Eat Like a Caveman? The Trouble With Paleo Living," Robert Herritt

"Finally, between 4 and 6 years of age, **evaluative** statements, which help to clarify 'why' an event is personally meaningful, become common."—*Awakening Children's Minds: How Parents and Teachers Can Make a Difference*, Laura E. Berk

Synonyms: appraising, assessing, calculating, discerning, evaluating, grading, weighing

To express a feeling, fact, or quality very clearly

Used in Context

"The preference for a state-run plan seems to **evince** a lack of understanding of the policy issues."—"What's the Public Option, Again?," Matthew Yglesias

"I shall be happy, on every occasion, to **evince** my regard for the Fraternity."—*Washington's Masonic Correspondence*, Julius F. Sachse

"His wife, once merely indifferent, was beginning to **evince** malice."—*Athalie*, Robert W. Chambers

"New contracts needed drawing up and old ones needed nullifying all with the astonishing goodwill that parties always **evince** in the company of rapid-firing machine pistols."—*Manderlay*

"So we have to **evince** at least a rudimentary level of understanding."—*DaVinci's Demons*, "The Vault of Heaven"

Synonyms: attest, declare, demonstrate, disclose, display, indicate, make clear, prove, reveal, show, verify

215. Exacerbate
verb (ex•*ass*•er•bate)

To worsen a problem or a situation

Used in Context
"Now I realize that Dick probably can't grasp the literature that you gave me. And the books you send him only… they only **exacerbate** the problem. They only heighten or intensify it."—*Capote*

"It will **exacerbate** the trend of publishers placing more resources on far fewer big bets."—"Why Random and Penguin Must Merge— And When They Almost Did," Gayle Feldman

"They can **exacerbate** bunions, cause arthritis in the knees, and some even believe high heels can cause headaches."—"Killer Heels!," Isabel Wilkinson

"We are in the process of compromising the climatic balance. More and more wildfires encroach on major cities. In turn, they **exacerbate** global warming. As the trees burn, they release carbon dioxide. The system that controls our climate has been severely disrupted."— *Home*

Synonyms: add insult to injury, aggravate, annoy, exasperate, fan the flames, inflame, intensify, irritate, make worse, provoke, rub salt in a wound

216. Exasperation
noun (ex•ass•per•*ay*•shun)

Frustration over a problem or annoyance that won't go away

Used in Context

"The shooting was very difficult. It seemed to be raining all the time. And once, in **exasperation**, I asked one of the young Norwegian kids, 'Hey, does it rain here all the time?'"—*Cameraman: The Life and Work of Jack Cardiff*

"Still, her **exasperation** over being a role model for the gay community seemed to be headed towards a breaking point."—"Michelle Shocked's Crazy Switch From Lesbian to Homophobe." Kevin Fallon

"His uneasiness, his **exasperation**, his scorn were blunted at last by all these trying hours."—*Under Western Eyes*, Joseph Conrad

"I realized how much we've lost. Somewhere along the line it changed from ecstasy to **exasperation**."—Remington Steele, "Molten Steele"

Synonyms: anger, annoyance, displeasure, enragement, fury, ire, irritation, pique, rage, resentment, vexation, wrath

217. Excoriate
verb (ex•*kor*•ee•ate)

To brutally criticize someone

Used in Context

"It teases and goads the wealthy to be fair rather than **excoriate** them for being rich."—"Obama Call for Buffett Rule Is Potent Politics but an Economic Pitfall," Zachary Karabell

"You're quite right to **excoriate** me."—*Lost in Space*, "The Deadly Games of Gamma 6"

"Its pamphlets went so far as to **excoriate** allied methods of warfare and to level accusations of inhumanity against the Belgians."—*Woodrow Wilson and the World War*, Charles Seymour

"Newspaper editorials continue to **excoriate** Netanyahu, even calling for his resignation—editorials written by his supporters."—"Why Did Netanyahu Release Palestinian Prisoners?," Abraham Katsman

Synonyms: abrade, attack, berate, censure, condemn, disparage, rebuke, take to task, upbraid

218. Exculpate
verb (*ex•cul•payte*)

To absolve someone of guilt or responsibility

Used in Context

"Your disdain for human interaction doesn't **exculpate** you, it inculpates you. You signed the charts. You're responsible for everything Chase does." – *House M.D.*, "The Mistake"

"Again he had endeavored to **exculpate** himself, yet she could not

believe that he was innocent."—*In the Roar of the Sea*, Sabine Bar-
ing-Gould

"And listen to you? Slander his good name to **exculpate** Martin
Odum, a man who has betrayed his country time and time again."—
Legends, "Identity"

"Miss Riley feels she has evidence which will **exculpate** her client."—
Suspect

Synonyms: acquit, clear, condone, discharge, dismiss, excuse, exon-
erate, free, pardon, release, vindicate

219. Execrable
adjective (*ex•uh•cruh•buhl*)

Terrible, of bad quality; deserving to be despised

Used in Context
"O thou sad Andronicus, give sentence on this **execrable** wretch. Set
him breast-deep in earth and famish him. There let him stand and rave
and cry for food."—*Titus Andronicus*, William Shakespeare

"Anything, for example, to take our minds off the **execrable** 'dining
experience.'"—"Your iPod (Most Likely) Won't Bring Down the
Plane," Clive Irving

"United with these **execrable** traits of character, there were others, to
which we have already alluded, which were alluring."—*The Adventures
of the Chevalier De La Salle and His Companions, in Their Explorations*

of the Prairies, Forests, Lakes, and Rivers, of the New World, and Their Interviews with the Savage Tribes, Two Hundred Years Ago, John S. C. Abbott

"Would you care to hazard a guess? I didn't think you would. Your essays, class, were **execrable**. I am likening your work to human bodily waste."—*Hiding Out*

Synonyms: abhorrent, abominable, appalling, atrocious, deplorable, despicable, disgusting, foul, heinous, obnoxious, odious, repulsive, revolting, vile, wretched

220. Exemplary
adjective (ex•*em*•pluh•ree)

Refers to an achievement or creation so well-done that others would use it as an example of how to succeed

Used in Context

"His behavior was not **exemplary** that season, but he must have been thinking, I'm not this guy."—"Why Manny Ramirez Hates Fans," Will Doig

"The man was in his prime, and had been of most **exemplary** habits."—"History of Circumcision from the Earliest Times to the Present," Peter Charles Remondino

"I checked on his record with the Bureau. It was **exemplary**. His accident was something of a mystery."—*The X Files*, "Duane Barry"

"Are you also aware that Ferris does not have an **exemplary** attendance record?"—*Ferris Bueller's Day Off*

Synonyms: admirable, commendable, consummate, correct, enviable, estimable, excellent, honorable, ideal, laudable, meritorious, not too shabby, perfect, sterling

221. Exigency
noun (ex•*ij*•en•see)

An urgent need; an emergency

Used in Context
"His speaking was unequal, and always rose with the subject and the **exigency**."—*Patrick Henry*, Moses Coit Tyler

"God is perfectly sufficient for every **exigency**, great or small, and we only want to trust Him to know that He is."—*The All-Sufficiency of Christ*, Charles Henry Mackintosh

"The army was entirely unprovided with any means of meeting this **exigency**."—*Woman's Work in the Civil War*, Linus Pierpont Brockett

Synonyms: contingency, demand, need, predicament, requirement, urgency

222. Exiguous
adjective (ex•*ij*•yoo•us)

Extremely scanty

Used in Context

Exiguous means scanty or bare, but it does not refer to clothing or nudity; it refers to quantity of the thing being discussed, as in "the school could not afford new computers due to its exiguous resources" or "they barely eked out an exiguous existence on the barren land."

"If our pecuniary resources be **exiguous**, let our resolution, Dick, supply the deficiencies of Fortune."—*Burlesques*, William Makepeace Thackeray

"With the broad spectrum of intermeshing functions and could be said to place an excessive burden on the office when considered in relation to the **exiguous** advantages of their overall centralization."—*Yes Prime Minister*, "The Key"

"These incredibly **exiguous** women. You know, those people who look like they can't support the weight of their own teeth and their head. Stalking in and out of fashionable restaurants."—*Dylan Moran: Like, Totally*

"Flora saw her father trembling in all his **exiguous** length, though he held himself stiffer than ever if that was possible."—*Chance*, Joseph Conrad

Synonyms: bare (as in a cabinet), meager, scarce

223. Expedient
adjective (ex•*pee*•dee•ent)

Proper under the circumstances; appropriate for the intended purpose

Used in Context

"It was the result of a chain of good decisions—wise, prudent, long-sighted, or, at the least, **expedient** choices."—"Why Does the USA Depend on Russian Rockets to Get Us Into Space?," P. J. O'Rourke

"That tape will prove far more persuasive than any **expedient** and mealy mouthed evasions."—"How Obama Will Cash In on Paul Ryan: Medicare, Taxes, Education & More," Robert Shrum

"And perhaps cheating on your French philosophers exam at the Groton School was an **expedient** way to get your diploma, and perhaps it wasn't."—*Meet Joe Black*

"The rapidly failing health of the missionary, rendered it **expedient** for him to endeavor to return to his friends at Green Bay."—*The Adventures of the Chevalier De La Salle and His Companions, in Their Explorations of the Prairies, Forests, Lakes, and Rivers, of the New World, and Their Interviews with the Savage Tribes, Two Hundred Years Ago*, John S. C. Abbott

Synonyms: advantageous, apt, commendable, consummate, convenient, correct, desirable, fitting, opportune, proper, utilitarian

224. Expiate
verb (ex-pee-ate)

To make amends, to undergo punishment for wrongdoings

Used in Context
"A lifetime of faithfulness, cost what it may, is not enough to **expiate** what I did."—*A Lady of Rome*, F. Marion Crawford

"These are autumnal deaths to **expiate** the sins of a people and appease the heavens so summer might return."—"Three Great Men Died That Day: JFK, C. S. Lewis, and Aldous Huxley," John Garth

"Can it, as the prophets suggest, **expiate** our sins and bring us closer to God?"—"The Enlightenment Diet," Bruce Feiler

"Big pharmaceuticals are right up there with the arms dealers. This is how the world fucks Africa, Mr. Black. Blood on their hands? It's how they **expiate** their guilt."—*The Constant Gardener*

Synonyms: absolve, amend, apologize, appease, atone, compensate, do penance, forgive, pay your dues, recompense, rectify, redeem, redress

225. Explicate
verb (ex•plih•kate)

To explain something in detail

Used in Context
"Science takes as its province mechanical causes, and leaves formal and

final causes to the philosopher to **explicate**."—*A Critical History of Greek Philosophy,* W. T. Stace

"I'm a hard-charging dutiful motherfucker, and I want to **explicate** the LAPD's somewhat hyperbolized misdeeds with true panache, regardless of my alleged transgressions."—*Rampart*

"An attempt to **explicate** them from the congruity and incongruity of Bodies: what those proprieties are."—*Micrographia,* Robert Hooke

Synonyms: amplify, clarify, elucidate, explain, expound, illuminate, illustrate, make clear, make plain, provide details, run down, spell out, untangle

226. Extemporaneous
adjective (ex•tem•per•*ayn*•ee•us)

Performed or carried out without any preparation; spontaneous

Used in Context
"Oh yeah, I figured I'd settle down here. Get away from all the zipper heads uptown, not get involved with all the **extemporaneous** bullshit."—*The Nine Lives of Fritz the Cat*

"But **extemporaneous** speech is not his strongest suit; Kanye expresses himself much better creatively than he does in conversation."—"In Defense of Kanye West," Rawiya Kameir

"It, of course, depended a good deal on the **extemporaneous** affidavit qualifications of the applicant."—*Remarks,* Bill Nye

"I'm not so great at **extemporaneous** speaking, so I've memorized some quick conversational facts I can whip out at a moment's notice."—The Gilmore Girls, "The Lorelais' First Day at Yale"

Synonyms: ad hoc, ad lib, by ear, casual, impromptu, improvisatory, informal, on the spot, unrehearsed

227. Extenuating
adjective (ex•*ten*•yoo•ate•ing)

Describes circumstances that could mitigate an accusation or situation and make it appear less serious than initially thought

Used in Context
"Due to **extenuating** circumstances, he may be released later tonight."—*Independence Day*

"The jury brought in a verdict of guilty with **extenuating** circumstances."—*The Cult of Incompetence*, Emile Faguet

"**Extenuating**, exschmenuating. We had a deal, a signed, written deal. Each grade, two weeks, or I get the company."—*Billy Madison*

"But really, you know, where are the **extenuating** circumstances?"—*A Tangled Tale*, Lewis Carroll

Synonyms: diminishing, explanatory, justifying, lessening, mitigating, palliating, softening

228. Extirpate
verb (*ex•tur•pate*)

To completely destroy something; to eliminate something undesirable

Used in Context

"To me, inveterate, hearkens my brother's suit. Which was, that he should **extirpate** me and mine out of the dukedom, and confer fair Milan on my brother."—*The Tempest*, William Shakespeare

"The gentry want to **extirpate** us by means of poison, we will **extirpate** them with fire and sword."—*The Day of Wrath*, Maurus Jkai

"Fire, avalanches, famine, and disease all did their best to **extirpate** the brotherhood."—*Tyrol and its People*, Clive Holland

"But this time we need to reach the roots. **Extirpate** it all. All."—*Fabiola*

Synonyms: abolish, annihilate, demolish, eradicate, erase, excise, expunge, extinguish, kill, wipe out

229. Extraneous
adjective (ex•*trane•*ee•us)

Not necessary; not important; not relevant

Used in Context
"Aren't we lucky we were there to get that information? It seemed **extraneous** at the time."—*Wayne's World*

"Actually, I'm highly logical, which allows me to look past **extraneous** detail and perceive clearly that which others overlook."—*Harry Potter and the Deathly Hallows, Part 1*

"The whole stack was re-evaluated—a 'one-time decision,' said a memo from the advisory council, due to '**extraneous**' circumstances."—"At This Creepy Libertarian Charter School, Kids Must Swear 'to Be Obedient to Those in Authority.'"—ProPublica

"I did it; and threw in a good deal of **extraneous** matter that hadn't anything to do with sugar."—*What Is Man? And Other Stories*, Mark Twain

Synonyms: immaterial, inappropriate, irrelevant, nonessential, not necessary, not pertinent, off point, peripheral, superfluous, unconnected, unrelated

230. Extrapolate
verb (ex•*trap*•oh•late)

To take known facts, ponder them, and to come to a previously unconsidered conclusion

Used in Context
"But he came across this old math book. And from this simple text, he was able to **extrapolate** theories that had baffled mathematicians for years."—*Good Will Hunting*

"A sound pension should plan for the time on the bottom, not **extrapolate** from the moment on top."—"Sorry, Folks: One Way or the

Other, You'll Never Be Able to Completely Count on Retirement," Megan McArdle

"What does the end feel like? It's like saying when you try to **extrapolate** the end of the universe. If the universe is indeed infinite, then what does that mean?"—*This is Spinal Tap*

"He saw his shortcoming, but could not do anything to help it: he was unable to **extrapolate** ahead."—*Starman's Quest*, Robert Silverberg

Synonyms: anticipate, assume, conclude, construe, deduce, envision, figure, figure out, foresee, foretell, guess, hypothesize, infer, interpret, make an educated guess, predict, project, theorize, work out

F

231. Facade
noun (fuh•*sod*)

A false appearance; also, a front, as in the face of a building

Used in Context

"In keeping with the **facade**, Williams showed himself to be dedicated preacher who 'knows his scripture.'"—"Exposed: The Gay-Bashing Pastor's Same-Sex Assault," M. L. Nestel

"I love a macho **facade**. It is such a turn-on."—*Clerks*

"We, like his various conquests, were seduced by his **facade** of invincibility and haunted past."—"What's Happened to Don Draper? Why Everyone's Favorite *Mad Men* Stud Needs His Mojo Back," Lizzie Crocker

Synonyms: deceit, deception, posturing, pretense, superficiality

232. Facetious
adjective (fuh•*sea*•shush)

Refers to "tongue-in-cheek-advice" characterized by wit and pleasantry; joking inappropriately; meant to be funny but definitely is not

Used in Context

"This is not by any means a **facetious** question: Do you think alcohol should also be made illegal?"—"Live Chat: Let's Talk About Drugs," David Frum

"Why the drawing? I don't know except that she often left drawings like that around with some kind of a **facetious** comment on them. I don't know what to make of that one. You think it was meant as a suicide note?"—*Black Widow*

"I know what **facetious** means, dick face."—*American Pie Presents: The Book of Love*

For example: If you're standing with a neighbor whose house has just burned down, a facetious remark would be, "Well, I guess you don't have to worry about that new roof anymore, right?"

Another example: "I was being facetious when I told my mother I wanted Brussels sprouts with every meal, but she took me seriously!"

"The feeble attempt to be **facetious** to the last utterly failed."—*The Giant of the North*, R.M. Ballantyne

Synonyms: comical, droll, funny, humorous, irreverent, jokey, sardonic, satirical, wisecracking, witty, wry

233. Facile
adjective (*faa*•syl)

Describes something superficially done with little effort

The Yorkshire Post blasted American election observers for comparing Donald Trump's election to Brexit. Don Burslam of Dewsbury wrote, "The attempt to draw a close parallel between Brexit and the election of Mr. Trump is facile, tenuous and superficial."

Used in Context

"They are not **facile** at expression, these same men of the soil."—*The Toilers of the Field*, Richard Jefferies

"If most of the McCarthy comparisons have been favorable, all of them have been **facile**."—"Compliments Are Nice, but Enough With the Cormac McCarthy Comparisons," William Giraldi

'A blind person has a better sense of feeling, of taste, of touch,' he writes, and speaks of these as 'the gifts of the blind.' And all of these, Lusseyran feels, blend into a single fundamental sense, a deep attentiveness, a slow, almost prehensile attention, a sensuous, intimate being at one with the world which sight, with its quick, flicking, **facile** quality, continually distracts us from."—"The Mind's Eye: What the Blind See," Oliver Sacks

Synonyms: adept, adroit, articulate, cursory, effortless, flip, glib, hasty, insincere, obvious, shallow, slick, smooth, superficial

234. Facilitate
verb (fuh•*sill*•uh•tate)

To make something possible; to make something easier to do

Used in Context

"Colonel, I'm sorry, but we cannot **facilitate** an evacuation for you or your men. Sir, there is nowhere else to evacuate to."—*World War Z*

"Here he was able to maintain a few poor scholars of theology and to **facilitate** their studies."—*Paris and its Story*, Thomas Okey

"That was when Mexico changes its laws so as to **facilitate** extradition to the United States."—"El Chapo on the Couch: Inside a Drug Lord's Therapy Sessions," Michael Daly

Synonyms: aid, assist, ease, expedite, forward, grease the wheels, help, make easy, open doors, promote, simplify

235. Fait accompli
noun (fate•ah•kom•*plee*)

An accomplished and presumably irreversible deed or fact

Used in Context

"Yet Woodward treats it as a **fait accompli** that Obama would pursue it."—"Woodward: The Juicy Bits," Bryan Curtis

"And this, of course, remains to you, since the marriage is a **fait accompli**?"—*Adventures of Sherlock Holmes*, A. Conan Doyle

Basically, this is French for "a done deal."

For example: "Based on the majority of polls, Mitt Romney's defeat was a fait accompli long before the polls closed."

"Decisive action would surgically remove the missiles, confronting the world with a **fait accompli**."—*The Kennedys*, "Cuban Missiles"

Synonyms: certainty, done deal, done deed, fact of life, irreversible deed, matter of fact

236. Fallacious
adjective (fuh•*lay*•shus)

Containing a deceptive statement; basing on a fallacy or misleading information

Used in Context

"They never went upstairs to visit the former tenants, so your characterization of their behavior as 'typical' is demonstrably **fallacious**."— *The Big Bang Theory*, "The Dead Hooker Juxtaposition"

"To suggest that we haven't refuted the very basis of socialism is **fallacious** and specious."—*Rocket Science*

"There has never been a religion too gross, too **fallacious**, to fail of followers."—*The Tyranny of the Dark*, Hamlin Garland

Synonyms: deceiving, erroneous, false, fraudulent, incorrect, invalid, mythical, phony, spurious, untrue, wrong

237. Fastidious
adjective (fuh•*stid*•ee•us)

Describes someone who is meticulous about the smallest details of whatever it is they're doing

Used in Context

"I'm actually quite **fastidious**. I put them in this box just to screw with you."—*Stranger Than Fiction*

"Very rarely, though, that **fastidious** and precise pulse deteriorates into a disorganized scramble."—"Heart Attack 101: What May Have Killed James Gandolfini," Kent Sepkowitz

"Emma made her toilet with the **fastidious** care of an actress on her debut."—*Madame Bovary*, Gustave Flaubert

"I wouldn't be as **fastidious** as you are for a kingdom!"—*Pride and Prejudice*

Synonyms: choosy, critical, demanding, discriminating, exacting, finicky, fussy, hard to please, hypercritical, nitpicky, particular, persnickety, picky

238. Fatuous
adjective (*fat•chu•us*)

Stupid and unaware

Used in Context

"That's the most **fatuous** lie you could possibly think up. Don't say any more. I know what you've been doing. You've been with this leading man of yours."—*Lolita*

"And 'alkalinizing' someone in an attempt to improve their health is simple-minded, **fatuous**, and dangerous."—"Alkalinizing Someone to Improve His or Her Health Is Simple-Minded, Fatuous, and Dangerous," Kent Sepkowitz

"He passed from fatuous credulity to equally **fatuous** distrust."—*The Argonauts of North Liberty*, Bret Harte

"Freedom. The **fatuous** jingle of our civilization. But only those deprived of it have the barest inkling of what it really is."—Cloud Atlas

Synonyms: absurd, asinine, birdbrained, boneheaded, brainless, childish, dense, dull-witted, dumb, foolish, idiotic, imbecilic, inane, lamebrained, meaningless, mindless, pointless, simpleminded, vacuous, witless

239. Feckless
adjective (*fek•less*)

Useless, incompetent

Used in Context
"It is because I am useless, **feckless**, hollowed out by failed ambitions, by failed loves."—*Vikings*, "The Usurper"

"Then there was the self-dramatizing and **feckless** suspension of his campaign over the financial crisis."—"Sorry, Dad, I'm Voting for Obama." Christopher Buckley

"Feckless" is a nice way (because many people don't know what it means) to tell someone they're worthless, if the occasion arises where you need to do such a thing, of course.

"My love is so **feckless**, that it is a shame to offer it to Him!"—*Letters of Samuel Rutherford*, Samuel Rutherford

"Steve is a thoughtless, **feckless**, feelingless, useless wanker!"—*Coupling*, "Nightlines"

Synonyms: feeble, good-for-nothing, hopeless, incompetent, ineffective, ineffectual, insignificant, irresponsible, of no use, valueless, worthless

240. Felicitous
adjective (feh•*lis*•ih•tus)

Appropriate, pleasingly suitable, well suited for a particular occasion

Used in Context

"What a **felicitous** choice of words: was it a coincidence that the Democratic opponent was a woman?"—"The Indispensable Nancy Pelosi," Robert Shrum

"There is one friend who declares that she has never had a **felicitous** dream in her life."—*The World I Live In*, Helen Keller

"But except for the **felicitous** pretense of deafness I had not tried to pretend anything."—*The Secret Sharer* Joseph Conrad

"You know, I have a hobby: I'm collecting rooms, **felicitous** rooms. That's why I put out this magazine. If I can't build houses according to my theories at least I can talk about them."—*Secret Beyond the Door*

Synonyms: applicable, apt, blessed, fortuitous, fortunate, germane, lucky, opportune, pertinent, propitious, relevant, timely, well-chosen

241. Feral
adjective (*fair*•uhl)

Describes animals that live in the wild, often after having been domesticated

Used in Context
"He's not really my cat. He's kind of **feral**. You know, wild."—*Coraline*

"As Jordan Belfort, a charismatic monster of a stockbroker, DiCaprio is a **feral** beast; the id incarnate."—"Why Leonardo DiCaprio, Who Wows in *The Wolf of Wall Street*, Deserves to (Finally) Win An Oscar," Marlow Stern

"He becomes an outlaw, to be dealt with as any other **feral** creature."—*Aphorisms and Reflections from the Works of T. H. Huxley*, T. H. Huxley

"Let me apologize for my **feral** son."—*The Nanny Diaries*

Synonyms: animal, ferocious, in their natural habitat, natural, tameless, uncultivated, undomesticated, untamed, wild

242. Filibuster
noun (*fill*•ih•bus•tur)

A political tactic in which someone delivers a long irrelevant speech without stopping in order to delay voting on, or passage of legislation

Used in Context
"It's our first **filibuster**, and I'm not a rules expert, but the rules of a

filibuster are simple enough: you keep the floor as long as you can hold the floor."— *The West Wing*, "The Stackhouse Filibuster"

"Rush Limbaugh compared Democrat-led **filibuster** reform to rape on his radio show on Friday."—"Rush Compares Filibuster Reform to Rape, Proving Yet Again He Is America's Worst Person," Jamelle Bouie

The record for the longest filibuster is held by Strom Thurmond, who spoke for 24 hours and 18 minutes in protest against pending legislation. What was he so adamant should not be passed? The Civil Rights Act of 1957. (Spoiler: It passed.)

"Republican Minority Leader John Boehner engaged in a rare House **filibuster** and read shocking section after shocking section from the legislation."—*Fall of the Republic: The Presidency of Barack H. Obama*

Synonyms: delay, hindrance, holding the floor, interference, opposition, procrastination, stonewalling, talkathon

243. Foment
verb (*fo•ment*)

To cause trouble, to stir up rebellion

Used in Context
"Herr Beethoven, there are many forces in Austria that **foment** revolt. I like a lively discussion as much as the next man, but I fear that these days we cannot allow quite so much."—*Immortal Beloved*

"He advocates instead quiet support for Iranian opposition groups that could **foment** regime change."—"Israel's Top Iran Expert: You Can't Out-Negotiate the Mullahs," Dan Ephron

"The Civil Guard can keep us from rogues, but they **foment** dissensions and cause the ruin of the country."—"The Grandee Armando," Palacio Valds

"Our provocateurs have been unable to **foment** so much as a border skirmish since the sultan issued a decree to his men to stand down under pain of death."—*Dracula*, "From Darkness to Light"

Synonyms: agitate, arouse, excite, fan the flames, fuel, goad, incite, instigate, provoke, rile up, stimulate, stir up, work up

244. Forbearance
noun (for•*bare*•ense)

Patience; good-natured tolerance of delay or incompetence

Used in Context
"You'd never think of pressing your advantage. **Forbearance** is the hallmark of your creed."—*Mary Poppins*

Forbearance can be used in a couple of ways; financially it means a bank agreeing to put off mortgage payments for a while.

In common usage it means good-natured patience.

"But selfies, like people, deserve our forgiveness, our **forbearance**, and our support."—"In Defense of the Selfie, Oxford English Dictionary's Word of the Year," James Poulos

"I tell you again that my **forbearance** will last but little longer."—*The Tinted Venus*, F. Anstey

"In that moment, I wanted to praise him for his generosity and letting me drag him to China. His **forbearance** for not murdering me, even his awful jokes."—*Hemingway & Gellhorn*

Synonyms: abstinence, indulgence, leniency, mercy, moderation, patience, restraint, self-control, temperance, tolerance, toleration

245. Fortuitous
adjective (for•*too*•uh•tus)

Happening by chance, fortunate

Used in Context
"A **fortuitous** turn of events brought Django and myself together."—*Django Unchained*

"It was a **fortuitous** decision, because the plaza's roof happened to be crammed with several hundred refugees."—"'The Extinction Parade': An Original Zombie Story by Max Brooks," Max Brooks

Fortuitous means lucky:
- "Winning the lottery was fortuitous, considering I was about to go bankrupt."
- "Fortuitously the library had a copy of the exact old computer manual I needed."

"But inwardly she thanked her guardian-angel for the **fortuitous** miracle by which intervening waiters formed a screen."—*Out of the Air*, Inez Haynes Irwin

"On the contrary, they are the richest, from one **fortuitous** circumstance."—*The Writings of Thomas Jefferson*, Thomas Jefferson

Synonyms: accidental, casual, felicitous, flukey, random, serendipitous, out of the blue, unexpected, unforeseen, unplanned

246. Fractious
adjective (*frak•shus*)

Inclined to be irritated, a whiner, and prone to complaint marathons

Used in Context
"The animals kept moving around and crying out. Cow got **fractious** and tried to kick out the side of the stall."—*The Twilight Zone*, "Jess-Belle"

"And you start to feel jittery, self-conscious, paranoid, and **fractious**."—"Susan Boyle Is Crying—and My Heart Bleeds," Piers Morgan

"In the American system, unlike parliamentary ones, opposition parties lack centralized leadership, and thus tend to be **fractious**."—"Mitch McConnell and John Boehner Lose Their Grip on the Republican Party," Peter Beinart

"Who would have thought that such an inexorable nurse as Miss Lambert should prove such a **fractious** invalid?"—*Heriot's Choice,* Rosa Nouchette Carey

"**Fractious** cracks have opened up in your relationships and in your testimony and we'll explore them in a later session."—*Veep*, "Testimony"

Synonyms: awkward, complaining, crabby, difficult, easily angered, huffy, intractable, irritable, ornery, peevish, petulant, quarrelsome, recalcitrant, scrappy, snappish, stubborn, testy, thin-skinned, touchy, unruly

Completion; when something has reached a desired outcome

Used in Context

"The energy breakthrough I was working on came to **fruition**. All these years, Jon was helping me replicate his power, unaware of how I planned to use it."—*Watchmen*

"One of the more fascinating projects I read about that never came to **fruition** was your Howard Hughes biopic starring Jim Carrey."—"Christopher Nolan Uncut: On *Interstellar*, Ben Affleck's Batman, and the Future of Mankind," Marlow Stern

"So, for a time, if such a passion comes to **fruition**, the man will get what he wants."—*The Good Soldier*, Ford Madox Ford

"Remember the information that I imparted to you about my imminent megabucks deal in the States? Well, it's about to come to **fruition**."—*Prêt-a-Porter*

Synonyms: achievement, actualization, attainment, completion, consummation, culmination, end, end result, final result, fulfillment, gratification, realization, refection, result, success

To express vehement criticism and/or condemnation

Used in Context

"We do not **fulminate** against a treatise on Quaternions because it lacks humor."—*The Dramatic Values in Plautus*, Wilton Wallace Blancke

"Mum, I am at job, right in the town of West Bank of Jordan, and you want to **fulminate** against my rotten woman?"—*Omar*

"I want you to stay here in this revered firm, in this historic downtown building. I want you to formulate and **fulminate** and fabricate."—*Son of Morning*

Synonyms: berate, blow up, bluster, castigate, censure, chide, condemn, curse, declaim, denounce, denunciate, fume, intimidate, inveigh against, menace, rage, rail, swear at, upbraid, vilify,

G

249. Galvanize
verb (*gal•vuh•nize*)

To motivate someone (or a group) into highly productive activity

Used in Context

"Witch hunters have always been the best way to **galvanize** witches."—*The Secret Circle*, "Family"

"The current firestorm should **galvanize** critics of education reform, but not in the way they think."—"De Blasio Misread His Mandate, Now Some of His Own Supporters are Fighting Back Over Charter School Cuts," Conor P. Williams

The word "galvanize" comes from the name of the Italian physician and scientist Luigi Galvani, who discovered animal electricity; i.e., the fact that electricity can be generated through chemical action.

"I am going to shake them out of their paralysis. I'm going to get them moving. I'm going to . . . I am going to **galvanize** them."—*Teen Wolf: Galvanize*

Synonyms: animate, encourage, fire up, incite, spur, stimulate, stir up

250. Gambit
noun (*gam•*bit)

Any move designed to gain an advantage

Used in Context
"It's a **gambit** designed to turn Fischer against his own subconscious."—*Inception*

"The Republicans' sly repeal-and-delay **gambit**—repealing the Affordable Care Act right away while delaying the effective date until after the midterms—wouldn't work."—"Let Republicans Fix What They Break," Froma Harrop

"This is no author's **gambit** to keep a reader's interest, although it does."—"William Trevor's Quiet Explosions," Marisa Silver

"He also did well with his Latino **gambit** since, once again, the media, including many conservatives, were sympathetic to amnesty."—"A Racially Polarized Election Augurs Ill for Barack Obama's Second Term," Joel Kotkin

Synonyms: maneuver, ploy, ruse, scheme, stratagem, strategy, tactic, trick

251. Gamut
noun (*gam•*ut)

The entire range or scope of something

Used in Context

"History will be made here today. For the first time, the so-called mutant cure will be available to the public. Reaction has run the **gamut** with mutants on both sides of the line; some are desperate for this cure while others are offended by the very idea of it."—*X-Men: The Last Stand*

"Notwithstanding the wide **gamut** of moods and drastic leaps in Tchaikovsky's score, nothing prepares the ear for the sweeping, beyond-candy grandeur of the music here."—"The Sugar Plum Fairy: An Enigma Wrapped in a Beautiful Dance," Alastair Macaulay

"Normally, her strongest expressions run the **gamut** from 'gee' to 'gosh.'"—"Amy Adams: 'I Thought, If I Can't Figure This Out, I Can't Work Any More,'" Hadley Freeman

"Anecdotes run the **gamut** from simple spills to drunken collisions with large vehicles."—"Biking While Drunk," Anneli Rufus

Synonyms: breadth, compass, continuum, extensiveness, extent, field, length, orbit, range, reach, scale, scope, spectrum

252. Garrulous
adjective (*gar•uh•lus*)

Extremely, annoyingly talkative

Used in Context

"In America, the death of an American star is really the occasion for a **garrulous**, obsessive, round-the-clock denial of death."—"How Constant Change Killed Jackson," Lee Siegel

"For this story has not been derived from hacked voicemails, an avaricious doctor, or a **garrulous** friend."—"Is Kate Preggers?," Tom Sykes

"No doubt there is justification enough for his suspicion in the exploits of pretentious and **garrulous** souls."—*Mankind in the Making*, H. G. Wells

"We got you a seat right next to him, and he's known to be somewhat **garrulous** in the company of thieves."—*Con Air*

"If you're going to be this **garrulous**, I shall have to ask you to be less familiar."—*Appointment with Death*

Synonyms: babbling, chatty, effusive, glib, long-winded, loquacious, mouthy, prolix, verbose, voluble, wordy

253. Gauche
adjective (gohsh)

Having no class, tact, or grace in a social situation

Used in Context
"The **gauche** boy gone from him, Milt took her hand, pressed it to his cheek."—*Free Air*, Sinclair Lewis

"Would it be terribly **gauche** of me to inquire if I might peek around upstairs?"—*The Diary of Ellen Rimbauer*

"In the academic confines of museums, such talk of marketing and the bottom line qualifies as **gauche**."—"Prada and Schiaparelli Exhibit Opens at the Metropolitan Museum of Art," Robin Givhan

"This **gauche** repression, this adolescent exhibitionism. No wonder you can't tell the difference between violence and passion."—*Six Feet Under*, "Tears, Bones & Desire"

Synonyms: awkward, coarse, crude, gross, maladroit, tacky, tasteless, vulgar

254. Glib
adjective (glib)

Shallow, superficial, and uninformed in conversation and attitude

Used in Context
"To stand up before men and pour forth a stream of **glib** words is generally to make yourself obnoxious to them."—*The Wisdom of Confucius*, Epiphanius Wilson

"Smart alecky, too wise for himself, too **glib**, too full of himself – that's how we felt about him."—"For Democrats, Anthony Weiner Makes an Unwelcome Return," Maggie Haberman, Alexander Burns

"But despite **glib** talk about 'pro-growth' economic policies, productivity growth is something over which governments have very little control."—"Why the Economy Doesn't Roar Anymore," Marc Levinson

"Cut to a video clip of an intense Cruise calling Lauer '**glib**.'"—"Tom Cruise's Career Rehab Secrets," Kim Masters

Synonyms: convincing, facile, fluent, loquacious, pat, persuasive, slick, smooth, superficial, voluble

255. Gratuitous
adjective (gruh•*too*•it•us)

Unnecessary and unwarranted; something done for its shock value

Used in Context

"These are real soldiers. They're living in a war zone. The language is not **gratuitous**. We're not instructing people to bleed off. These obscenities, it's just their life."—*This Film is Not Yet Rated*

"Even shorn of all that **gratuitous** nudity, though, *Drive He Said* would be far from a masterpiece."—"Jack Nicholson Deserves a Better Biography Than This," Christopher Bray

"Renting videos, that's **gratuitous**, and illogical, since you work at a video store."—*Clerks*

Synonyms: groundless, needless, redundant, superfluous, uncalled for, unjustified

256. Gregarious
adjective (greg•*ar*•ee•us)

Outgoing, friendly, sociable

Used in Context

"The surprise choice was the **gregarious** rotund 77-year-old patriarch of Venice."—"The Catholic Church Is Insular and Intolerant," Robert Shrum

"He may not be **gregarious** but Petraeus wields a bony and ascetic charm which he combines with practical intelligence."—"Petraeus, a Master of Spin," Ellen Knickmeyer

"Street photographers tend to be **gregarious** in the sense that they can go out on the street and they're comfortable being among people."— *Finding Vivian Maier*

"He was one of the **gregarious** sort, a loud talker, nervy really, very familiar with all the passengers."—*Sea and Sardinia*, D. H. Lawrence

Synonyms: affable, companionable, convivial, extroverted, fun, genial, social, sociable,

257. Guile
noun (giy•ul)

Deceitful behavior commonly used to trick people

Used in Context
"Studying his nature as one can do on the Road, I perceived also that in him there was no **guile**."—"The Mahatma and the Hare," H. Rider Haggard

"Emmy Lou was pink-cheeked and chubby and in her heart there was no **guile**."—*Emmy Lou*, George Madden Martin

"Probably, by the time he reached the tenth green, he was too intent upon his game to remember how **guile** had won him freedom."—*Seeing Things at Night*, Heywood Broun

"She's quite wonderful. No training, no craft to speak of. No **guile**, just pure instinct. She's astonishing."—*My Week with Marilyn*

Synonyms: artfulness, artifice, chicanery, craftiness, cunning, deception, deviousness, dishonesty, disingenuousness, duplicity, fraud, slyness, treachery, trickery

H

Habeas corpus
noun (*hay*•bee•us•cor•pus)

Latin for "deliver the body;" a legal writ demanding the presentation of someone in custody

Used in Context

"Now, if you please, Senator McCain, in the spirit of **habeas corpus**, show me the body."—"Why My Former Hero Shouldn't Be President," Christopher Brownfield

"Is an outrage! I demand you release my client immediately. I have here the **habeas corpus**."—*On the Beat*

"In hearings for a writ of **habeas corpus**, an immediate decision is mandated, but I propose to consider the issues carefully."—*Whose Life Is It Anyway?*

Synonyms: action, arraignment, case, citation, claim, counterclaim, court action, cross-examination, hearing, impeachment, indictment, lawsuit, litigation, prosecution, seizure, suite, tribunal

259. Hackneyed
adjective (*hak*•need)

Trite, made boring by overuse

Used in Context
"Under normal circumstances, a politician being grilled by fifth-graders is **hackneyed** political theater."—"Biden Grilled by Fifth-Graders," Alex Pasternack

"It was slit-your-wrists dull, but in a **hackneyed** avant-garde manner."—"Whitney Museum's Biennial: A Big Yawn," Blake Gopnik

"His anger thrilled out in a feeble stream of **hackneyed** profanities."— *The Wonder*, J. D. Beresford

"Now, I know it's an old **hackneyed** expression, but it's the truth: you've got to start at the bottom."—*The King of Comedy*

Synonyms: banal, clichéd, commonplace, corny, overdone, overused, pedestrian, quotidian, stale, timeworn, tired, unoriginal, worn-out

260. Haiku
noun (hy•*koo*)

A form of Japanese poetry consisting of 17 syllables in 3 unrhymed lines of 5, 7, and 5 syllables

Used in Context
"I wrote little **haiku** poems. I emailed them to everyone."—*Fight Club*

"They only want a few words, more a **haiku** than a work of fiction."—"Rich People Want You to Work for Free," Ted Gioia

"So we get to her house, we have some kind of a weird argument, about the number of syllables in a **haiku**."—*Anger Management*

> Another similar form of Japanese poetry is the cinquain, which consists of 5 (usually unrhymed) lines in this order, 2, 4, 6, 8, and 2 syllables.

Synonyms: lyric, poem, verse

261. Halcyon
adjective (*hal•cee•on*)

Peaceful, undisturbed, and happy

Used in Context

"I remember when it used to flow every Wednesday. Those were **halcyon** days. Must be a reason she quit on us."—*Rango*

"In retrospect, 2009 and 2010 were **halcyon** days in the Middle East, now that we seem just one horseman short of an apocalypse."—"The Myth of the Central Park Five," Edward Conlon

> There's a reason Pfizer named its very popular sleeping pill "Halcion." They spelled it H-a-l-c-i-o-n—no "y," but it's obvious they were going for an association with this adjective.

"Can you be suggesting that these **halcyon** honeymoon days and nights, just the two of us alone together... should ever end?"—*Marnie*

Synonyms: calm, carefree, quiet, pacific, placid, serene, still, tranquil, untroubled

262. Harangue
verb (huh•*rang*)

To criticize someone in a hostile, aggressive manner

Used in Context
"The occasion was a gala dinner during which Pinter began to **harangue** some unfortunate guest for his political views."—"Antonia Fraser on Her Wild Marriage," Amanda Foreman

"Harangue" can also be used as a noun.

"The MIT Commencement Speech is in June. Please, don't **harangue** me about stuff that's way, way down."—*Iron Man*

"In a wild outburst that followed his gaming license denial, Rothstein followed several stunned commissioners into the hallway where he continued his **harangue** until his own lawyers and friends urged him to leave."—*Casino*

Synonyms: admonish, berate, criticize, rant, rebuke, scold, shout at, tell off, yell at

263. Harbinger
noun (*har*•bin•jer)

Something that foreshadows a future event

Used in Context
"Anyway, Mr. NBE One here, aka Megatron, that's what they call him, who's pretty much the **harbinger** of death, wants to use The

Cube to transform human technology to take over the universe."—
Transformers

"Cyberexperts say attempts to hack into the computer systems of several German political parties this summer were likely a **harbinger** for similar problems for Europe."—"Russia Aims to Disrupt Other Western Elections, U.S. Officials Say," Alan Cullison

"Al Gore's surprising failure there in 2000 was an overlooked factor in his narrow Electoral College loss, and a **harbinger** of the future."—"Hillary Clinton and the Populist Revolt," George Packer

"Whether this three-day system is a **harbinger** of seasonal weather changes is uncertain."—"A Cloud Forms Over Saturn's Mysterious Moon," Matthew R. Francis

Synonyms: herald, indication, omen, portent, precursor, predictor

A Note from Prof. Spignesi: Singer/songwriter Paula Cole's first album is titled *Harbinger*. It's excellent, and well worth your time.

264. Hedonist
noun (*hee*•duh•nist)

Someone devoted to self-pleasure of all kinds

Used in Context
"She knew him to be a **hedonist**, a materialist, a man who had very few scruples."— "From Out the Vasty Deep," Mrs. Belloc Lowndes

"Hedonist" can also be used as an adjective.

"After years in which he gave the impression of being a **hedonist**, Prince said he had a spiritual rebirth."—"Prince, Mysterious, Inventive Chameleon of Music, Dies at 57," Matt Schudel, Emily Langer

"Casting against type, he sent me to a **hedonist** camp in Jamaica, where I sat fully clothed on a nude beach."—"*Wigwag*: The Magazine That Lex Built," Mary Norris

"But I like me this way. You are a **hedonist**, a lover of the physical world."—*American Horror Story*, "Blood Bath"

Synonyms: degenerate, narcissist, pagan, playboy, pleasure-seeker, reprobate, sensualist

265. Histrionic
adjective (his•tree•*on*•ik)

Ridiculously overdramatic

Used in Context
"His coworkers would describe him as **histrionic**, paranoid, and secretive."—*Criminal Minds*, "Amplification"

"'Overall, alcohol and drug use disorders were most strongly related to antisocial, **histrionic**, and dependent personality disorders,' the organization said of its findings."—"Links Between Addiction and Mental Illness: Myths vs. Facts," Robert Yagoda

"She was a woman with mental illness who refused to be painted as a hysteric, a **histrionic**; sexist archetypes beloved by the early psychoanalyst set."—"Forget the Gold Bikini. For People with Mental Illness Carrie Fisher was a Queen," Hannah Jane Parkinson

"Silver Linings Playbook allowed her to explode, playing a woman unhinged, **histrionic**, and emotionally volatile."—"How Jennifer Lawrence Took Over Hollywood. (It's Not Just Because of Her Charm.),"
Kevin Fallon

Synonyms: exaggerated, hysterical, insincere, melodramatic, overacting, unrestrained

"Histrionic" can also be used as a noun.

266. Hobson's Choice
noun (*hob•*suns•choic)

A choice between what is being offered or nothing at all

Used in Context
"I felt for you, and I thought you showed great restraint. For a servant in that situation, restraint is **Hobson's Choice.**"—*Downton Abbey*, "A Moorland Holiday"

"**Hobson's Choice.** Lose our land or would you prefer to lose your home?"—*Father Brown*, "The Pride of the Prydes"

This phrase come from a 16th century Cambridge stable manager named Thomas Hobson, who gave his customers one choice regarding which horse they could take: they could have the one closest to the stable door, or none at all.

"It does seem fitting that a creation of Moloch's would inflict such a **Hobson's Choice** on an innocent family."—*Sleepy Hollow*, "Go Where I Send Thee..."

Synonyms: lack of choice, no alternative, no choice, only choice, zero options

267. Holistic
adjective (ho•*lis*•tik)

An approach to healing that takes into consideration a person's complete being; i.e., their physical, mental, and spiritual selves

Used in Context

"Jackson lived a **holistic** life when Chopra met him, and the wellness guru taught him how to meditate."—"Chopra: Michael Jackson Could Have Been Saved," Gerald Posner

"The appeal of this **holistic** medicine culture does need to be understood better by the modern medical establishment."—"Why Smart People Are Dumb Patients," Jean Kim

"Education needs to shift from the atomistic view that isolates subjects from the whole of reality to a **holistic** perspective."—"The Civilization of Illiteracy," Mihai Nadin

"There are no Russians. There are no Arabs. There are no Third Worlds. There is no West. There is only one **holistic** system of systems! One vast and immense, interwoven, interacting multi-variant, multinational dominion of dollars!"—*Network*

"You probably read in *People*, I was on Zoloft, but this is **holistic**."—*America's Sweethearts*

Synonyms: aggregate, comprehensive, entire, full, integrated, total, universal, whole

268. Homogeneous
adjective (huh•*moj*•eh•nus)

Comprising elements that are alike, or the same

Used in Context

"I grew up in an idyllic society, really. Homogeneous, no crime. Everything was basically perfect."—*Until the Light Takes Us*

"As elsewhere in Italy, voters who backed the no campaign in Catania were not a homogenous group."—"'This Was A Protest Vote': Sicilian City Where 75% Said No to Matteo Renzi," Angela Giuffrida

Example:

"All the members of my book club share a homogenous taste in reading so we never have any issues agreeing on a book."

"If our country is to defeat terrorism, we must stand as one homogenous people instead of as separate races."

"Much of Boston seems to be extremely racially **homogenous**, and the parts that do not fall under this characterization seem to be experiencing gentrification."—"A Student View of Boston's Gentrification: 'We Are Ruining the Lives of City Residents,'" Paige Smith

"The last thing we want is a **homogenous** workroom."—*Project Runway*

Synonyms: akin, alike, all the same, analogous, consistent, harmonized, identical, kindred, like, standardized

269. Hubris
noun (*hyoo*•bris)

Excessive pride; arrogant and egotistical self-confidence

Used in Context
"The god-king has betrayed a flaw: **hubris**. Easy to taunt, easy to trick."—*300*

"What were his weaknesses as a military commander: was it **hubris**?"—"Napoleon Was a Dynamite Dictator," J. P. O'Malley

"Her **hubris** was in part, at all events, the result of ignorance."—*Before the War*, Viscount Richard Burton Haldane

"Well, it is this kind of **hubris** that brought the wrath of God in the first place."—*The Mist*

"Ron, you're a good man. But you have fallen victim to your own ego and your own **hubris**. And before others can forgive you, you must learn to forgive yourself."—*Anchorman 2: The Legend Continues*

Synonyms: arrogance, audacity, chutzpah, cockiness, contemptuousness, disdain, loftiness, nerve, pompousness, pretentiousness, self-importance

270. Hyperbole
noun (hi•*per*•buh•lee)

Conscious, extravagant exaggeration

Used in Context

"**Hyperbole** aside, this is a heinous crime that requires swift resolution."—*LA Confidential*

"Exaggeration and **hyperbole** are constant campaign companions, as useful and expected as hammers and saws on a construction site."— "When Campaign Spin Becomes Fact," Stuart Stevens

"While some may say that our exploding obesity epidemic is a **hyperbole**, fat does beget fat."—"Will Your Baby Be Obese?," Joyce C. Tang

"It was so ever-present with him that there was neither paradox nor **hyperbole** in his words: I am never alone when I am alone."—*The Life of Ludwig van Beethoven*, Alexander Wheelock Thayer

"When someone says we got people everywhere, you expect it to be **hyperbole**. Lots of people say that. Florists use that expression. Doesn't mean that they've got somebody working for them inside the bloody room."—*Quantum of Solace*

Synonyms: amplification, big talk, distortion, embellishment, hype, laying it on thick, overstatement, PR

These are all examples of hyperbole:

- I'm so hungry I could eat a horse.
- I have a ton of homework.
- If I told you once, I told you a thousand times!

271. Hypothesis
noun (high•*poth*•uh•sis)

A tentative explanation that has not been proven; the first step toward further investigation hopefully resulting in a proof

Used in Context

"Let's say for a moment that I accept the Bath Item Gift **Hypothesis**, I now lay the conundrum at your feet: which size?"—*The Big Bang Theory*, "The Bath Item Gift Hypothesis"

"It's no more valid than my gut—a good **hypothesis** withstands testing. That's what makes a good **hypothesis**."—*Bones*, "Pilot"

"Each idea begins with a **hypothesis**, to put it into scientific terms."—"Barbara Kingsolver: How I Write," Noah Charney

"He talks with doctors and scientists who study cognition, and cites a raft of research that bolsters his **hypothesis**."—"The Unpersuadables: Why Smart People Believe Crazy Theories," Kevin Canfield

"But for this, the **hypothesis** would be but a curious scientific theory."—*The Other Side of Evolution*, Alexander Patterson

Synonyms: assumption, axiom, conclusion, conjecture, deduction, derivation, extrapolation, guess, induction, inference, interpretation, generalization, position, premise, proposition, rationale, suggestion, supposition, theorem, theory

I

272. i.e.
adverb (eye-ee)

Id est (that is)

Used in Context

"If you weren't sure you wanted to marry her today of all days; **i.e.**, your wedding day, then it must be the right decision, mustn't it?"—*Four Weddings and a Funeral*

"Sandra Bullock is the new Will Smith (**i.e.**, a star who can single-handedly carry a blockbuster)!"—"Hollywood's Christian Blockbuster," Nicole LaPorte

"I.e." adds information that further explains or makes an additional point. Yes, we know it happened in September, but the writer wants to remind you that September was three months ago from the time of his writing.

"Then you believe in spirits; **i.e.** in the existence of spirits?"—*Zones of the Spirit*, August Strindberg

Synonyms: especially, explicitly, in other words, namely, particularly, specially, specifically, that is, that is to say, to be exact

273. ibid
(adverb) (*ih•*bid)

Abbreviation of ibidem meaning the citation is the same as the one previously cited

Used in Context
"A letter from Adam to Senchia, Richards wife, is extant, **ibid.**"—*The Grey Friars in Oxford*, Andrew G. Little

"Of the mode in which the capital withdrawn from circulation is disposed of—**ibid.**"—*An Inquiry Into the Nature and Causes of the Wealth of Nations*, Adam Smith

"'You see that the heavens are not idle, nor do they observe the Sabbath' (**ibid**, chap, xxiii)."—*The Christian Sabbath*, J. E. Remsburg

"And when it cannot take a long breath, laws are girded too tight. Without liberty, man is a syncope. . . . **Ibid.**, Your Honour"—*Good Will Hunting*

Synonyms: as previously

274. Iconoclast
noun (eye•*kon*•oh•klast)

One who attacks and seeks to overthrow traditional or popular ideas

Used in Context
"Bruce was an **iconoclast** and a rebel in that he thought traditional martial arts were way too bound by tradition."—*Bruce Lee: A Warrior's Journey*

"Concerned and kind, he was also the ultimate risk taker, an **iconoclast** with an edgy, hard charging quality about him."—"They Murdered My Friend," Sandra McElwaine

"The **iconoclast** that is in the heart of this poet is rampant."—*Egoists*, James Huneker

"He's also [an] **iconoclast** with a brilliant mind and an outsized ego who has flaunted the conventional wisdom, and tweaked the staid scientific establishment at every turn."—Shameless, "Frank the Plank"

> John Lennon was an iconoclast with his "give peace a chance" and "all you need is love" ideology (not to mention his "The Beatles are bigger than Jesus" and "Christianity will die" comments).

Synonyms: critic, cynic, disbeliever, dissenter, dissident, doubter, doubting Thomas, heretic, nonbeliever, nonconformist, questioner, radical, rebel, revolutionist, skeptic

275. Ideology
noun (eye•dee•*ahl*•oh•gee)

The combined beliefs and ideas forming a coherent philosophy

Used in Context
"But what I hear about the role of women is often inspired by an **ideology** of machismo."—"The Secret Pope Francis Haters," Barbie Latza Nadeau

"But think more deeply: Congress could make all kinds of laws that aggressively establish an **ideology** that is not a religion."—"Gay Marriage Vs. the First Amendment," James Poulos

"The world of fact in the Confucian **ideology** does not correspond with the beliefs accepted as fact by the dominant West."—*Government in Republican China*, Paul Myron, Anthony Linebarger

"Has a war been staged for us, complete with weapons and **ideology** and patriotic drum beating?"—*Star Trek*, "Day of the Dove"

"At an abandoned monastery, Chenkov and other boys and girls learned English long before they learned Russian. Drilled in idiom, idiosyncrasy. And **ideology**. And by methods of rigorous physical and psychological programming. The spy master made warriors of iron."—*Salt*

Synonyms: beliefs, credo, creed, culture, dogma, ideas, outlook, philosophy, principles, system, tenets, view

276. Idiom
noun (*ih*•dee•um)

A particular style of speaking common to groups or certain people. Also, a clever saying that is purely metaphoric and that expresses an idea, but makes no literal sense based on the words actually used; e.g., "You have a chip on your shoulder."

Used in Context
"Yet he seemed interested only in recasting GOP concepts in his own **idiom**."—"Obama's Speech Took Ideas From the GOP and Rhetoric From Madison Avenue," Lee Siegel

"Both films quite seriously question and call out the cretinous conception of 'black masculinity' pushed in the **idiom**."—"The Hip Hop Inauguration," Stanley Crouch

"The folk **idiom** is so widespread that you could take any part of it and rework a song."—*American Masters: No Direction Home: Bob Dylan*

"We are unfamiliar with this particular **idiom**. What does crap mean?"—*Wonder Woman*

Synonyms: argot, colloquialism, dialect, expression, jargon, lingo, locution, phrase, saying, street talk, turn of phrase, vernacular

277. Idiosyncratic
adjective (*ih•dee•oh•sin•krat•ik*)

Describes a unique, and often odd or unusual way of behaving

Used in Context
"They stormed in with shotguns, and after liberating the place of all the firearms they could carry, and various personal **idiosyncratic** knickknacks, they killed every customer without hesitation."—*Natural Born Killers*

"Her smart, **idiosyncratic** genre movies go all the way back to the sly vampire flick *Near Dark* in 1987."—"The Best Action Film and the Woman Who Directed It," Caryn James

"We tracked dogboy88 through **idiosyncratic** phrases in his e-Mail messages, comparing his writing to the other 231 Relevant screen names we've gathered. People have habits of speech and writing that they're unaware of."—*Numb3rs*, "Animal Rites"

"They were organized by **idiosyncratic** subject categories, and alphabetical by author within those categories."—*Someone Comes to Town, Someone Leaves Town*, Cory Doctorow

"But anyone who holds that view cannot be a juror in a federal death penalty case. This isn't just weeding out people with **idiosyncratic** opinions. This is weeding out the majority, It's strategic."—*Boston Legal*, "Trick or Treat"

Synonyms: all your own, characteristic, distinctive, individual, particular, peculiar, personal, quirky

278. Ignoble
adjective (ig•*no*•bull)

Describes someone's dishonorable behavior

Used in Context
"Well, with wit and grit and no small amount of courage, we accomplished something on that day, a feat of derring-do, an enterprise not **ignoble**. We merry band, unbound by the constraints of society and the prejudices of the common ruck."—*The Ladykiller*

"But I certainly do believe that Bashar, if facing defeat, prefers guaranteed safe-passage into exile rather than an **ignoble** death."—"Be Careful What You Wish For In Syria," Theodore Kattouf

"An ambition that confessedly overleaps all bounds is at least not an **ignoble** one."—*The Doomsman*, Van Tassel Sutphen

"We all have thoughts. We all have sexual thoughts. We have **ignoble** thoughts. I just don't want those to be who I am to people, especially not to my wife."—*House, MD*, "The Social Contract"

Synonyms: base, contemptible, corrupt, craven, dastardly, degraded, despicable, disgraceful, dishonorable, heinous, ignominious, immoral, inferior, lewd, low, reprehensible, shameful, vulgar, wicked

Describes someone's total humiliation and loss of
dignity

Used in Context

"[T]hen suddenly, less than one week before election . . . defeat.
Shameful, **ignominious**. Defeat that setback for 20 years the cause of
reform in the US, forever cancelled political chances for Charles Foster
Kane."—*Citizen Kane*

"A repatriation ceremony would help bury the **ignominious** squabbles
of the past."—"Incontrovertible Evidence Proves the First Americans
Came From Asia," Doug Peacock

"Bayh seems to have a very different reason for cutting and running
than the specter of **ignominious** defeat."—"Evan Bayh's Shameful
Retreat," Lee Siegel

"Peter Blood was sold to Colonel Bishop—a disdainful buyer—for the
ignominious sum of ten pounds."—*Captain Blood*, Rafael Sabatini

"He was granted the dignity of early retirement. But the humiliation of
half a pension. It was an **ignominious** end to an illustrious career."—
Gone Baby Gone

Synonyms: despicable, discomfiting, discreditable, disgraceful, dishonorable, disreputable, embarrassing, humiliating, ignoble, inglori-
ous, shameful

280. Imminent
adjective (im•min•ent)

Describes something is about to happen, or could happen immediately

Used in Context

"Perhaps you refer to the **imminent** attack of your rebel fleet."—*Star Wars Episode VI: Return of the Jedi*

"So what about the colossal intelligence failure of 9/11—how could the CIA not have known an attack was **imminent**?"—"Hands Off the CIA," Joseph Finder

"While she was waiting, she one day received a letter from Toby, announcing his **imminent** arrival in London."—*Coquette*, Frank Swinnerton

"People, listen up! This is a national security emergency. We have an **imminent** threat."—*The Bourne Ultimatum*

"Now you try. Concentrate. The ring will inform you where there is an **imminent** threat."—*Green Lantern*

Synonyms: about to happen, approaching, brewing, coming up, fast approaching, forthcoming, highly likely, immediate, impending, inescapable, inevitable, in the offing, in the pipeline, just around the corner, likely, looming, on the horizon, pending, probably, unavoidable

281. Immutable
adjective (ih•*myoo*•tuh•bull)

Describes something that can not be changed or someone who will not be changed

Used in Context

"Six wardens have been through here in my tenure, and I've learned one **immutable**, universal truth: Not one born whose asshole wouldn't pucker up tighter than a snare drum if you ask for funds."—*The Shawshank Redemption*

"I think it was born out of a desire to have something beautiful and **immutable** in their lives."—"Anne Rice on *Sparkly Vampires, Twilight, True Blood,* and Werewolves," Marlow Stern

"The outraged grammar stickler mistakes a convention for an **immutable** and fundamental law of the universe."—"Go Ahead, End With a Preposition: Grammar Rules We All Can Live With," Nick Romeo

"And I did not know that **immutable** Truth sometimes has the ring of a curse and makes you cry, and yet is Truth."—*Woman,* Magdeleine Marx

"Now there's a theory in time physics that time is **immutable**. It's like a river, you can throw a pebble and it will create a ripple but the current always corrects itself. No matter what you do, the river just keeps flowing in the same direction."—*X-Men: Days of Future Past*

Synonyms: abiding, absolute, changeless, enduring, incontrovertible, indisputable, inflexible, invariable, permanent, perpetual, sacrosanct, steadfast, unalterable, unchallengeable

282. Implacable
adjective (im•*plak*•uh•bull)

Impossible to appease or mollify; intractable

Used in Context
"Cold, **implacable**, the triple killer remains at ease, calm in the lair of his enemy."—*Castle*, "3XK"

"But he had soldiered on, bound by loyalty to Hillary and an **implacable** sense of duty."—"An American in Full," Jonathan Alter

"He has a will of iron, dauntless resolution, and an **implacable** temper."—*Cord and Creese*, James de Mille

"Duty. A starship captain's life is filled with solemn duty. I have commanded in battle, negotiated peace between **implacable** enemies. I have represented the Federation in first contact with 27 alien species."—*Star Trek: Nemesis*

Synonyms: coldhearted, cruel, inexorable, inflexible, merciless, pitiless, relentless, rigid, ruthless, unappeasable, uncompromising, unforgiving, unyielding

283. Imprimatur
noun (*im*•prim•muh•tur)

The authority to say or print something; also the authority to carry out a specifically delineated task

Used in Context
"You've operated behind the scenes to suborn the trust of a man who

has stamped you with his **imprimatur** of class, elegance, and stature. I've had the opportunity to be witness to every kind and degree of deception."—*Meet Joe Black*

"What makes CEOs think that putting their **imprimatur** on a political movement will increase public pressure on the two parties?"—"Starbucks' Effort to Solve the Fiscal Cliff Probably Won't Work," Daniel Gross

"He took a small case from his pocket, and presented a card to him, and also papers which revealed the **imprimatur** of the company."—*The Man Who Rose Again*, Joseph Hocking

"There's the basic framework, but then every comedian puts his own **imprimatur** on the joke."—*The Aristocrats*

Synonyms: approval, blessing, charter, (the) okay, permission, permit, sanction, support

284. Impugn
verb (im•*pyoon*)

To cast doubt upon someone's work or reputation; to slander someone by suggesting that they are duplicitous and cannot be trusted; to accuse someone of vile deeds

Used in Context
"Rose and I differ somewhat in our definition of fine art. Not to **impugn** your work, sir."—*Titanic*

"Defense lawyers will look for inconsistencies in the same records as they try to **impugn** her credibility further."—"The Evidence That Could Doom DSK," Christopher Dickey, John Solomon

"What we have to do is an act of justice, and I don't wish that anyone should be able to **impugn** my motives."—*Jack Harkaway and His Son's Escape From the Brigand's of Greece,* Bracebridge Hemyng

"I, in no way wish to **impugn** his veracity, but I would have Mr. Swearengen understand that for her try on my life, I ought to see that the whore has paid with her own."—*Deadwood,* "Tell Him Something Pretty"

Synonyms: accuse, asperse, attack, cast aspersions on, censure, challenge, charge, criticize, malign, smear, tar

285. Impute
verb (im•*pyoot*)

To attribute to someone an (often undesirable) trait; to ascribe an action to someone

Used in Context

"As a former rock critic, Ms. Maslin should know better than to **impute** bad intent here."—"The Maslin Stain: A Writer Defends Himself Against the NYT Critic," William Stadiem

"People will **impute** responsibility on them for the actions of the family member."—"Wisconsin Spa Shooting Brings Back Painful Memories for the Moms of Mass Killers," Winston Ross

"You will rather believe all ill of him and will most likely **impute** things to him he never did."—*The Rider of Waroona,* Firth Scott

"I am too fond. Therefore pardon me, and not **impute** this yielding to light love, which the dark night hath so discovered."—*Romeo and Juliet,* William Shakespeare

"Look, I will not **impute** the genetic anomaly with the acts of a vengeful deity. This is a matter of science, not religion, Father."—*Revenge*, "Sin"

Synonyms: accredit, accuse, adduce, assign, blame, brand, charge, credit, indict, insinuate, intimate, pin on, stigmatize

286. In medias res
(adverb) (in•*mee*•dee•uh•ray)

Beginning in the middle of things rather than at the beginning

Used in Context
"**In medias res** is a quick and easy way to have an action sequence at the beginning of an episode."—"TV Tropes"

"As it happens, Blake is not only a candid memoirist but a well-connected one; for half a century he sat **in medias res** in modern architecture."—*No Place Like Utopia: Modern Architecture and the Company We Kept*, Peter Blake

"Most people are familiar with his biggies, like *Crime and Punishment* or *The Brothers Karamazov*, but it's his lesser-known work, *The Gambler*, that makes use of **in medias res**."—"5 Great Examples of In Medias Res," David K. Israel

This adverbial phrase is most commonly used to describe a scene in a movie, book, or TV show that picks up in the middle of events, suggesting that much has already happened of which the reader or viewer has no awareness of.

Synonyms: at once, directly, immediately, instantly, without delay

287. Inalienable
adjective (in•a•lee•en•uh•bull)

Describes a right or a protection that is unable to be taken away because it is protected by law

Used in Context

"We hold these truths to be self-evident, that all men are created equal. That they are endowed by their creator with certain **inalienable** rights, among these are life, liberty, and the pursuit of happiness."—*The Declaration of Independence*

"We would exercise our right to go anywhere at any time, as **inalienable** in the modern world as the right to freedom of speech."—"Ciao, Roma! Hello, Newark!," James Atlas

"The fascist state recognizes no **inalienable** right, and needs no consent from its people."—"Proclaim Liberty!," Gilbert Seldes

"No qualms of conscience troubled her as to her **inalienable** right to fly from him."—*Browning and His Century*, Helen Archibald Clarke

"We do believe all planets have a sovereign claim to **inalienable** human rights."—*Star Trek IV: The Undiscovered Country*

"And, last time I heard, speech in the United States of America is protected. You can't limit my advocacy just because it works. I have a sovereign, **inalienable** right to petition my government. And why is it some dirty little secret that it's in America's interest to do business overseas?"—*Syriana*

Synonyms: absolute, immutable, indisputable, inherent, inviolable, unassailable, unchallengeable, undeniable

288. Inchoate
adjective (in•*ko*•it)

Describes something partially, but not fully in existence or operation

Used in Context
"I am reminded of a verse: 'the painter's brush touched the **inchoate** face by ends of nimble brushes and with the blush of first color rendered her lifeless cheek living.'"— *The Grand Budapest Hotel*

Inchoate means partially complete: After the Big Bang, the universe was an inchoate enormity that would expand and evolve to where we are today.

"William Morris is so **inchoate** that you can't even really describe their culture."—"Hollywood's Coming Culture Clash," Kim Masters

"Ideas as they first present themselves are **inchoate** and incomplete."— *How We Think*, John Dewey

Synonyms: amorphous, embryonic, formless, incipient, nascent, rudimentary, shapeless, undeveloped, unformed

289. Incipient
adjective (in•*sip*•ee•ent)

Describes something that is beginning to develop

Used in Context
"Well, your eyes are one of your best features, but we can do something about the **incipient** crow's feet."—*Burn After Reading*

"Similarly, much of the policy rhetoric coming from Washington focuses on fears of **incipient** inflation that have yet to pan out." —"Chill Out About the Debt," Justin Green

"Well, the autopsy revealed nothing out of the ordinary beyond signs of malnutrition and **incipient** anemia. Whatever young Fenton was, he wasn't entirely preternatural."—*Penny Dreadful*, "What Death Can Join Together"

"It seems inarguable that the donation has something to do with the **incipient** arrival of the unflattering film."—"Insider: Zuckerberg Wanted to Delay $100 Million Donation," David Kirkpatrick

Synonyms: beginning, budding, developing, early, embryonic, inchoate, initial, introductory, nascent

290. Incognito
adjective (in•cog•*nee*•toe)

When an identity is disguised or hidden; using a false name

Used in Context
"This was a good idea, Lunch Box. In these outfits, we're totally **incognito**."—*Jay and Silent Bob Strike Back*

"Celebrities like Paris Hilton and an **incognito** Selena Gomez mingle in the elevated VIP area by the main stage."—"Miami Music Week: Florida's Epic DJ Dance Party," Marlow Stern

"He might have been **incognito** except for that unmistakably resonant voice of his."—"Edgar Oliver, Actor and Raconteur, Hews to His East Village Past," Laura Collins-Hughes

"Leery of running into one of their many friends in Manhattan, he squired her away to Brooklyn, where they could go **incognito**."—"For a King of Night Life, a Sunny Bride," Alex Williams

Synonyms: anonymously, clandestine, disguised, in disguise, secretly, under another name, undercover, using another name

291. Incongruous
adjective (in•*kon*•groo•us)

Out of place within a particular context

Used in Context
"Looks like Sumoto is ticklish. This is **incongruous**, inconceivable, inexcusable." —*Samurai Jack*, "Jack and the Smackback"

One incongruous blunder appeared in the 1960 movie *Spartacus*, starring Kirk Douglas. Several Roman slaves are wearing wristwatches.

"Berliners for the most part simply lived with it, **incongruous** and sinister as it was."—"Scaling the Berlin Wall," Michael R. Meyer

"I must say, running diagnostics on a computer seems **incongruous** for a man of action."—CSI, "Skin in the Game"

"Even those who were not already republicans wanted the royals to be more aware of how **incongruous** their profligacy seemed."—"Imagining Prince Charles as King Makes All of Britain Wish They Could Leave Like Scotland," Clive Irving

"Two **incongruous** metaphors should not be used in the same sentence."—*Elementary Guide to Literary Criticism*, F. V. N. Painter

Synonyms: absurd, alien, anachronistic, bizarre, conflicting, contradictory, contrary, discordant, discrepant, disparate, foreign, improper, inappropriate, incompatible, incongruent, inconsistent, inharmonious, mismatched, odd, ridiculous, unsuitable

292. Incorrigible
adjective (in•*kor*•uh•je•bull)

Describes someone who cannot be made to change or cease their nefarious ways

Used in Context
"'I gotta tell you, you guys in the press are **incorrigible**,' the president said."—"Hillary Clinton and Barack Obama's Lovefest on *60 Minutes*," Lauren Ashburn

"No one wins when the political field is populated exclusively by the **incorrigible** right and the bemused left."—"Resolved: This is Not the Road to a Two-State Solution," Elisheva Goldberg

"This naturally tries the temper of high-spirited mistresses—as does also the **incorrigible** carelessness of some servants."—*Six Months at the Cape*, R. M. Ballantyne

"I give up. I have had it with men. They are **incorrigible**."—*Charmed*, "Little Monsters"

Synonyms: hardened, hopeless, incurable, intractable, irredeemable, persistent, uncorrectable, wicked

293. Incredulity
noun (in•kreh•*dool*•ity)

Being in a state of disbelief

Used in Context

"It was the epoch of belief, it was the epoch of **incredulity**. It was the season of light, it was the season of darkness."—*A Tale of Two Cities*

"Informed of the great interest in his new beard, he responded with **incredulity**."—"Political Tensions Takes Center Stage at World Economic Forum," Daniel Gross

"When we were in China, my father here was always waxing lyrical about his wee home in the glen. But being Oriental-born myself, like my brothers and my sister here, I suffered from a natural **incredulity**. But looking about me now, the heather and the hills, I can see he was right. It's very special."—*Chariots of Fire*

"I will make no attempt to set down for you his surprise nor his **incredulity**."—*The Iron Pirate*, Max Pemberton

"Do forgive our **incredulity**, but I wonder how you can be certain you've achieved transparency?"—*Mystery Men*

Synonyms: disbelief, doubt, misgivings, skepticism, unbelief, uncertainty, wonder

294. Inculcate
verb (*in*•kul•kate)

To place or embed ideas in someone's mind through repetition that they ultimately embrace

Used in Context
"The reason they studied so intensely history, philosophy, literature, grammar, rhetoric, was to **inculcate** in the human being the seeds of moral excellence."—*The Historian*

"Although a body professing to **inculcate** pure spiritual truths, the church teaches the grossest form of materialism."—*Woman, Church & State*, Matilda Joslyn Gage

"The poet was to labor for the advancement of what he felt to be unholy—he was to **inculcate** what would lower the perfection of man."—*Complete Prose Works*, Walt Whitman

"It is the consensus. Your girls are said to be vastly informed in subjects irrelevant to the accepted curriculum. Most heinous of all, you are said to **inculcate** no team spirit."—*The Prime of Miss Jean Brodie*

Synonyms: brainwash, convince, drum into, educate, impart, implant, impress, indoctrinate, ingrain, inspire, instill, plant, program, teach

295. Indefatigable
adjective (in•dih•*fat*•ih•guh•bull)

Tireless, unrelenting

Used in Context

"We sing from the diaphragm a lot. In war we're touch and able, quite **indefatigable**, between our quests, we sequin vests and impersonate Clark Gable."—*Monty Python and the Holy Grail*

"A few enterprising college students, myself included, were inspired by Andrew's **indefatigable** pace and his success."—"What Liberal Bloggers Can Teach the Right," Reihan Salam

"I wrote the book precisely to memorialize my mom and her courage, her **indefatigable** will to live."—"My Problem With The *NYTBR*," Sean Manning

"What have l done? What have l done, Smee? Agreed to a preposterous plan? An absurd war? Now I'm bound by my **indefatigable** good form to wait."—*Hook*

"The man's **indefatigable**. No wonder he's held sway for coming on 50 years."—*The West Wing*, "Ninety Miles Away"

Synonyms: assiduous, determined, diligent, dogged, energetic, inexhaustible, inexorable, nose to grindstone, persevering, steadfast, stop at nothing, tireless, unfaltering, unflagging, unflinching, unremitting, untiring, unwavering

296. Indolent
adjective (in•doh•lent)

Avoiding labor and exertion; lazy

Used in Context

"It's not exactly my business, de Laage, but you've only been here a year.

Whereas I, **indolent** wretch, have spent a pitifully long time on these islands."—*The Hurricane*

"Indolence" is a synonym for "laziness;" If someone accuses you of indolence they are saying you are lazy and don't want to do what you're supposed to be doing.

"This kind of cancer can be so **indolent** that patients often die with it than from it."—"Jobs's Unorthodox Treatment," Sharon Begley

"I had a loose box, and might have been very comfortable if he had not been too **indolent** to clean it out."—*Black Beauty*, Anna Sewell

"Good-for-nothing, kickable creatures. I hate people! I abhor them when I see the **indolent** classes sitting on their indolent arses, gulping ale from **indolent** glasses! I hate people!"—*Scrooge*

Synonyms: apathetic, idle, inactive, inert, languid, lethargic, listless, slothful, slow, sluggish, torpid

297. Ineffable
adjective (in•*eff*•uh•bull)

Describes something so monumental that it essentially cannot be expressed in words

Used in Context

"These past three weeks have been great. I should be in love with her, but I'm not feeling that thing. It's **ineffable**."—*How I Met Your Mother*, "Return of the Shirt"

"This whole thing has an **ineffable**, dreamlike quality. Like I've been here before."—*Castle Keep*

"The passages where Phillips articulates that **ineffable** transport that comes from a particular song are the best in the book."—"Love in the Time of iPod," Taylor Antrim

"He threw up his hands in **ineffable** scorn, and shuffled away into the house."—*The Night Riders*, Ridgwell Cullum

"Would you not have, too, your brother Charlie resurrected? Would you stipulate your envy of him be purged? Surely, you'll insist that Charlie retain certain defects, his **ineffable** self-deceptions, for example, and purpose, so far as you had one. I suppose you would see removed those qualities which caused you to love him, and the obliviousness to danger which allowed you to shed his blood."—*Deadwood*, "Amalgamation and Capital"

Synonyms: beyond words, deep, incommunicable, indescribable, inexpressible, overwhelming, transcendent, unspeakable

298. Inestimable
adjective (in•*est*•uh•muh•bull)

Describes something so great its worth cannot be calculated

Used in Context
"I must simply content myself to form part of this belligerent expedition, hurry past **inestimable** wonders, bent solely on destruction."—*Master and Commander: The Far Side of the World*

"I am glad you were so careful of your **inestimable** eyes as not to write to me yesterday."—*Love Letters of Nathaniel Hawthorne*, Nathaniel Hawthorne

"A brilliant researcher and a dedicated botanist. And now, properly nurtured, he can be of **inestimable** value to science."—*Doctor Who*, "The Seeds of Doom, Part 4"

"The shores were strewed with articles of **inestimable** value to these poor Indians."—*The Adventures of the Chevalier De La Salle and His Companions, in Their Explorations of the Prairies, Forests, Lakes, and Rivers, of the New World, and Their Interviews with the Savage Tribes, Two Hundred Years Ago*, John S. C. Abbott

Synonyms: beyond measure, enormous, fathomless, great, immeasurable, immense, incalculable, infinite, invaluable, limitless, precious, tremendous

299. Inexorable
adjective (in•*ex*•or•uh•bull)

Describes something that cannot be stopped; also, someone who is not persuaded no matter what

Used in Context
"The memory of the night before hit her with full force. **Inexorable**. Swift. Like fast water moving over rocks."—*Motherhood*

"They are also correct that Tocqueville anticipated the **inexorable** spread of equality around the globe."—"Today's Wonky Elite Is in Love With the Wrong French Intellectual," James Poulos

"Why this usually tolerant and always sensible emperor should have been so **inexorable** on this occasion is a mystery."—*Roman Women*, Alfred Brittain

"But as for help, you must put it from your minds, all of you. I have summoned all my will to the task, and it's no use. My feet are on the **inexorable** path to destruction. A man may sometimes retrace his steps. Not from the fiendish coils of drug addiction. No man can do it."—*The Seven-Per-Cent Solution*

Synonyms: implacable, inescapable, inevitable, inflexible, merciless, relentless, set in stone, severe, single-minded, unavoidable, unbending, unchangeable, unstoppable, unyielding

300. Inimical
adjective (in•*im*•eh•kul)

Describes something that can have a harmful effect

Used in Context
"You're telling me that these things are **inimical** to the whole animal creation?"—*Doctor Who*, "The Seeds of Doom, Part Two"

"There is a general impression in England, that the people of the United States are **inimical** to the parent country."—*The Sketch Book of Geoffrey Crayon, Gent.*, Washington Irving

"Of all the tribes I believe the Sioux to be the most **inimical** to the Americans."—*Diary in America*, Frederick Marryat

"Sensors reveal nothing which is **inimical** to human life."—*Star Trek*, "The Deadly Years"

Synonyms: adverse, antagonistic, contrary, damaging, dangerous, destructive, detrimental, disadvantageous, hostile, injurious, noxious, pernicious, unfavorable

301. Injudicious
adjective (in•joo•*dish*•us)

Describes someone who lacks judgment or who behaves without discretion

Used in Context
"She said she didn't, but I took it for granted she was lying. Not an **injudicious** thing to do."—*The Maltese Falcon*

"The business world provides us with numerous examples of beliefs that are as widespread as they are **injudicious**, or misinformed."—"Ignorant America," Tunku Varadarajan

"Besides, threatening me is **injudicious**, for it rouses a spirit of resistance in me not easy to break down."—*Records of a Girlhood*, Frances Ann Kemble

"Would it be **injudicious** to run like hell?"—*Remington Steele*, "Steele Trying"

Synonyms: careless, foolish, gauche, ill-advised, imprudent, impulsive, inadvisable, indiscreet, lacking judgment, rash, unwise

302. Innate
adjective (in•*ate*)

Describes traits, skills, talents, or qualities that a person or an animal is born with

Used in Context

"The winner is Mr. Diggory, who showed **innate** command of the Bubble-Headed Charm."—*Harry Potter and the Goblet of Fire*

"The city keeps taking these blows and, in spite of the repeated attacks, continues to maintain its **innate** sense of decency."—"Mumbai's Stoic Courage," Salil Tripathi

"They had grown as they could, not as their **innate** proclivities would have led them."—*The Foot-path Way*, Bradford Torrey

"And Phil's **innate** wisdom of what people want and need has never failed to date."—*Elizabethtown*

Synonyms: congenital, hereditary, inborn, inbred, indigenous, ingrained, inherent, instinctive, intrinsic, natural

303. Insular
adjective (*in•*suh•lar)

Completely self-involved socially, politically, or personally; personally distanced from others

Used in Context

"After a while, I realized it's not that they're all total snobs, it's just that they are **insular**."—*The L Word*, "Last Word"

"The Cheney team was **insular** and close-knit, not usually ones for gossip."—"The Cheney You Don't Know," Matt Latimer

"He could see no place for himself in that **insular** world if he lived as an openly gay man."—"Gay Orthodox Jews Sue Over Therapy That Claims to 'Cure' Them," Zoë Blackler

"That made him angry, and he said that **insular** envy made me unresponsive."—*American Notes*, Rudyard Kipling

"The **insular** world of the samurai was in decay. To find a cure for its ills, some would begin to look in an unlikely direction."—*Japan: Memoirs of a Secret Empire*, "The Return of the Barbarian"

Synonyms: alienated, blinkered, circumscribed, closed, inward-looking, isolated, limited, narrow, narrow-minded, parochial, provincial, self-involved, sequestered

304. Interlocutor
noun (in•tur•*lok*•uh•tur)

Any person who participates in a conversation

Used in Context
"I guess what struck me most was she didn't mince words: between brain and mouth, there was no **interlocutor**."—*The Sopranos*, "Proshai, Livushka"

"They might also be unwilling to work with the **interlocutor** picked by the government to lead the talks."—"Pakistan's Drone Dilemma," Jahanzeb Aslam

"My hesitation and prevarication had apparently not inspired my **interlocutor** with confidence in me."—*Miss Mehetabel's Son*, Thomas Bailey Aldrich

"But not to put too fine a point on it, the individual in question is, it may surprise you to learn, one whom your present **interlocutor** is in the habit of defining by means of the perpendicular pronoun."—*Yes Minister*, "The Skeleton in the Cupboard"

Synonyms: conversationalist, debater, dialogist, interrogator, interviewer, narrator, orator, questioner, speaker

305. Intractable
adjective (in•*trak*•tuh•bull)

Describes someone or something (a situation) that is completely resistant to change, correction, or improvement; also describes someone notoriously difficult to deal with

Used in Context
"It was announced today, after almost 30 years of bloody and seemingly **intractable** civil conflict in Northern Ireland, that a peace agreement has been reached."—*Ronin*

"The father of the child says that at home he is violent, overbearing, and **intractable**."—*Spontaneous Activity in Education*, Maria Montessori

"His temper is said to have been moody, impetuous, and **intractable**."—*Paul and Virginia*, Bernardin de Saint Pierre

"After repeated conversations with Beijing, they remain **intractable** in their position. This morning I gave orders for a carrier group to reposition near Okinawa."—*House of Cards*, "Chapter 24"

Synonyms: adamant, arrogant, bullheaded, contrary, dogged, headstrong, immovable, inflexible, intransigent, noncompliant, obdurate, obstinate, pigheaded, stubborn, unbending, uncompromising, undisciplined, ungovernable, unyielding, willful

306. Inure
verb (inn•*yoor*)

> To make someone get used to circumstances that are unpleasant; to happen; to come into effect

Used in Context

"Case law shows that contracts with minors are voidable only to protect the minor and should such contract **inure** to the benefit of the minor, they are fully enforceable."—*Franklin & Bash*, "You Can't Take It With You"

"He's going to live on deck to **inure** himself to the rigours of the Arctic climate."—*The Trail of '98*, Robert W. Service

"The czar now found himself amply repaid for the immense pains he had taken to **inure** his troops to strict discipline."—*The History of Peter the Great, Emperor of Russia*, Voltaire

"Mrs. Florrick, but everything that you're feeling now will be used against you later. So it's important to **inure** yourself."—*The Good Wife*, "Oppo Research"

Synonyms: acclimate, adapt, adjust, become accustomed to, familiarize, habituate, harden, make ready, orient, prepare, season, toughen, train

307. Inveigle
verb (inn•*vay*•guhl)

To coax someone into doing something

Used in Context
"He tried to **inveigle** me also into it, but I remained glum and silent."— *Youth*, Leo Tolstoy

"We will **inveigle** ladies fair, and wed them in our secret cavern."— *Barnaby Rudge*, Charles Dickens

"You don't understand that there's a macabre conspiracy to **inveigle** me into a loveless marriage."—*Arthur*

"There's no possibility, is there, that Brian would be so hard up for money that he would sacrifice one of his own fingers in an attempt to **inveigle** funds out of his big brother?"—*Beautiful Creatures*

Synonyms: allure, bait, bamboozle, beguile, cajole, charm, con, convince, deceive, ensnare, ensorcell, entice, entrap, induce, influence, lure, persuade, rope in, seduce, trick, wheedle

308. Inveterate
adjective (in•*vet*•ur•it)

Describes a habit or behavior, often not a good one, that is fixed and hard to break; firmly established

Used in Context
"An **inveterate** networker, he managed to get Tennessee Williams as

One of the most common uses of "inveterate" is in the phrase "inveterate gambler."

the chief signatory on one letter-writing campaign.—"Sean Strub: Sex, AIDS, Politics and Survival," Tim Teeman

"The father was hardly a model citizen, we knew that he served a prison term and that he was an **inveterate** gambler and a consistent loser."—*12 Angry Men*

"This **inveterate** list maker also loved minutiae; in his copious account books, he kept track of every cent he ever spent."—"Companies Discover Untapped Brainpower: Autistics," Joshua Kendall

"Austria, on the other hand, had been an old and **inveterate** rival of France in the race for territorial extension."—*The Life of Napoleon Bonaparte*, William Milligan Sloane

"One job in Vegas isn't going to turn me back into an **inveterate** gambler."—*Lie To Me*, "Fold Equity"

Synonyms: abiding, chronic, confirmed, deep-rooted, deep-seated, entrenched, fixed, habitual, hard-core, hardened, incorrigible, ingrained, lifelong, obstinate, persistent, seasoned, set, stubborn

309. Invidious
adjective (inn•*vid*•ee•us)

Describes an action or words that can slight or insult someone and, thus, cause ill will or resentment

Used in Context
"No, Your Honor, it was a case brought on trumped-up charges. At

its best, Your Honor, this was an **invidious** effort by Ms. Lockhart to undermine the credibility of a decorated Chicago police detective."— *The Good Wife*, "Winning Ugly"

"The drive toward nihilism is **invidious**, and it adds a substantial layer of risk to the financial world and markets."—"More Mania in the Markets," Zachary Karabell

"Of course no offense is intended and no **invidious** comparison is aimed at."—*An Inquiry Into The Nature Of Peace And The Terms Of Its Perpetuation*, Thorstein Veblen

"The task would be an **invidious** one and one beyond my poor powers."—*The Dead*

Synonyms: defamatory, detestable, discriminatory, libelous, maligning, obnoxious, odious, offensive, repugnant, scandalous, slanderous, slighting, undesirable, unpleasant, vilifying

310. Inviolable
adjective (inn•*vy*•oh•luh•bull)

Secure from infringement, violence, attack, or violation

Used in Context
"He told me that in business dealings a handshake was **inviolable**."—"What the Richest Men in the World Don't Know," Barbara Goldsmith

"As far as I know, once a werwolf always a werwolf is an **inviolable** rule."—*Werwolves*, Elliott O'Donnell*

"Moreover, every form, every deformity even, has there a sense which renders it **inviolable**."—*Notre-Dame de Paris*, Victor Hugo

"Well, the question he does pose is if God created the world, how do we know what things we can change, and what things must remain sacred and **inviolable**?"—*Cloud Atlas*

*The "werwolves" mentioned in the "Used in Context" quote above does not refer to werewolves. It refers to a Nazi plan, developed in 1944, to create a resistance force which would operate behind enemy lines as the Allies advanced through Germany. The plan's propaganda value far outweighed its actual achievements.

Synonyms: firm, holy, incorruptible, sacred, sacrosanct, unassailable, unbreakable, unchallengeable, uninfringeable

311. Irredeemable
adjective (ear•reh•*deem*•uh•buhl)

Cannot be repaired or reformed once lost or corrupted

Used in Context
"If you're so far gone and so **irredeemable**, then why would they know you by such a beautiful name?"—*Arrow*, "Streets of Fire"

"Concetta left him and went home to God. In the two weeks that followed, Nicolo struggled without her, finally succumbing to

irredeemable loss. The enormity of his grief can hardly be imagined."—*The Sopranos*, "In Camelot"

"Someone took the kid and manufactured the monster, as the same time as an adult, he is **irredeemable**. He butchers whole families to pursue trivial fantasies."—*Manhunter*

"I do not believe in comforting the families of **irredeemable** mortal sinners."—*The Last Supper*

Synonyms: absolute, beyond recall, complete, hopeless, immitigable, impossible, incorrigible, incurable, inveterate, lost, past hope, pointless, useless

312. Itinerant
adjective (eye•*tin*•er•ant)

Traveling from place to place, either for work, or as part of a roving enterprise, like a carnival, or musical tour

Used in Context
"A respectable English lady traveling through the Scottish countryside, posing as an **itinerant** performer."—*Outlander*, "The Search"

"From there, Leo lived an **itinerant** childhood, eventually winding up in England."—"Melissa Leo Breaks Oscar Silence," Jacob Bernstein

"Some of these **itinerant** writing craftsmen had professional fame."—"In Our Town," William Allen White

"Itinerant" can also be used as a noun.

"Born in New Delhi, the third son of an **itinerant** gynecologist, I showed early signs of genius."—*The Big Bang Theory*, "The Tenure Turbulence"

Synonyms: ambulatory, floating, gypsy, journeying, migratory, nomadic, peripatetic, riding, the rails, roaming, roving, traveling, unsettled, wandering, wayfaring

J

Language and vocabulary specific to a particular
group, trade, culture, profession, hobby, or pursuit

Used in Context

"Elections make sense; central-bank announcements replete with **jargon**, arcane policies, and acronyms do not stir souls."—"Mario Draghi May Become the Man Who Saved Europe—and the World," Zachary Karabell

"The way she spoke. She kept repeating these words, this **jargon**. I didn't know what she was getting at, and she just disappeared."—*Criminal Minds*, "The Tribe"

"Write up a brief summary and have it to me by the end of the day. Layman's terms. None of that inside, bullshit **jargon** that nobody understands."—*Christmas Vacation*

"Above all, she felt, there was a more pressing need for it than ever before, with **jargon** steadily taking over the world."—"Will Jargon Be the Death of the English Language?," John Preston

"This piece of **jargon** is pretty common on mainstream movie sets: 'director of photography,' or 'head cinematographer.'"—"Six Words That Mean Something *Very* Different to Porn Stars," Aurora Snow

Synonyms: argot, babble, doublespeak, drivel, insipidity, lingo, gibberish, gobbledygook, mumbo jumbo, newspeak, palaver, parlance, patois, slang, terminology

314. Jingoism
noun (*jin*•go•izm)

Bellicose patriotism commonly expressed with hostility and vile language toward other nationalities and countries

Used in Context

"It just sounds to me like **jingoism** and self-deception and armchair quarterbacking. Any time you lose a war, you just wait a few years and you'll hear from everyone."—*Babylon 5*, "And Now For a Word"

"Visiting China, you are struck, sometimes troubled, by sentiments you hear that come close to **jingoism**."—"China, Rising," Blake Gopnik

"Can we fight back against deceptive news, massive media concentration? Can we fight back against **jingoism** posing as journalism?"—*WMD: Weapons of Mass Deception*

"The pseudo-national spirit of **jingoism** is the meanest and the most dangerous."—*The Earl of Beaconsfield*, James Anthony Froude

"I figured that sort of reductive **jingoism** might be beneath you."—*Covert Affairs*, "Horse to Water"

Synonyms: bellicism, chauvinism, ethnocentricity, fanatical patriotism, fanaticism, narrow-mindedness, narrowness, nationalism, patriotism, xenophobia, zealotry

315. Joie de vivre
noun (*jwah•deh•veev*)

French for "love of life" or "joy of living"

Used in Context
"We think that this thing has something to do with his excessive **joie de vivre**. . . . It's some drug."—*Gotham*, "Viper"

"Libyans are by and large charming, charismatic, humorous people with a Mediterranean **joie de vivre**."—"It's Not the USA that Made Libya the Disaster it is Today," Ann Marlowe

"The whole work is a convincing example of Brahms's vitality and **joie de vivre**."—*Music: An Art and a Language*, Walter Raymond Spalding

"You're so provincial, Bill. Do you know what your problem is? You have no **joie de vivre**."—*Coffee and Cigarettes*

Synonyms: delight, energy, enjoyment, enthusiasm, gaiety, happiness, high spirits, joviality, joy, joyousness, lightheartedness, merriment, zeal

316. Judicious
adjective (joo•*dish*•us)

Showing good judgment in the carrying out of action or in the making of decisions

Used in Context

"Now, this overdone, or come tardy off, though it make the unskillful laugh, cannot but make the **judicious** grieve."—*Hamlet*, William Shakespeare

"The retired general made a stand for **judicious** self-control in the face of the ongoing evil of racial profiling."—"Obama Needs Bubba," Tina Brown

"He did not answer immediately, for he had to be **judicious** and not truthful."—*Adam Bede*, George Eliot

"Here's to **judicious** cowardice."—*Head in the Clouds*

Synonyms: astute, careful, cautious, circumspect, clear-sighted, considered, discerning, efficacious, enlightened, expedient, farsighted, informed, judicial, keen, perceptive, perspicacious, politic, prudent, rational, reasonable, sage, sane, sensible, sharp, sound, wary, well thought out, wise

317. Juxtapose
verb (jux•tuh•*pohz*)

To place two or more things together, commonly to contrast them and highlight their differences

Used in Context

"While suggesting the free treatment of form attributed to Fauvism, this quite inappropriately attempts to **juxtapose** the disparate cubistic styles of Picasso and Leger."—*Star Trek: The Next Generation*, "A Matter of Perspective"

"The premiere attempts to **juxtapose** the good and the bad of heterosexual male online daters."—"Bravo's *Online Dating Rituals* Reveals American Males Are Creepy and Want Sex," Emily Shire

"It occurred to me. You know, you could serve them on that green platter we bought yesterday. The colors would **juxtapose** nicely."— *Gilmore Girls*, "The Nanny and the Professor"

"I believe I shall begin by making use of this map. I have the distance and bearing which were provided by Commander Uhura. If we **juxtapose** our coordinates, we should be able to find our destination. I think we'll find what we're looking for at the Cetacean Institute in Sausalito. A pair of humpback whales, named George and Gracie."—*Star Trek IV: The Voyage Home*

Synonyms: appose, bring together, connect, contrast, pair, place in proximity, set side by side

K

318. Ken
noun (kehn)

Perception; understanding; body of knowledge

Used in Context

"I believe there are powers beyond our **ken**, beyond what we can see and hear and touch."—*Outlander*, "The Way Out"

Ken means a base of knowledge and understanding:

- The theory of relativity is beyond a child's ken.
- The primitive phases of many of the world's religions are beyond the ken of historical investigation.

"The life they had nourished was dropping into the abyss out of **ken**—they remained."—*Robert Elsmere*, Mrs. Humphry Ward

"The grandeur of the achievement was quite beyond the **ken** of the generation that witnessed it."—*Christopher Columbus and His Monument Columbia*, John Fiske

"Timid and shy and scared are you, of things beyond your **ken**."—*The Sound of Music*, "Sixteen Going on Seventeen"

Synonyms: acumen, apprehension, awareness, cognizance, comprehension, consciousness, grasp, knowledge, understanding

319. Kinetic
adjective (kih•*net*•ik)

Pertaining to motion; caused by or producing motion

Used in Context
"Meeting Chelsea was a major thing, and we have a very **kinetic** relationship. It's very positive. I'm sure you'd be pleased."—*On Golden Pond*

"It is an impressive film: crisp, beautiful, **kinetic**, with humor as dark as its lighting."—"*The Social Network*'s Female Props," Rebecca Davis O'Brien

"With all the enthusiasm and energy of his **kinetic** personality, he went about laying the foundations for the new society."—*Christianity and Problems of Today: Lectures Delivered Before Lake Forest College on the Foundation of the Late William Bross*, John Huston Finley

"Water doesn't compress under pressure. A shockwave carries a long distance without losing **kinetic** energy. And if you're still within the blast radius when the bomb goes off, that **kinetic** energy will shatter every bone in your body."—*Burn Notice*, "Nature of the Beast"

Synonyms: animated, dynamic, lively, peppy, unflagging, vigorous, zippy

320. Knell
noun (nell)

The sound of a bell; also used to describe a harbinger or signal of death, tragedy, or the end of something

Used in Context

"Then the ague? The head stammers? The pain in your joints when you take your man, or **knell** to the God?"—*Penny Dreadful*, "The Night-comers"

"Lincoln's face was terrible in its strain, for the words 'in the moment of victory' had rung the **knell** of his hopes."—*The Path of the King*, John Buchan

"I owed Shoddy three pounds, and this summons fell on my ear like a **knell**."—*My Friend Smith*, Talbot Baines Reed

"In what prosecutors are calling a death **knell** for organized crime, indictments have been handed down across the board."—*Knockaround Guys*

Synonyms: bell, proclaim, ring, signal, sound, toll, warning

L

321. Laconic
adjective (luh•*kon*•ik)

Describes someone who uses very few words; taciturn

Used in Context
"She's terse. I can be terse. Once in flight school, I was **laconic**."—*Firefly*, "Objects in Space"

"In an unfinished high-rise in the middle of Caracas, a **laconic**, cynical 'doctor' operates on his new patient."—"Damian Lewis Spills On *Homeland*'s Shocking Plot Twist and Brody's Return," Andrew Romano

"Ramsey was **laconic** in response to inquiries upon this subject."—*Ramsey Milholland*, Booth Tarkington

Calvin Coolidge was one of America's more laconic presidents. The story goes that a woman walked up to the president at a society gathering and said, "Mr. President, I bet my husband I could get you to say more than two words this evening." Silent Cal (that was actually his nickname) looked her in the eye and said, "You lose."

"You know, you're taking this **laconic** thing way too far."—*Crossing Jordan*, "Second Chances"

Synonyms: blunt, brief, concise, direct, economical, pithy, short, succinct, terse, to the point

322. Lambaste
verb (*lam•*baist)

To severely criticize someone; to harshly reprimand someone

Used in Context
"Did it, perchance, have anything to do with the fact that I continue to **lambaste** Detective Hip Flask?"—*Elementary*, "On the Line"

"He will go on the stump and **lambaste** Republicans for holding out on tax cuts."—"Who Wins a Fiscal Cliff Showdown?," Megan McArdle

"This was the first time he had ever touched a book—when he picked up one to **lambaste** these boys with it."—*The Librarian at Play*, Edmund Lester Pearson

"He wants things to get so bad down there that you have to put the troops in. Then he'll **lambaste** you for invading his sovereign state and that's how he'll save himself."—*Path to War*

Synonyms: berate, bludgeon, castigate, censure, cudgel, denounce, excoriate, rebuke, scold, to rake over the coals, upbraid

323. Laudable
adjective (*law•duh•buhl*)

Praiseworthy; commendable

Used in Context
"I would very much like to commend you for the charitable face you have shown Mr. John Merrick, the Elephant Man. It is **laudable** that you have provided one of England's most unfortunate sons with a safe and tranquil harbor, a home."—*The Elephant Man*

"These are telling remarks, and they show how **laudable** exercises in empathy can end up hurting those they intend to help."—"Stop Moping! The Marathon Is Exactly What New York Needs Right Now," Jay Michaelson

"He attached himself to the king's interest during the war with the parliament, with **laudable** fidelity."—*The Memoirs of Count Grammont*, Anthony Hamilton

"Your talk is all well and good, sir, but your own past is far from **laudable**."—*The League of Extraordinary Gentlemen*

Synonyms: admirable, brave, commendable, courageous, creditable, deserving, deserving of praise, estimable, impressive, meritorious, praisable, thankworthy, valiant

324. Lethargic
adjective (leh•*thar*•jik)

Physically slow due to illness, drugs, depression, or exhaustion

Used in Context

"Anybody would say right now that you're sick. If you're fatigued with this, you'll feel **lethargic** with this, you'll feel run-down with this."— *Super Size Me*

"Compared with the **lethargic** figure of two weeks ago, it was as if the Obama campaign had sent a body double."—"Barack Obama Seizes the Upper Hand Over Mitt Romney at Second Debate," Howard Kurtz

"He was a large, **lethargic** man, who had commonplace views on all subjects."—*The Secret House*, Edgar Wallace

"Oscar is not good. He's just **lethargic** as can be and his bark is like, emasculated. You think it's from the incident?"—*Curb Your Enthusiasm*, "Wandering Bear"

Synonyms: apathetic, debilitated, dilatory, dormant, drowsy, dull, exhausted, indolent, lackluster, languid, languorous, lazy, listless, passive, sleepy, sluggish, tired, torpid, weary, wimpy

325. Lexicon
noun (*leks•ih•kon*)

Terms used in a particular profession or subject; a topic-specific vocabulary

Used in Context

"This week I also gave a lot of thought to many of the sayings in our **lexicon** that need updating."—"Some 4 a.m. Brainstorming on How to Make Obama Tougher Than Putin," Annabelle Gurwitch

"*Star Trek* is a cultural icon, and it's part of the **lexicon** now. As a psychotherapist, I have *Star Trek* stuff in my office, and I use *Star Trek* metaphors that everyone understands, even if they're not a fan."—*Trekkies*

"When you can make a dollar off it, it gets uploaded into the cultural **lexicon**, the slang becomes your normal patois of the day."—*Punk: Attitude*

There are music lexicons, Civil War lexicons, *Harry Potter* and *Lord of the Rings* lexicon, law lexicons, etc.

My book, *The Complete Stephen King Encyclopedia* has an alphabetical entries part that is a lexicon since it only contains words specific to the works of Stephen King.

"You have it in you, and in your **lexicon** there is no such word as fail."—*Dorothy's Triumph*, Evelyn Raymond

"This is widely considered by my peers to be the Holy Grail of dead languages, but we haven't deciphered the entire **lexicon**."—*The Fourth Kind*

Synonyms: concordance, dictionary, glossary, thesaurus, vocabulary, word list

326. Liaison
noun (lee•*ay*•zon)

Communication between people of different organizations; the person responsible for such intercourse; also, a romantic get-together, often illicit

Used in Context
"As a **liaison** to Stark Industries, I've had the unique privilege of serving with a real patriot."—*Iron Man*

"I was on the plane with LBJ, **liaison** to the Kennedy entourage."
—"JFK's Intellectual Remembered," Bill Moyers

"The operation was jointly commanded by a CIA man and the British **liaison** officer Kim Philby."—"The Charmed Life of a Traitor," Harold Evans

"Staff Sergeant Dignam is our **liaison** to the undercover section. His undercover work is extensive. He's here to give us his report."—*The Departed*

"I was on the plane with LBJ, **liaison** to the Kennedy entourage."
—"JFK's Intellectual Remembered," Bill Moyers

Synonyms: association, connection, contact, cooperation, interchange, interface, intermediary, relationship

327. Libel
noun (*lie*•bell)

A demonstrably false statement in print; a written statement intended to do harm to someone's reputation

Used in Context
"Slander is spoken. In print, it's **libel**."—*Spider-Man*

"American **libel** law does not require a reporter to be fair, balanced, or necessarily even accurate."—"Don't Drink and Jive," Eric Dezenhall

Libel is also a verb; i.e., "Do not libel me in your newspaper or I will sue."

"For a public figure (which Mann is), it is extremely difficult to win a **libel** suit against a publication."—"Climate Scientist

Michael Mann Sues *National Review*," Megan McArdle

"You will be called as a witness on your own side to prove the **libel**."—*Cousin Henry*, Anthony Trollope

"The lawyers have asked us to tone down the cover on Serbia. It might invite charges of **libel**."—*Shattered Glass*

Synonyms: aspersion, defamation, denigration, disparagement, insult, lie, slander, smear, vilification, vituperation

328. Litigious
adjective (lit•*ij*•us)

Relating to litigation; also used to describe someone who is sue-crazy; i.e., they'll sue over anything

Used in Context
"Three years in Singapore: another alien identity card and immense red tape in that fussy, **litigious** bureaucracy."—"Arizona, Show Your Papers? So What!," Paul Theroux

"I don't even want to think about the **litigious** possibilities. We could be up to our ears in lawsuits."—*Network*

"It was not a company to sympathize deeply with such a **litigious** spirit."—*Barrington*, Charles James Lever

"Legal got back to me about her lawsuit. Turns out she's pulled this stunt in the workplace before, **litigious** little weasel."—*Dead Like Me: Life After Death*

"Yes, there is fiction in every fact. But you know what I hate? I think I know what he hates. Our **litigious** society and a world where lawyers find cleverer and cleverer ways to make end runs around the First Amendment."—*The Good Wife*, "Net Worth"

Synonyms: argumentative, belligerent, combative, confrontational, contentious, debatable, disputatious, factious, having a chip on your shoulder, pugnacious, quarrelsome

329. Logistics
noun (luh•*jis*•tix)

The planning, coordination, and implementation of a business plan or a complex project

Used in Context
"We are supplying not only the **logistics**, but the bulk of the weaponry, the crucial technology, and the more important personnel."—"Why Libyan War Is America's War," Stephen L. Carter

"The **logistics** are a pain in the ass, packing stuff for two days spending time at his place—will it rain, should I take boots?"—"Is Sleeping Apart Good for Your Relationship?," Tim Teeman

"In **logistics**, even as commander of the Army of the Potomac, he deserves high praise."—*The Campaign of Chancellorsville*, Theodore A. Dodge

"And obviously, Jesse and I have manufacture covered. But there's still distribution, support, **logistics**, that sort of thing. For instance, we'll need a steady supply of precursor."—*Breaking Bad*, "Madrigal"

Synonyms: engineering, masterminding, planning, plans, strategy, tactics

Argument over the definition of words

Used in Context

"Our difference as to pity I suspect was a **logomachy** of my making."—*The Works of Robert Louis Stevenson*, Robert Louis Stevenson

"Originating from the Greek 'Logos' for word and 'Makhia' for fighting, **Logomachy** is a game where players fight or compete for the forming of words."— "1874 McLoughlin Bros. Game of Logomachy or War of Words," Jenny Kyle

One of the most prevalent examples of logomachy in modern society had been the fight over one particular word. *Gay*. When the gay community first began insisting that media refer to them as "gay," there was a logomachy over whether or not this should happen.

"While perfectly willing to watch the **logomachy** when it should arrive, I had no wish to take part."—*A Woman Tenderfoot*, Grace Gallatin Seton-Thompson

"This **logomachy** of vituperation [abuse] was opened by President Wheelock who wrote an unsigned attack upon the Trustees."—*The Life of John Marshall*, Albert J. Beveridge

"If this sort of **logomachy** pleases you as an intellectual exercise, well and good, if it goes no further."—*The Real Jesus of the Four Gospels*, J. B. Atwater

Synonyms: argument, debate, deconstruction, discussion

331. Loquacious
adjective (low•*qway*•shush)

Very talkative

Used in Context

"Actually, we don't really talk at all. Viktor's more of a physical being. I just mean he's not particularly **loquacious**."—*Harry Potter and the Goblet of Fire*

"The singer was not nearly as **loquacious** as she was on the subject of her son's lost baby lamb toy or the new family puppy."—"The Perils of Celebrity Pregnancy," Nicole LaPorte

A pop culture example of a loquacious chap would be the guy Elaine got stuck sitting next to at a party in a *Seinfeld* episode. He knew everything there was to know about the peanut. And he delighted in regaling her with the details.

"A **loquacious** advocate is more likely to gain his case than a taciturn one."—*The Proverbs of Scotland*, Alexander Hislop

"Oh, Lillian, you **loquacious** provocateur. Just admit it, I look scary smart."—*Hannah Montana*, "Wherever I go"

"Any conversation with Kevin Smith, the **loquacious** filmmaker/geek god, tends to go to interesting places."—"Kevin Smith's Marijuanaissance: On *Tusk*, 'Falling Out' with Ben Affleck, and 20 Years of *Clerks*," Marlow Stern

Synonyms: babbling, chatterbox, chatty, effusive, fluent, gabby, garrulous, long-winded, motormouthed, prolix, rambling, talkative, verbose, voluble, wordy, yacking

M

The creation of a secret, cunning plan, often with several "moving parts"

Used in Context

"The villain's **machination**, the lover tied to the railroad track, the train dashing to within two inches of its victim."—*The Shadow*, Mary White Ovington

"He rails about the **machinations** of power-hungry billionaires, as if referring not to the text in a teleprompter but to a mirror image of himself."—"What Clinton and Trump Should Do After the Election," Amy Davidson

"Machination" is often used in the plural form, i.e. "machinations."

Example:
"After being caught running a machination against his political rival, the ruthless candidate lost the election."

"The sheer volume of roster **machinations**—from trades and minor-league call-ups to stints on the disabled list—has been growing steadily for years."—"Don't Recognize Half the Players on Your Baseball Team? You're Not Alone," Brian Costa, Jared Diamond

"His elevation to the presidency was the act of his fellow-citizens—not the **machination** of himself."—*Thirty Years' View*, Thomas Hart Benton

Synonyms: conspiracy, device, intrigue, means, plan, plot, ploy, set-up, stratagem

333. Magnanimous
adjective (mag-nan-ih-mus)

Very generous and kind, forgiving

Used in Context
"The colossal prick even managed to sound **magnanimous**."—*The Shawshank Redemption*

"The opening of the film was exactly as I expected—grand and **magnanimous** as films like these tend to be."—"What *Lincoln* Gets Wrong About Black Leaders and the 13th Amendment," Allison Samuels

"Yet it was but modesty and respect in the author, not to bring so **magnanimous** a hero on the scene, to speak bad poetry."—*The Grecian Daughter*, Arthur Murphy

Synonyms: altruistic, beneficent, fair, forbearing, giving, high-minded, munificent, noble, ungrudging, worthy

334. Magnum opus
noun (mag•num•*oh*•puss)

An artist's greatest creation

Used in Context
"*It* is the book I and many other King researchers and fans consider to be his **magnum opus**. It is the greatest manifestation of his many narrative gifts, and the book that may very well be the definitive, quintessential 'Stephen King' novel—if we make the questionable leap that such a thing can even be defined."—*The Essential Stephen King*, Stephen Spignesi

"For years, it was her dream to create an illustrated '**magnum opus**' that addressed shortcomings in American sex education."—"'Oh Joy Sex Toy': The Internet's Most Radical Sex-Fueled Comic Strip," Rich Goldstein

"His **magnum opus** is an elementary chemistry in verse for use in schools."—*Confessions of Boyhood*, John Albee

Synonyms: crowning achievement, masterpiece, masterwork

335. Maladroit
adjective (*mal*•uh•droyt)

Clumsy or bungling in behavior or speech

Used in Context
"Are you such a **maladroit** that you can't keep a firearm without discharging it advantageously?"—*Anything Else*

"He proceeded honestly to pay it, but with a **maladroit** manner, as one unaccustomed to the currency."—*The King of Schnorrers*, Israel Zangwill

"Mitt Romney has received much (deserved) criticism for his **maladroit** comments on the 9/11 embassy attacks."—"Obama's Foolish Embrace of Egypt's Muslim Brotherhood," David Frum

Synonyms: all thumbs, awkward, floundering, gauche, gawky, inelegant, inept, klutzy, two left feet, ungainly, ungraceful, unskillful

336. Malaise
noun (muh•*layz*)

A general feeling of illness and weakness whether or not attached to a diagnosis of disease or sickness

Used in Context
"There was no Jimmy Carter–style '**malaise**' in his upbeat vocabulary."—"The Catch in *Catch-22*," Morris Dickstein

On July 15, 1979, President Jimmy Carter gave a speech in which he described Americans as undergoing a "crisis of confidence." The speech was depressing enough that it is now known as Carter's "malaise speech."

"Sometimes he would accuse chestnuts of being lazy, the sort of general **malaise** that only the genius possess and the insane lament."—*Austin Powers: International Man of Mystery*

"But repeated tests create a uniform sort of busywork, which can turn quickly into **malaise**."—"How Space Agencies Are Preparing for a Mission to Mars," Josh Dzieza

"The next morning we had very little appetite, no ambition, and a miserable sense of **malaise** and great fatigue."—*Inca Land*, Hiram Bingham

"I'm impressed, Bailey. It usually takes people 35 years to work up a good holiday **malaise**."—*Party of Five*, "Christmas"

Synonyms: angst, anxiety, debility, decrepitude, depression, despair, disquiet, dissatisfaction, distress, doldrums, enervation, feebleness, lassitude, melancholy, sickliness, unease

337. Malapropism
noun (*mal•uh•prop•izm*)

Using the wrong word in way that is often very funny due to the misused words sounding alike

Used in Context
"I was self-conscious about the lyrics of 'Tomorrow Never Knows,' so I took one of Ringo's **malapropisms** like 'Hard Day's Night' to take the edge off the heavy philosophical lyrics."—John Lennon, *The Beatles Anthology*

Synonyms: blooper, blunder, error, faux pas, gaffe, mistake, misuse, solecism

Comedian Norm Crosby is known as the King of Malapropisms.

The following are examples of malapropisms:

- "That skinny dog looks emancipated."

- "Wilt Chamberlain is an insulation to young people all over the world. Wherever he appears, after every game the kids give him a standing ovulation."

338. Malcontent
noun (*mal*•kun•tent)

Someone who is displeased and/or dissatisfied with a specific set of circumstances, often the conditions of a workplace, the policies of a government or political system, or just life in general

Used in Context

"Every **malcontent** in Paris knew that Napoleon held the key of the situation."—*Talleyrand*, Joseph McCabe

"The **malcontent** radicals who have turned them out are not going to bring them in."—*Sybil*, Benjamin Disraeli

"Majesty, these superstitious ramblings of this Jewish **malcontent** should have no impact on your decision."—*Book of Esther*

"And now let me tell you something about us. Let me explain the difference between you and me. You are a **malcontent**, major. You can never accept that which is ordained. I, on the other hand, I adapt to my situations."—*The Twilight Zone*, "The Jeopardy Room"

Synonyms: complainer, curmudgeon, demagogue, faultfinder, grouch, grumbler, moaner, nitpicker, whiner

339. Malevolent
adjective (mal•*ev*•oh•lent)

Describes someone who wishes evil upon others; someone or something that has a harmful or evil influence on people, circumstances, or situations

Used in Context

"Basically, they're these **malevolent**, evil spirits that only exist to cause pain and commit evil for their own amusement."—*Paranormal Activity*

"Instead, it makes me appear capricious, **malevolent** and cruel."—"Pediatrician: Don't Make Me the Bad Guy By Teasing Your Kid About Shots," Russell Saunders

"In the absence of facts, it is always easy to jump to conclusions; to find bread crumbs and assign a **malevolent** purpose."—"Titillation Over Tiffany's," Lauren Ashburn

"The speaker's tone was so **malevolent** that Hamilton was impressed, in spite of himself."—*Making People Happy*, Thompson Buchanan

"What do I mean by all this, people? I mean that inside all of us there lurks a dark, **malevolent** figure."—*Halloween: Resurrection*

Synonyms: evil-minded, hostile, malicious, malignant, mean, nasty, pernicious, rancorous, sinister, spiteful, vengeful, vicious, wicked

340. Maverick
noun (*mav•er•ik*)

Someone who refuses to accept or conform to orthodox or mainstream thinking; a dissenter and independent thinker

Used in Context

"I'm no ordinary fortress guy. I'm a visionary. A **maverick**, just like you."—*Superjail*, "Lord Stingjay Crash Party"

"He has always been more of a **maverick** by auto-conceit than by political record."—"McCain's Embarrassing Last Act." Tunku Varadarajan

"Listen closely to **maverick** entrepreneurs…and you quickly realize that they don't sound like traditional executives."—*Mavericks at Work: Why the Most Original Minds in Business Win*, William C. Taylor and Polly G. Labarr

"**Maverick** is a word which appeals to me more than misfit. **Maverick** is active, misfit is passive."—"Alan Rickman's Quotes," Alan Rickman

"This man who was once bigger than life, a **maverick**. It's obscene."—*Boston Legal*, "The Mighty Rogues"

Synonyms: bohemian, eccentric, iconoclast, individualist, malcontent, nonconformist, radical, rebel, unconventional person

341. Mendacious
adjective (men•*day*•shush)

Describes someone who is an unrepentant liar

Used in Context
"No, I'm pretty sure I'm a snake. I remember because I'm determined, self-possessed, and **mendacious**."—*Community*, "Mixology Certification"

"Everybody had eventually accepted that narrative as being accurate, but Mathieu now felt that it was **mendacious**."—*Fruitfulness*, Emile Zola

"Ran into Nora in the elevator. She no longer thinks we're gay. Now she thinks we're **mendacious** dirt bags."—*House M.D.*, "The Down Low"

"I think he wants you all to himself. But he's naturally **mendacious**. If he had $100, he'd steal a stick of chewing gum."—*Capote*

Synonyms: deceitful, deceptive, dishonest, duplicitous, equivocating, fallacious, false, fibbing, fictitious, fraudulent, insincere, lying, misleading, perfidious, prevaricating, shifty, unreliable, untrue, untruthful, wrong

342. Meritorious
adjective (mair•eh•*tor*•ee•us)

Deserving honor, recognition, and reward; praiseworthy

Used in Context
"Therefore, for your **meritorious** conduct, extraordinary valor, and conspicuous bravery against wicked witches, I award you the Triple Cross."—*The Wizard of Oz*

"The reforms that Howard advocates, **meritorious** as they are, require political support to be enacted."—"Just Use Your Common Sense," Henry Stern

"The Queen was so impressed that she had a watch inscribed to Miss Eagle for '**meritorious** and extraordinary clairvoyance.'"—"How Queen Victoria's Affection For John Brown Sprang From His Contact With Dead Albert's Shade," Tom Sykes

"To Special Agent Joseph D. Pistone, in grateful recognition for **meritorious** service. Allow me to present you with this medal and this check for $500."—*Donnie Brasco*

Synonyms: admirable, commendable, creditable, deserving, estimable, excellent, exemplary, laudable, meritable, praisable, top drawer, worthy

343. Metaphor
noun (*met•uh•for*)

A literary device used to compare one thing to another, stating that is not *like* another thing, it *is* another thing

Used in Context

"Kirkman does dip into **metaphor** here, as telephones are a symbol of our connection with one another."—"*The Walking Dead*'s Luke Skywalker: Rick Grimes Is the Perfect Modern-Day Mythical Hero," Regina Lizik

Examples:
My heart *is* a block of ice; love *is* a battlefield; death *is* a door.

Metaphors are often confused with similes. A simile compares something by stating that something is *like* something else. (See "simile.")

Bad metaphors abound on the Internet: "He fell for her like his heart was a mob informant and she was the East River."

"Well, yes, interesting rhythmic devices, which seemed to counterpoint the underlying **metaphor** of the humanity of the poet's soul."—*The Hitchhiker's Guide to the Galaxy*

"The fall of the Berlin Wall was of course no accident, either as fact or **metaphor**."—"Do National Writers Still Exist?," Colum McCann

"I'm suggesting that love will be the key by which they acquire a subconscious never before achieved. An inner world of

metaphor, of intuition of self-motivated reasoning, of dreams."—*Artificial Intelligence: AI*

Synonyms: allegory, figure of speech, image, symbol

"The revelation that his marriage of 30 years had disintegrated because of his wife's infidelity came as a rude shock, like a surcharge at a formerly surcharge-free ATM."

344. Milieu
noun (mill•*yer*)

Environment, setting

Used in Context
"She doesn't talk very much, but if you'd like to meet her, I can arrange a more personal **milieu**."—*The Matrix*

"That was the **milieu** he came from: the paid-by-the-word grind of the hack writer."—"Elmore Leonard Was the Cool King of Crime Fiction," Malcolm Jones

A milieu is the physical location or setting where something occurs.

The milieu of Stephen King's *The Shining* is a haunted hotel during the winter.

The milieu of *Great Expectation*s is 18th century London; etc.

"I think space tourism is the venue in which sex in space will be addressed more comfortably and more openly and I think that that will be the **milieu** in which it will finally be comfortably dealt with."—*The Universe*, "Sex in Space"

Synonyms: ambience, background, climate, environment, locale, location, mise-en-scene, neighborhood, place, scene, setting, sphere, surroundings

345. Misanthrope
noun (*miss*•ann•thrope)

Someone who hates mankind; a curmudgeon who distrusts everyone and avoids any human interaction whatsoever

Used in Context

"I don't think I like people, period. You guys are OK. I'm just trying to be honest about being a **misanthrope**."—*Dazed and Confused*

"The **misanthrope** once more retired to the pantry for shelter, and the rest of the guests were evidently disconcerted."—*The Adventures of Sir Launcelot Greaves*, Tobias Smollett

"Losers love company. And if even a **misanthrope** like me has a chance at happiness, it's gonna be pretty lonely."—*House M.D.*, "Selfish"

Synonyms: cynic, detractor, disparager, doubter, egoist, egotist, hater, loner, misanthropist, pessimist, recluse, skeptic

346. Misbegotten
adjective (miss•bee•*got*•enn)

Badly conceived or carried out, badly planned; gotten illegally or dishonestly

Used in Context

"Well, there was a **misbegotten** adventure with a waitress who lives across the hall. It ended as inexplicably as it began."—*The Big Bang Theory*, "The Plimpton Simulation"

"And a sorry figure they make out there in the sun, like **misbegotten** yew-trees!"— *Essays of Travel*, Robert Louis Stevenson

> "Misbegotten" is also used to describe the child of unmarried parents."

"The day that I celebrate this **misbegotten** marriage is the day that I ride a goat to Kmart."—*Dharma & Greg*, "And the In-Laws Meet"

"My only aim in life is to help the **misbegotten**, the downtrodden, and the members of my parish."—*The Battle of Cable Hogue*

Synonyms: dishonest, disreputable, illegal, spurious, stolen, unlawful, unrespectable

347. Misconstrue
verb (*miss*•kun•strew)

To misinterpret and/or misunderstand something

Used in Context
"Certain people might **misconstrue** some of the mean and hurtful things you say and do to them."—*The Hot Chick*

"I acted on the impulse of affection, and I am sure you will not **misconstrue** my motives."—*Frederic Chopin*, Moritz Karasowski

"But the trappers were too wise to **misconstrue** the action of the Blackfeet."—*The Life of Kit Carson*, Edward S. Ellis

"If I'm romantically involved with their father, and I advise them to go to college out of state, they could **misconstrue** my intentions."—*10 Things I Hate About You*, "Changes"

Synonyms: distort, exaggerate, get the wrong idea about, misapprehend, miscomprehend, misjudge, misread, mistake, pervert, take the wrong way

348. Misnomer
noun (mis•*nome*•er)

An unsuitable or wrong name for something or someone; an inappropriate designation

Used in Context
"Part of the reason for the bid-ask gap stems from the fact that calling Miramax or MGM a 'studio' is a **misnomer**."—"Why No One Wants Miramax," Peter Lauria

"When we call this a village it is only out of courtesy that we are guilty of such a **misnomer**."—*Fern Vale*, Colin Munro

"In my FBI profiling seminar, we learned that the notion of 'thinking like a criminal' is actually a **misnomer**, because criminals are sociopaths, and in order to match wits with them, you actually have to think contrary to your normal thought process."—*Numb3rs*, "Checkmate"

"Have you ever done a peer review before? Peer's a **misnomer**. These are your bosses. This could cost you some money, some privileges or it could cost you your career."—*House M.D.*, "The Mistake"

Synonyms: alias, nickname, nom de guerre, nom de plume, sobriquet

349. Misogynist
noun (miss•*oj*•en•ist)

Someone who hates, mistrusts, or mistreats women

Used in Context

"I don't know, Jean. I read *Madame Bovary* in grad school. It's a pretty **misogynist** text."—*Little Children*

"Because **misogynist** monsters always implicate themselves in crimes to protect women."—"Prosecuted for Standing Her Ground," Kirsten Powers

"How often before and since the **misogynist** has asserted that women have no conscience."—*Balzac*, Frederick Lawton

> "Misogynist" can also be used as an adjective, as in some of the quotes listed.

"You have given the reader the distinct impression that I'm a **misogynist**. Actually, I don't dislike women. I merely distrust them."—*The Private Life of Sherlock Holmes*

"It would be incorrect to describe him as a **misogynist**, but he successfully withstood all attempts to marry him."—*Lord Lyons: A Record of British Diplomacy*, Thomas Wodehouse Legh Newton

"I think you're a sexist, **misogynist** dinosaur. A relic of the Cold War, whose boyish charms, though lost on me, obviously appealed to that young girl I sent out to evaluate you."—*GoldenEye*

Synonyms: antifeminist, male chauvinist, misanthrope, sexist

verb (*mitt*•ih•gate)

To make something less serious, like a crime, an insult, a mistake

Used in Context

"And they seem hell-bent on making the rest of us lay down, too. That's why we need to **mitigate** the damages."—*Private Practice*, "Something Old, Something New"

"The deafening klaxons can leave one feeling helpless, but there are still steps you can take to **mitigate** the damage."—"How to Mitigate the Damage of the Heartbleed Security Hole," Joshua Kopstein

"My backlog of open cases doesn't **mitigate** the fact that your client tried to kill his brother-in-law."—*Fracture*

"He did not attempt to absolve himself or **mitigate** his offense by telling her that he loved her."—*Blow The Man Down*, Holman Day

"The more and more we put mandates on the school, to be very myopic in their focus, we **mitigate** against all of these other areas where they should be devoting time and energy, including phys ed, nutrition, health."—*Super Size Me*

Synonyms: allay, alleviate, assuage, blunt, calm, diminish, dull, ease, lessen, moderate, mollify, palliate, reduce, relieve, smooth, soften, subdue, take the edge off, temper, tone down, weaken

A mental trick, rhyme, or technique to help remember something

Used in Context

"Physical content accesses **mnemonic** data. I can see your memories."—*Green Lantern*

"And I observed that forgetfulness was a common negative condition of **mnemonic** illusion."—*Illusions*, James Sully

"We'll be using a basic alphabet technique with a **mnemonic** multiplier."—*House M.D.*, "Man of the House"

"Hard Artichokes Rarely Keep Norwegian Elephants Singapore Sleep Singapore Sleep. Harkness is a library at the law school . . . the song is a **mnemonic**, yes?"—*Fringe*, "Johari Window"

Synonyms: catchword, clue, hint, idea, lead, prompt, reminder, suggestion

Here are some good examples that illustrate the mnemonic concept:

Medical:
ABC = Airway, Breathing, Circulation

Geography:
HOMES (names of the Great Lakes) = Huron, Ontario, Michigan, Erie, Superior

Science:
My Very Educated Mother Just Served Us Nine Pizzas (names of the planets) = Mercury, Venus, Earth, Mars, Jupiter, Saturn, Uranus, Neptune, Pluto

352. Modicum
noun (mod-ih-kum)

A small amount, commonly used to describe something abstract, as a quality, a trait, or a behavior

Used in Context

"Your Honor, would you please instruct counsel to proceed with a **modicum** of sensitivity?"—*I Am Sam*

"A salty pragmatism runs throughout, and only a **modicum** of introspection is encouraged."—"Advice From the Oldest Americans," Casey Schwartz

"The lawyer's jauntiness dropped off, as if a **modicum** of respect for this man had found its way into his calculating soul."—*The Mayor of Warwick*, Herbert M. Hopkins

"Excuse me, but I think a **modicum** of gratitude would not be outta line here….I mean it's your ass, not mine. I think you should be grateful."—*My Cousin Vinny*

Synonyms: bit, crumb, degree, fraction, fragment, iota, jot, little, pinch, scrap, shred, smidge, speck

353. Moribund
adjective (*mor•*ih•bund)

Almost dead; also, describes the loss of all sense of purpose

Used in Context

"She thought about restarting her **moribund** career with a kickstarter campaign, but the potential for further humiliation was daunting."— *Veronica Mars*

"It's no secret that many European states are disenchanted with the **moribund** peace process."—"How Europe Will Vote And Why," Fatima Ayub

"Surely it was time to infuse new blood into the veins of the **moribund** art."—*The Reef*, Edith Wharton

"Her father is a self-made millionaire. He modernized factories and resurrected the **moribund** Belgravian transportation equipment industries. Then turned to politics."—*NCIS*, "Defiance"

Synonyms: at death's door, declining, dissipated, dying, fading, going, mortally ill, one foot in the grave, on its last legs, on the way out, seen better days, waning

354. Motif
noun (moe•*teef*)

A recognizable and recurring theme, design, idea, shape, or pattern

Used in Context

"Thank you, Miranda. I was going for a refugee **motif**. Fleeing-my-homeland kind of thing."—*Mrs. Doubtfire*

"This **motif** has been a classic of anti-modernism for two centuries in Europe."—"Sorry, Naysayers, But America Isn't Over Yet," James Kirchick

"It is all based on the **motif** of the Wagner drama and of the Liszt symphonies, and it is carried to quite as fine a point."—*Symphonies and Their Meaning*, Philip H. Goepp

"I need to find a **motif** that's about movement."—*Cape Fear*

Synonyms: concept, decoration, image, logo, notion, pattern, shape, structure, subject, theme

355. Multifarious
adjective (mul•tih•*fair*•ee•us)

Including elements from many different sources

Used in Context
"Hey, only my Uncle Harvey is **multifarious**. When he sang 'Somewhere Over The Rainbow,' you'd swear Judy was in the room."—*The Nanny*, "Schlepped Away"

"This book intimately and expertly covers his **multifarious** activities during each of these great crises."—"Inside Kissinger's Brain," Andrew Roberts

"His sympathies are **multifarious** and diverse; he loves everything."—*The Book of Masks,* Remy de Gourmont

"I think we've exhausted the many, indeed the **multifarious** merits of our two candidates. I suggest we now move to the election of the new Master of Courtenay College."—*Inspector Morse*, "Ghost in the Machine"

Synonyms: assorted, different, divers, diverse, diversified, manifold, many, miscellaneous, mixed, multiple, myriad, numerous, varied, various

356. Myopic
adjective (my•*op*•ik)

A lack of discernment or long-range perspective in thinking or planning; shortsighted

Used in Context
"I don't want to be **myopic**, but this looks like a straight-up terrorist act for the ATF."—*The X Files*, "Hollywood AD"

"But trying to impose such order by chasing away informal commerce and culture is **myopic**."—"Great Cities are Born Filthy," Will Doig

Myopic is a "dual-service" word: it is a medical term and a description of behavior.

Myopic actually means nearsighted, but as an adjective it can be used to describe shortsighted decisions.

"It is they who are **myopic**, because the end of peace is worse than war."—"Daniel Gordis Has It Backwards," Mark Baker

"The risk with collage is that it can seem slapdash or **myopic**, its meaning opaque to anyone but the artist."—"Is Fiction Worthless? David Shields Think So," Jacob Silverman

"The point of view is too **myopic**, too tight and close to take in the inductive argument."—*Essays in Radical Empiricism*, William James

"Yet, I find it strangely exciting standing here in a grungy hovel with a **myopic** insurance clerk."—*The Curse of the Jade Scorpion*

"You know, Matthews has this locked up, but conservatives on the Hill are saying he's gonna return to Harrisburg with the same **myopic** deficit growing mentality."—*House of Cards*, "Chapter 14"

Synonyms: astigmatic, bigoted, clueless, intolerant, nearsighted, prejudiced, shortsighted

357. Myriad
adjective (*meer•*ee•ad)

A huge amount that cannot be accurately counted; something made up of many different components and elements

Used in Context
"We capture things, photograph them, record them, on **myriad** social platforms."—"Memory Porn: America's Obscene Anniversary Obsession," Tim Teeman

"Who wouldn't be? War, terror, disease, there were a **myriad** of problems which conspired to corrupt your reason and rob you of your common sense."—*V for Vendetta*

"It is a night of **myriad** stars, shining from a dome of deepest blue."—*The Call Of The South*, Louis Becke

"Myriad" can also be used as a noun.

"To me, though, suicide is the natural answer to the **myriad** of problems life has given me."—*Heathers*

"And 'In Your Eyes' by Peter Gabriel. Which gives one pause to think of the **myriad** of ways a man can be obsessed by a woman, and what is she doing in bed to inspire that kind of obsession, and can she teach us? Because I want to know."—*Criminal Minds*, "Zugzwang"

Synonyms: boundless, countless, endless, gobs, heaping, immeasurable, infinite, innumerable, multiple, no end of, numberless, numerous, uncounted, untold

N

358. Nadir
noun (*nay•*dur)

The lowest possible point

Used in Context
"Hades sits at the **nadir** of the Lower Planes, halfway between two races of fiends bent on the others' annihilation."—*The Dungeon Master's Guide: Version 3.5*

"Nadir" can also be used metaphorically, in a non-physical sense, as in, "His self-pride reached its nadir after she broke up with him."

"The debt debacle of 2011 was far and away the **nadir** of his first term."—"Michael Tomasky on Obama's Republican Revenge Over the Debt Limit," Michael Tomasky

"The **nadir** is the lowest point in the heavens and the zenith is the highest."—*Keats: Poems Published in 1820*, John Keats

"Today you've sunk below even yourself. This is the sewer, the **nadir** of good manners."—*Unfaithfully Yours*

"I could have worked a hundred years, she never would have absorbed it all. She was the most unexciting thing God ever created. The absolute **nadir** of passion. A sexual civil service worker."—*The Opening of Misty Beethoven*

Synonyms: all-time low, base, bottom, depths, depths of despair, floor, lowest point, low point, pits, record low, rock bottom, zero level

359. Nefarious
adjective (nuh•*far*•ee•us)

Describes extremely wicked behavior and personal traits

Used in Context
"You devised the murder of the heads of The Five Families in New York to assume and consolidate your **nefarious** power?"—*The Godfather: Part II*

"He has warned about a **nefarious** gay plot he uncovered that proves gays are planning to turn 'your sons' into 'minions' of gay men."—"Meet the Man Running for Congress on an Anti-Muslim Platform," Dean Obeidallah

The key word is "extreme."
Examples:
- Screwing poor people out of money.
- Genocide.

"Her **nefarious** brother killed her man in the hopes of stealing his great fortune."—"Virgil, Jane Austen and Other Authors Can Teach Us About Love," Maura Kelly

"They do treat 'em **nefarious** down thah on the wholesale plantations."—*The Crisis*, Winston Churchill

"Ladies and gentlemen, this tall drink of water headed my way is a pillar of the shopping community who informed me today of a **nefarious** plan of his to screw my girlfriend in a very uncomfortable place."— *Mallrats*

"Fear, intimidation, violence—these are the tools of this **nefarious** scoundrel known as the modern-day criminal."—*Boardwalk Empire*, "Friendless Child"

Synonyms: abominable, atrocious, corrupt, criminal, degenerate, depraved, despicable, detestable, disreputable, dreadful, evil, execrable, foul, gross, heinous, horrible, immoral, iniquitous, monstrous, odious, opprobrious, putrid, reprehensible, rotten, shameful, treacherous, vicious, vile, villainous, wicked

360. Nemesis
noun (*nem•uh•sis*)

A bitter enemy, commonly someone who seems invulnerable and unbeatable

Used in Context
"Oh my, does he hate us! He thinks I'm his **nemesis**."—*The Silence of the Lambs*

"And that wasn't even the first time Franco had put a **nemesis** on Twitter blast."—"The James Franco Backlash," Chris Lee

"A number of reporters and bloggers have tirelessly catalogued all this mendacity, particularly Palin **nemesis** Andrew Sullivan."—"Palin's Ego Trip," Michelle Goldberg

"I have nothing to compare it to. You're the only real friend I've ever had, Clark. And somewhere along the way, you saw me as your **nemesis**, turned your back on me."—*Smallville*, "Nemesis"

"Scott, I want you to meet Daddy's **nemesis** Austin Powers."—*Austin Powers: International Man of Mystery*

Synonyms: adversary, antagonist, archenemy, archrival, challenger, competitor, foe, opponent, opposition, rival, scourge

361. Nihilism
noun (*nee•hil•ism*)

The philosophy that states that life is meaningless and human cultural, social, and moral values are worthless

Used in Context
"God help me, I killed innocent people to prove to you that I loved you, but it was pure **nihilism**."—*True Blood*, "Release Me"

"It's arguably the best film of the '90s—a postmodern pop culture smorgasbord awash in **nihilism** and dripping with retro cool."—"The Secrets of *Pulp Fiction*: 20 Things You Didn't Know About the Movie on Its 20th Anniversary," Marlow Stern

"The very faults which **nihilism** seeks to remedy are kept alive by its existence."—*Princess Zara*, Ross Beeckman

Synonyms: abnegation, agnosticism, anarchy, denial, disbelief, nonbelief, renunciation, skepticism

362. Nonplussed
adjective (non•*plust*)

To render someone completely puzzled or confused

Used in Context

"All I can say is that this is a coincidence that leaves me embarrassed and **nonplussed**. I wouldn't convict a dog on circumstantial evidence. And yet, it's as broad as it is long."—*Dimple*

"Then he's quiet, while I, **nonplussed**, just stare until he adds, 'The camera must never move.'"—"Alfred Hitchcock's Fade to Black: The Great Director's Final Days," David Freeman

"Pinder, 29, appears to be **nonplussed**, telling the website, 'The shoot is meant to be fun and very tongue-in-cheek.'"—"Catholics Pissed Over Busty Model's Topless Pics Mocking Pope," Marlow Stern

"He looked at her, **nonplussed** for the moment, and suddenly Chloe's face softened."—*Afterwards*, Kathlyn Rhodes

"Now, all your talk of the FDA and Florida laws didn't explain why my Oxy sales have dropped off in my voting district. And frankly, I'm **nonplussed** by your lack of motivation, Johnny, 'cause it ain't just my bottom line being affected."—*Justified*, "Hole in the Wall"

Synonyms: at a loss, baffled, befuddled, bewildered, boggled, confounded, disconcerted, dumbfounded, flummoxed, muddled, mystified, perplexed, speechless, stumped, stymied, thwarted

363. Non sequitur
noun (non•*sek*•wi•tour)

A statement that makes no sense relative to something that was said before it

Used in Context

"This is not a breakfast. This is an afternoon at Dodger Stadium, and that is a **non sequitur**."—*Star Trek: Voyager*, "Future's End, Part 2"

"He said he was living in a valley in Montana, which seemed a **non sequitur** in that setting."—"Faulkner of Oil Country: Rick Bass Talks New Novel," Jane Ciabattari

"Curran said he was a perfect human personification of a **non sequitur**."—*Club Life of London*, John Timbs

"It doesn't work on K-PAX the same way it works here, Mark. On K-PAX, we don't have families in the way that you think of them. In fact, a family would be a **non sequitur** on our planet, as it would on most others."—*K-PAX*

"The key is you have to make a strong impression, so you want to have a picture taken, you want to say some peculiar **non sequitur** that people remember, you want to note something unique, a talking point, for later."—*The Office*, "Pool Party"

Synonyms: fallacious statement, illogical response, invalid argument, ridiculous response

Examples:
- "It's starting to rain. I forgot to brush my teeth this morning."
- "A brown dog barked at me. When will dinner be ready?"
- "My feet hurt. What if Sally doesn't go?"

364. Nota bene
(interjection) (*no•ta•ben•*ay)

"Note well"(Latin). Commonly abbreviated as "NB."

Used in Context

"Now, look, mark them well. **Nota bene.** Here is the medulla of a malinger, the hippocampus of a hypochondriac."—*Kingdom Hospital,* "Death's Kingdom"

"This emphatic word has not escaped the watchful eye of Dr. Warton, who has placed a **nota bene** at it."—*The Works of Samuel Johnson, LL.D. in Nine Volumes,* Samuel Johnson

"It's the mad bull and the china shop, and, **nota bene**, we are the china shop."—*The Letters of Elizabeth Barrett Browning, Volume II,* Elizabeth Barrett Browning

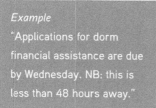

Example
"Applications for dorm financial assistance are due by Wednesday. NB: this is less than 48 hours away."

Synonyms: admonition, annotation, caution, caveat, notation, warning

O

To intentionally and needlessly complicate something (an explanation, a description, an excuse) so as to make it unclear and hinder someone understanding it

Used in Context

"They lie, they **obfuscate**, and then if that weren't enough, on top of it all, they think they can get away with it."—*Girls*, "Sit-In"

"You're not psychic Charles. Using the copycat killer as an excuse to get out of prison or using Vicki to **obfuscate** the investigation, I mean, come on, admit it."—*Blood Ties*

"What I've learned, the truth is surprisingly easy to **obfuscate**."—*Boardwalk Empire*, "You'd Be Surprised"

"Obfuscation" is the noun to describe an act of obfuscating.

"Spaziano pretended to be Hutch in order to **obfuscate** time of death?"—*Bones*, "The Purging of the Pundit"

Synonyms: baffle, becloud, befuddle, bewilder, cloud, complicate, conceal, confound, confuse, muddle, obscure, perplex, rattle, stupefy

366. Oblivious
adjective (oh•*bliv*•ee•us)

Unmindful, completely unaware of something happening or someone's presence

Used in Context
"And my lazy, lying cheating, **oblivious** husband will go to prison for my murder."—*Gone Girl*

"How dare we wax holy about 'their' culture of violence while pretending to be **oblivious** of our own?"—"What's Wrong With the Discourse About Throwing Rocks?," Moriel Rothman

"You've gone nose deaf. You're **oblivious** to your effect on other guests."—*Ocean's Thirteen*

"It seemed as if he preferred to have her angry rather than **oblivious** of him."—*The Convert*, Elizabeth Robins

Synonyms: distracted, heedless, ignorant, inattentive, insensible, preoccupied, unconscious, unobservant

367. Obsequious
adjective (ob•*see*•kwee•us)

Describing behavior that is excessively fawning and deferential; also, servile and sycophantic

Used in Context
"And the survivor bound in filial obligation for some term to do **obsequious** sorrow."—*Hamlet*, William Shakespeare

"All week, the nation has been gripped by a classic tale—a powerful yet married man meets a younger, hot, **obsequious** woman."—"Paula Broadwell, Eminem, & More Spurned Lovers Who Went Ballistic," Paula Froelich

"With a flattering and **obsequious** bow our guide leads the way."—*In Eastern Seas*, J. J. Smith

Synonyms: brownnosing, compliant, dutiful, flattering, ingratiating, kowtowing, menial, slavish, submissive, toadying, unctuous

368. Obtuse
adjective (ob•*toose*)

Slow to understand; unobservant, dull-minded

Used in Context
"People find the Bible **obtuse**, even hokey."—*Dogma*

"The energy is clearly growing to rid this country of the fear-based rule of **obtuse**, aged white men."—"The Gun Battle Since Newtown," Cliff Schecter

"Now, my friends, are any of you **obtuse** enough to swallow that?"— *The Papers And Writings Of Abraham Lincoln*, Abraham Lincoln

Synonyms: dopey, dull-witted, dumb, imperceptive, slow on the uptake, stupid, thickheaded, uncomprehending, unintelligent

369. Obviate
verb (*ob*•vee•ate)

To negate; make unnecessary; do away with

Used in Context
"If I mistake it not, the wristwatch of Mademoiselle Nick will **obviate** the necessity for a trial, because it is there, is it not, that you conceal the cocaine?"—*Agatha Christie's Poirot*, "Peril at The End House"

Examples:

- Visiting a nudist camp obviates the need for clothes.
- Being highly intelligent does not obviate the need to study for exams.
- The new medical treatment obviates the need for surgery.

"But that does not **obviate** the U.S. from its statutory obligation to cancel its $1.3 billion aid to the Egyptian military."—"Egypt: That Was A Coup," Ali Gharib

"To **obviate** this discrepancy in building with uneven logs, we can fill in the chinks with clay."—*Girl Scouts at Dandelion Camp*, Lillian Elizabeth Roy

Synonyms: avert, counter, hinder, interpose, intervene, preclude, prevent, stave off

370. Odious
adjective (*oh*•dee•us)

Deserving or causing hatred; describing something detestable; something that inspires contempt

Used in Context
"Tonight is that loathsome party hosted by the **odious** Mr. Shreck. May we RSVP in the resounding negative?"—*Batman Returns*

"The chief had come forward with that **odious** smiling face of his."—*The Exploits Of Brigadier Gerard*, Arthur Conan Doyle

"He will be **odious**, insufferable for all the world besides, except for me; and for me he will be heaven."—*Robert Elsmere*, Mrs. Humphry Ward

Synonyms: abhorrent, despicable, detestable, disgusting, hateful, horrible, loathsome, objectionable, obnoxious, repellent, revolting

371. Oeuvre
noun (*ooo*•vra)

The complete work of a single writer, painter, artist, etc.

Used in Context

"He worked very little, he died very early, so if they're added to a few paintings a few drawings, it's not going to destroy his **oeuvre**."—*F for Fake*

"Regardless of whether or not you consider King's **oeuvre** 'literary' is beside the point."—"Remedial Reader: The Essential Stephen King Back List," Jessica Ferri

Synonyms: body of work, composition, creation, opus, piece

372. Officious
adjective (oh•*fish*•us)

Describes someone who is eager to offer advice, and this counsel is usually unwanted

Used in Context

"Jack Torrance thought: **officious** little prick."—*The Shining*, Stephen King

Example:
"While the officious sales clerk may have believed he was giving me some helpful advice, he was just wasting my time by telling me things I already knew."

"How is it possible, continued the **officious** old man, that any thing relating to two dogs can give your majesty trouble?"—*The Brownie of Bodsbeck, and Other Tales*, James Hogg

"The constant advertisements and hail of yellow flags from overly **officious** officials make a PBS series seem fast-moving, with a clearer story line."—"The

NFL is Becoming More Disturbing Than Appealing, and TV Viewers Are Tuning Out," Sally Jenkins

"The help tended to be **officious**, the rules, if heeded, restrictive, and the management meddlesome."—*Catch-22*, Joseph Heller

Synonyms: bossy, bureaucratic, fussy, interfering, intrusive, meddlesome, overbearing, self-important

373. Oligarchy
noun (*oh•li•gar•key*)

A small group of people who control a nation or an organization, often for their own benefit and goals; government by the few

Used in Context
"And what is the word for when a few clerics are in charge? Religious **oligarchy**."—*Parks and Recreation*, "Flu Season"

"The franchises of the people were all taken away and the **oligarchy** left supreme."—*A Short History of Italy*, Henry Dwight Sedgwick

"'Some say America is an **oligarchy** for the multinationals,' he said."—"Vatican Science on Christmas and Creationism," Christopher Dickey

Synonyms: authoritarianism, autocracy, despotism, fascism, high-handedness, reign of terror, totalitarianism

374. Onerous
adjective (*oh*•ner•us)

Burdensome, troublesome; a duty that causes hardship of some sort

Used in Context

"This is a criminal proceeding, and these defense subpoenas are **onerous**, unreasonable, and designed merely to harass the victim of a crime."—*Law & Order*, "Blackmail"

"If he was stern, exacting the utmost, and holding them to a strict accountability for violations of law, they knew that his least word of promise was certain of fulfillment. They did not find his rule too **onerous** under those conditions."—*Lewis and Clark*, William R. Lighton

"The position of an umpire in a baseball match is one marked by **onerous** and important duties."—*Every Boy's Book: A Complete Encyclopedia of Sports and Amusements*

Synonyms: arduous, burdensome, cumbersome, difficult, exhausting, galling, grueling, heavy, intolerable, irksome, oppressive, tedious, tiring, time-consuming

A responsibility, a duty, a burden of proof

Used in Context
"You're getting the triple freeze from her. It's nice. Takes the **onus** off her daughter."—*Gilmore Girls*, "Die, Jerk"

"He ought to have thrown the **onus** of proof on him, instead of acknowledging his identity by that childish exclamation."—*A Crooked Path*, Mrs. Alexander

"Trying to put the **onus** onto someone else for your own decisions is really cowardly and kind of dishonest."—"Speed Read: Terry Richardson on Sex, Lies, and Lindsay Lohan," Justin Jones

Synonyms: burden, duty, encumbrance, liability, obligation, responsibility

P

376. Panacea
noun (pan•uh•*see*•uh)

A remedy that could cure all diseases

Used in Context
"I know somewhere that is truly tranquil, peaceful, restful. A **panacea** for the cares of the mind."—*Doctor Who*, "Revelation of the Daleks: Part Two"

"Even a ban on semi-automatics is no **panacea** in a world full of powerful shotguns."—"There's Little We Can Do to Prevent Another Massacre," Megan McArdle

"Government interference, the **panacea** of cranks and schemers."—*The Railroad Question*, William Larrabee

"Panacea" can also be used metaphorically as in, "Winning the lottery would be a panacea for all your financial woes."

"Do you honestly believe that you're the personal **panacea** to my lesbianism, that I'm suddenly gonna realize I'm straight and want to jump on top of you?"—*Mental*, "A Beautiful Delusion"

"The Common Core standards are not a **panacea**; much depends on the curricula that states and districts select to implement them."—"The Incredibly Stupid War on the Common Core," Charles Upton Sahm

Synonyms: answer, cure, cure-all, elixir, magic potion, medication, medicine, nostrum, patent medicine, relief, solution, universal remedy

377. Pecuniary
adjective (peh•*kyun*•ee•airy)

Relating to money

Used in Context
"Mr. Modell, for reasons more **pecuniary** than patriotic, stole a sample of a new biological agent from an arms dealer in Montenegro."—*Alias*, "Ice"

"Yet according to Hamilton, 'it was quickly apparent that other than **pecuniary** consolation would be acceptable.'"—"Should the U.S. Really Pay a Kim's Ransom?," Kevin Bleyer

"They saw in it, in the first place, a means of **pecuniary** gain."—*The Story of the Mormons*, William Alexander Linn

"While his client's **pecuniary** affairs were still unsettled, the lawyer had his claim to be taken into her confidence."—*The Evil Genius*, Wilkie Collins

Examples:
- Anything financial can be described by the adjective "pecuniary."
- You are in a pecuniary relationship with your bank, and your school, and probably your parents.
- It's a synonym for "fiduciary" and "financial."

"Well, nothing like the sting of over-oxygenated air and endless **pecuniary** promise."—*Numb3rs*, "Double Down"

Synonyms: economic, financial, fiscal, monetary

378. Pedantic
adjective (peh•*dan*•tik)

Characterized by a narrow, ostentatious concern for book learning and formal rules

Used in Context

"The problem was that Sorkin did too much (**pedantic**, predictable) telling and not enough showing."—"*The Newsroom* Season 2 Premiere: How Aaron Sorkin Saved the HBO Drama," Andrew Romano

Examples:
- Someone who makes a show of knowledge in front of other people.
- This word can also be used as an adjective to describe a piece of writing.
- "Even her family considers her somewhat pedantic with her obsessive need to expound on every subject."

"He's a **pedantic**, pontificating, pretentious bastard! A belligerent old fart! A steaming pile of cow dung! Figuratively speaking."—*Liar, Liar*

"Sprinkled with Paul's original theology, his letters were as often **pedantic** (whether Christians should eat meat or be vegetarian) as they were esoteric."—"The Truth About Jesus," Rev. Madison Shockley

"Nor am I suggesting that every film become a **pedantic** diatribe on class barriers; one Michael Moore in the world is plenty."—"Sofia Coppola's *Somewhere*: Boring Rich People in Hotels," Richard Rushfield

"I was just curious to know whether this kind of relentless, **pedantic** chat is a big hit with the other chicks."—*The Inbetweeners Movie*

"The **pedantic** type might note that Hippolytus makes no prophetic mention of the cinema or the Internet."—"St. Hippolytus' Careers Christians Should Never Have," Candida Moss

Synonyms: abstruse, academic, arcane, arid, didactic, doctrinaire, dry, dull, erudite, finicky, learned, nit-picking, obscure, ostentatious, pedagogic, plodding, pompous, punctilious, schooled, schoolish, sententious, sophistic, stilted

379. Pejorative
adjective (peh•*jor*•uh•tiv)

Disparaging, belittling

Used in Context
"So, you're a 'faith healer.' Or is that a **pejorative**?"—*House M.D.*, "House vs. God"

"The only **pejorative** aspect I intend by 'very liberal' is their spending."—"The GOP Should Let Obama Self-Destruct," Christopher Buckley

> "Pejorative" can also be used as a noun.

"You're a tough nut to crack…and, of course, I don't mean 'nut' in the **pejorative** sense."—*The Zero Theorem*

"I have a problem with 14. 'Do you think the president puts the needs of average people first?' 'Average' is **pejorative**."—*The West Wing*, "Lies, Damn Lies, and Statistics"

"Matter of fact, I have the transcript here. Transcript evinces a **pejorative**."—*CSI: Miami*, "Deadline"

Synonyms: critical, debasing, deprecatory, depreciatory, derogatory, insulting, irreverent, negative, reproachful, rude, slighting, sneering, sniping, uncomplimentary, unpleasant

380. Penury
noun (*pen•*yur•ee)

Horrible poverty

Used in Context
"If it were so successful, why would he exchange it for a life of aristocratic **penury**?"—*The Adventures of Sherlock Holmes*, "The Speckled Band"

"Or perhaps the plague of Strawberry Quick-flavored meth that was luring children into a life of addiction and **penury**."—"Parents Panic Over Old Fake Smarties Snorting Craze," Lizzie Crocker

"And $550 is a relatively small price to pay for the knowledge that I had nothing to do whatsoever with your financial downfall. You have brought yourself to **penury** entirely on your own."—*A New Leaf*

"For Care and **penury**, Night changes not with the ticking of the clock, nor with the shadow on the dial."—*Night and Morning, Complete*, Edward Bulwer-Lytton

"Just the travails that plague every poor widow who endures a life of **penury** and want, who's friendless and alone, whose bed is cold and unwelcoming, whose very existence is as devoid of love as a desert is of orchards and peach trees."—*Oliver Twist*

Synonyms: barrenness, dearth, destitution, hardship, impoverishment, indigence, insolvency, misery, need, neediness, pennilessness, privation, scarcity, want

381. Perfidious
adjective (per•*fid*•ee•us)

Describing someone who is guilty of vile betrayal or treachery; intentionally faithless

Used in Context
"Who will take you now with a fallen sister? Poor Mr. Bennet will now have to fight the **perfidious** Wickham and then be killed."—*Pride and Prejudice*

"*The American Spectator* proclaimed: 'It is unlikely Republicans shall soon forget your **perfidious** betrayal.'"—"Obama Escapes Scandals in New Jersey, but What's in It for Christie?," David Freedlander

"Hatto is said to have been ambitious, heartless, and **perfidious**, as well as cruel towards the poor."—*Legends of the Rhine*, Wilhelm Ruland

"And I witnessed the both of them, drunk with lust bring their **perfidious** horrors to completion in the very vortex of delight."—*Justine* de Sade

Synonyms: base, betraying, deceitful, deceptive, dishonest, disloyal, double-crossing, double-dealing, false, low, misleading, two-timing, traitorous, treacherous, treasonous, unfaithful, untrue, untrustworthy, two-faced

382. Pernicious
adjective (per•*nish*•us)

Deadly, fatal

Used in Context

"He's just a part, a piece, a pixel. There is a bigger, **pernicious**, Abu-Nazir-worthy plot out there, and we have little time."—*Homeland*, "Marine One"

"Every one is now convinced of the **pernicious** effects of gambling."—*A Journal of a Young Man of Massachusetts*, Benjamin Waterhouse

Cancer can be pernicious; poison can be pernicious; satire can be pernicious; etc.

"The biggest problem is not that such unfounded theories are ludicrous but that they are **pernicious**."—"Who Really Killed JFK? Experts Pick the Wildest Conspiracy Theories," Thomas Flynn

"Cancer is the most **pernicious**, insidious, disgusting disease of life."—"Pierce Brosnan's Life After Bond: From Action Hero to Losing His Daughter to Cancer," Tim Teeman

"I thought you started out the day with that **pernicious** caffeine."—*State and Main*

"Death is no respecter of youth. Death is a painful intruder and a **pernicious** reminder of our human condition. But I stand before you today to declare that we have a living hope and that causes us to rejoice greatly."—*Courageous*

Synonyms: baneful, damaging, dangerous, deleterious, destructive, detrimental, devastating, fatal, harmful, iniquitous, injurious, insidious, lethal, maleficent, malevolent, malicious, malign, nefarious, noxious, poisonous, sinister, spiteful, toxic, venomous, virulent, wicked

383. Perpetuity
noun (per•peh•*too*•it•ee)

Continuing indefinitely

Used in Context

"Perpetuity" is commonly used with the preposition "in," as in "in perpetuity."

"The next morning, Herr Becker received a peculiar, last-minute notice from the office of Deputy Kovacs, postponing their scheduled meeting in **perpetuity**."—*The Grand Budapest Hotel*

"It's a problem for people who see double digit increases and think they'll come for **perpetuity**."—"Here Comes the Farm Bubble," Justin Green

"Then she settled in **perpetuity** in front of the television, knitting overtight stripy jumpers."—"I'm Not The Sort of Man Who Goes To Prostitutes," Louis Bernières

"Whether or not that income was hers in **perpetuity**, or only for life, he had not positively known when he made his offer."—*The Eustace Diamonds*, Anthony Trollope

"Breakfast is, uh, my treat. In **perpetuity**."—*Dead Like Me: Life After Death*

Synonyms: ceaseless, continuing, eternal, eternity, everlasting, infinity, interminable, perpetual, timeless, time without end, undying, unending

384. Pique
noun (peek)

A feeling of resentment or anger; a bad mood or irritation brought on by an insult or a loss of pride

Used in Context
"You told me you only wanted to show me one trick that'd **pique** my interest."—*The Prestige*

"The **pique** will fade in time, but it will inhibit diplomacy for a while."—"WikiLeaks' Harmful New Dump," P. J. Crowley

"When you married Reginald Maitland, it was not because you loved him, but to gratify a feeling of **pique**."—*By Force of Impulse*, Harry V. Vogt

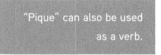
"Pique" can also be used as a verb.

"He may be unhappy, but he isn't stupid enough to withdraw the number one show on television out of **pique**."—*Network*

Synonyms: annoyance, displeasure, offense, temper, umbrage, vexation

385. Pithy
adjective (pih•thee)

Terse, meaningful, and somewhat forceful

Used in Context
"You know, instead of all the funny, **pithy** dialogue, everybody's just pissed off and tense. Marriage is like an unfunny, tense version of *Everybody Loves Raymond*."—*Knocked Up*

"She was always alert to what was going on, and her comments were **pithy** and to the point."—"Margaret Thatcher and Ronald Reagan: The Ultimate '80s Power Couple," George Shultz

"Pithy" is commonly used to describe a statement of retort that sums up a situation quite powerfully.

"I particularly enjoyed the **pithy** judgment in about five words on Comte."—*More Letters of Charles Darwin*, Charles Darwin

"How am I supposed to come up with something **pithy** and dynamic to say about cinnamon blends?"—*He's Just Not That Into You*

"NANCY: 'I was just saying to someone the other day that the Scandinavians seem to have such an instinctive feel for the human condition.' FIELDING: 'That's very wise. It was **pithy**. It had great pith.'"—*Bananas*

"I like the way you express yourself, too. **Pithy**, yet degenerate. You get many dates? I don't think so."—*Manhattan*

Synonyms: brief, cogent, concise, condensed, crisp, curt, down to brass tacks, effective, laconic, pointed, short and sweet, significant, succinct, to the point, trenchant, witty

386. Plenary
adjective (*plen•uh•ree*)

Full, entire, complete

Used in Context
"This **plenary** session of the Pennsylvania Athletic Commission is convened in order to consider the application of Rocky Balboa for the issuance of the discretionary boxing license."—*Rocky Balboa*

> The Catholic Church used to use the word "plenary" when it sold "indulgences," which forgave people for their sins; people could essentially buy a complete spiritual do-over with a "plenary" indulgence.

"A **plenary** session features a keynote address on 'unleashing creativity' from the founder of a promotions site called ePrize."—"The Perils of Borrowing Online," Gary Rivlin

"For him the blow was about to fall—not for his safety, but for his **plenary** authority."—*Lectures on the French Revolution*, John Emerich Edward Dalberg-Acton

"The full **plenary** indulgence absolved a person of all the sins that they had committed up to that time."—*Revelation: The Bride, the Beast & Babylon*

"We grant to all who contribute to St. Peter's pence a **plenary** indulgence from the pain and suffering of Purgatory."—*The Borgias*, "The Beautiful Indulgence"

Synonyms: absolute, complete, entire, full, inclusive, sweeping, unqualified

387. Plutocracy
noun (ploo•*tok*•ruh•see)

The rule of a society by its wealthiest citizens

Used in Context
"The White House is really in the pockets of the banks. It's a **plutocracy**, basically. It's not about the money and how much money people have. It is about people not having their voices heard."—*Inequality for All*

"The **plutocracy**, by contrast, still lives in the *Mad Men* era, and family life becomes more patriarchal the richer you get."—"Why Are There So Few Female Plutocrats?," Chrystia Freeland

"In the large cities the urbanized working class were slaves to a **plutocracy**."—"How Dickens and Scrooge Saved Christmas," Clive Irving

"American **plutocracy** has never got itself respected like English aristocracy."—*What I Saw in America*, G. K. Chesterton

"In the end, the only power that any of these institutions of empire or **plutocracy** or whatever have are the power that we as citizens yield to them. And they remain in power because we accept their legitimacy. And if we withdraw that legitimacy, they lose their power over us."—*The Economics of Happiness*

Synonyms: society ruled by the one-percent

388. Precipitate
verb (pree•*sip*•ih•tate)

To make something happen quickly

Used in Context
"And the fact I've got 'Desert Eagle .50' written on the side of mine should **precipitate** your balls into shrinking, along with your presence."—*Snatch*

"Anger, alcohol, drugs, economic hopelessness, reckless driving—they can all **precipitate** tragedy."—"Why I Love Guns," Meghan McCain

"If NATO withdraws, those forces will almost certainly sweep into Kabul and **precipitate** another protracted civil war."—"The Right and Left Are Wrong About My Movie," Sebastian Junger

"Toward the last he did **precipitate** a slump and sold at sacrifice."— *The House of Pride*, Jack London

"Let's remember what the real problem was: That we learned how to **precipitate** mass death before we got past the neurological disorder of wishing for it."—*Religulous*

Synonyms: accelerate, dispatch, expedite, further, hasten, hurry, push forward, quicken, rush, send forth, speed up, trigger

389. Precocious
adjective (pree•*koh*•shush)

Describes when a child is more advanced than their age would suggest; gifted

Used in Context
"She's a very **precocious** five. She announced the other day that she'd be less lonely if we were to buy her a baby brother."—*The Hunt for Red October*

"He is only 47 years old, but to me seemed older than that: a man of **precocious** aspect and judgment."—"Bonfire of the Inanities," Christopher Buckley

"Her mother tried to frighten her; but the child was too **precocious**."—"L'Assommoir," Emile Zola

"It's supercalifragilisticexpialidocious, even though the sound of it is something quite atrocious. If you say it loud enough you'll always sound **precocious**. Supercalifragilisticexpialidocious"—*Mary Poppins*

Synonyms: ahead of time, bold, bright, cheeky, cocky, flip, intelligent, mature, premature, presumptuous, pushy, quick, sassy, talented

390. Precursor
noun (*pree•kur•ser*)

Something that comes before and is usually necessary for something to proceed; i.e., to lead to the next stage of development

Used in Context
"That domed main terminal is the first of its kind, a **precursor** of everything from JFK to de Gaulle."—*Up in the Air*

"What could audiences possibly gain from watching Hollywood personnel go through the motions of adhering to an Asian **precursor**?"—"What Asian Film Remakes Like *Oldboy* Get Wrong," Jimmy So

Breaking Bad fans heard the word "precursor" frequently throughout the series as Walter White constantly sought sources for the precursor he needed to make his trademark Blue Sky crystal meth.

"It was the **precursor** of free trade—the stepping-stone to commercial liberty in these regions."—*The Philippine Islands*, John Foreman

"If the DEA's tracking her barrels, there goes our **precursor** connection."—*Breaking Bad*, "Fifty-One"

Synonyms: ancestor, antecedent, forerunner, foretaste, foundation, harbinger, herald, originator, pioneer, predecessor, sign, usher, vanguard

391. Predilection
noun (preh•dih•*lek*•shun)

A preference for something; partiality toward something

Used in Context

"I am puzzled by the human **predilection** for plotting vehicles at unsafe velocities."—*Star Trek: Nemesis*

"Readers who might feel shame about their **predilection** for tawdry paperbacks can now enjoy them discreetly."—"How *Fifty Shades of Grey* Is Shaking Up the Business of the Romance Genre," Chris Berube

"I made some success, and the students had a **predilection** for me."—*My Double Life*, Sarah Bernhardt

"This lady has a **predilection** for operations. She's had five surgeries, all completely unnecessary."—*ER*, "You Bet Your Life"

"I find myself intrigued by your sub-vocal oscillations, a singular development of cat communications that obviates your basic hedonistic **predilection** for rhythmic stroking of your fur to demonstrate affection."—*Star Trek: The Next Generation*, "Schisms"*

Synonyms: bent, bias, cup of tea, druthers, fondness, inclination, leaning, liking, penchant, predisposition, proclivity, propensity, taste, tendency, weakness

*This quote has the distinction of containing three of our 499 vocabulary words: **hedonistic**, **obviates**, **predilection**. But then again, there's never been any question that *Star Trek* is an intelligent show (and Data is one smart android!).

392. Prevaricate
verb (pree•*var*•ih•kate)

To depart from or evade the truth

Used in Context
"This is not a social call. I will not **prevaricate**."—*Rome*, "Heroes of the Republic"

"They can dodge or **prevaricate** or just hang up when dealing with a voice on the phone."—"Florida's Midterm Warm Up," Ben Jacobs

"How could she **prevaricate** to the good old woman who had been so kind to her?"—*Sheila of Big Wreck Cove*, James A. Cooper

"Sometimes I think: 'Oh, I hate you' and I'll leave you today. But then I **prevaricate**, involuntarily, and of course I still remain."—*Cuba Cabana*

Synonyms: beat around the bush, beg the question, belie, con, distort, dither, equivocate, exaggerate, fabricate, falsify, fib, garble, hedge, invent, jive, lie, misrepresent, misstate, put off, quibble, shift, stall,

To lie. To distort the truth to make a deceptive point.

393. Probity
noun (*proh*•bih•tee)

Honesty, uprightness

Used in Context
"I give you a new delegate from Massachusetts, a man whose prudence and **probity** are well known to you all, Mr. John Adams!"—*John Adams*

"But it clearly would have cast those shadows over the question of her general judgment and **probity**."—"Mitt's Mormon Predicament," Michael Tomasky

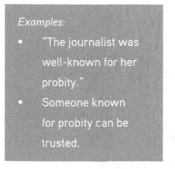

Examples:
- "The journalist was well-known for her probity."
- Someone known for probity can be trusted.

"Public life was then not only a possible but even the most natural career for a man of talent and **probity**."—*The Teaching of Epictetus*, Epictetus

"You need a wife with the strength of character and the highest moral **probity**."—*Downton Abbey*, "Season 6, Episode 9"

"This is a maximum security vault. No one's admitted unless they've undergone a complete **probity** check. There's no record of you ever having completed such a check."—*Doctor Who*, "Sentence of Death"

Synonyms: decency, fidelity, goodness, honesty, honor, integrity, rectitude, righteousness, sincerity, trustworthiness, truthfulness, virtue

394. Profligate
adjective (*prof*•lih•gate)

Wasteful; extravagant; also having low moral standards

Used in Context
"He will be equally resolute in the fight against runaway spending and **profligate** management at the highest levels of government."—*Homeland*, "Representative Body"

"The same day, one of the most reckless and **profligate** home lenders reported far less impressive results."—"Freddie Mac's Profits Obscure Housing-Boom Damage," Daniel Gross

"All the personages in this piece are of an abandoned and **profligate** character."—*Thoughts on Man*, William Godwin

"*Citizen Kane* catapulted the 26-year-old to worldwide fame. But everyone's favorite was becoming a burden. Hollywood thought him too **profligate**, rebellious and eccentric. Before long, no one in America wanted to hire him anymore. He chose to go into exile in Europe."—*Orson Welles: One-Man Band*

> "Profligate" can also be used as a noun, i.e., "He was a despicable profligate."

Synonyms: abandoned, decadent, degenerate, depraved, dissolute, iniquitous, lewd, libertine, licentious, promiscuous, reckless, reprobate, shameless, spendthrift, squandering, unprincipled, wanton, wild

395. Promulgate
verb (*prom•ul•gate*)

To talk about an idea and make it widely known and understood; also, state that a new law is in effect

Used in Context

"With that kind of authority, they felt it to take themselves seriously. And they tend to try and **promulgate** some concepts they basically make up."—*This Film is Not Yet Rated*

"The federal and state governments, at their core, establish laws and **promulgate** rules."—"How Cities Are Fixing America," Bruce Katz, Jennifer Bradley

"It is the Powers themselves who **promulgate** contemporary opinion, as they develop in apparent circles."—*The Road to Damascus*, August Strindberg

"In the first place, I hate music, which doesn't relieve me from having to snore through every confounded soiree that you **promulgate**."—*Unfaithfully Yours*

Synonyms: advertise, advocate, announce, annunciate, broadcast, circulate, declare, decree, disseminate, issue, make public, notify, pass the word, proclaim, propagate, publicize, spread, teach, transmit, trumpet

396. Propagate
verb (*prop•uh•gate*)

To reproduce; to spread ideas or customs

Used in Context

"I have to warn them. He'll **propagate**, Clyde. He will increase his number."—*The Witches of Eastwick*

"Anti-abortion organizations tend to **propagate** the idea that the procedure is dangerous and unproven."—"Abortion Complications Are Rare, No Matter What the Right Says," Samantha Allen

"A missionary is one who is sent on a mission; especially one sent to **propagate** religion."—*Orthography*, Elmer W. Cavins

"Maybe we should put in two flies and see if they'll **propagate** in orbit."—*The Apartment*

"Oak trees grow to be hundreds of years old. They only have to produce one single tree every hundred years in order to **propagate**."—*Antichrist*

Synonyms: broadcast, circulate, disseminate, proliferate, promulgate, publicize, transmit

397. Propitiate
verb (pro•*pih*•shee•ate)

To regain someone's favor or support through conciliation

Used in Context
"Yet the Brahman needed the Sudra, and had to **propitiate** him in order to use him."—*A Tour of the Missions*, Augustus Hopkins Strong

"And they being created, **propitiate** the dwellers of heaven by offerings made to the gods and the names of departed forefathers."—*The Mahabharata of Krishna-Dwaipayana Vyasa*, Krishna-Dwaipayana Vyasa

"The whole idea of this sacrifice was to **propitiate** Kroll and get him on their side. That's why I said it was political."—*Doctor Who*, "The Power of Kroll, Part 2"

"Then she told her tale, suppressing carefully all tears, for she was anxious to **propitiate** the red-haired boy."—*Sue, A Little Heroine*, L. T. Meade

"I told him I did, and it was because I did and meant to do so to the last, that I would not stoop to **propitiate** any of them."—*Little Dorrit*, Charles Dickens

"Percival had not even time to breathe into her ear the 'Forgive me' with which he meant to **propitiate** her."—*Under False Pretences*, Adeline Sergeant

Synonyms: appease, assuage, atone, endear, mollify, pacify, patronize, placate, redeem, satisfy

398. Prosaic
adjective (pro•*zay*•ik)

Commonplace, unimaginative, dull; also used to describe something having the characteristics of prose

Used in Context
"It's a good line, but I wonder whether they're really about reassuring platitudes, a **prosaic** sense of the familiar."—*1408*

"**Prosaic** needles and thread assumed a mysterious charm in the dimpled hands of the girl he loved."—*The Shadow of Victory*, Myrtle Reed

"'Out of the Past' was the name of the store, and its products consisted of memories. What was **prosaic** and even vulgar to one generation, had been transmuted by the mere passing of years to a status at once magical and also camp."—*Midnight in Paris*

"Cabernets can be powerful and exalting too, but they seem **prosaic** to me, for some reason, by comparison."—*Sideways*

Synonyms: banal, bland, boring, characterless, drab, everyday, hackneyed, humdrum, lackluster, lifeless, monotonous, mundane, ordinary, pedestrian, stale, tedious, tiresome, uninteresting, vapid, workaday

399. Proselytize
verb (*pross•eh•leh•tize*)

To try to convert someone to either a religious or political ideology or doctrine; it can also be used to describe pushing for a specific commercial purpose; i.e., proselytize for sugar-free beverages

Used in Context

"So Ted Haggard filed a counter suit on behalf of the 30-million strong National Association of Evangelicals, insisting that they be allowed to **proselytize** whenever, wherever, and to whomever they want in the US Military."—*Constantine's Sword*

"Convince them to write Macintosh versions of their software, as well as hardware manufacturers, to create peripherals. So it was basically to

proselytize Macintosh to the third party developer community."—*Welcome to Macintosh*

"When it became clear that this one would do little more than **proselytize**, I scanned his herd and realized that Aria was having second thoughts about being here."—*Elementary*, "A Stitch in Time"

"In sports medicine, we try to determine what the potential of an athlete is and then do all we can to help him or her achieve it. We analyze, theorize, **proselytize**, sometimes we even sympathize, but we never, never rationalize."—*American Flyers*

Synonyms: advocate, convince, defend, encourage, persuade, preach, sway

400. Provenance
noun (*prov•*uh•nance)

The place of origin of something, often used to describe the history of a work of art, literature, or artifacts

Used in Context
"The **provenance** of this journal is clear and under no doubt. And it's written in Angier's own hand, for which we have numerous examples."—*The Prestige*

"Today, a lack of **provenance** often means one of two things: an artifact is forged or an artifact was illegally acquired."—"Dismembering History: The Shady Online Trade in Ancient Texts," Candida Moss

"Proving that in this case, **provenance**—and prescience—can be quite lucrative."—"Kate Middleton's Charity-Auction Dress Auctioned in London." Robin Givhan

"When there is any doubt the history and **provenance** of the work should be carefully studied."—*Aubrey Beardsley*, Robert Ross

"Master Geoffrey Tipps, who, with great bravery, has saved us from a deadly assassin of unknown **provenance**."—*The League of Gentlemen's Apocalypse*

Synonyms: attribution, derivation, home, inception, origin, source

401. Puerile
adjective (*pyur•aisle*)

Displaying a lack of maturity

Used in Context
"The results were strange, compelling, **puerile**, trashy and slightly brilliant—laser-targeted towards young Israeli males."—"Israel's Sperm Clinic Crisis," Alastair Sloan

"Who would have the gall to send this? Someone with a **puerile** brain! These are both signed OG, who the hell is he?!"—*The Phantom of the Opera*

Childish, immature, juvenile—this is a good adjective to describe truly infantile behavior.

"This attempt to divert the conversation was too **puerile**, and Mrs. Honeychurch resented it."—*A Room with a View*, E. M. Forster

"Well, I can understand why you act like this, and Sam stooping to such **puerile** behavior. But I don't know why everyone else jumps in."—*Cheers*, "Diane Chambers Day"

Synonyms: babyish, callow, foolish, immature, inane, infantile, silly, trivial

402. Punctilious
adjective (punk•*till*•ee•us)

Very strict in complying with conventions of proper behavior; very attentive to specific details

Used in Context

"Your courtesy is always so **punctilious**, Doctor."—*Doctor Who*, "The Time Monster: Episode Six"

"Denis Thatcher got on well with the Queen Mother, enjoyed a drink as much as she did, and was **punctilious** about royal protocol."—"Margaret Thatcher and Queen Elizabeth's Complicated Relationship," Andrew Marr

"An old, gray-haired butler stood on the threshold, and greeted them with rather pompous respect and **punctilious** deference."—*Patty's Friends*, Carolyn Wells

"When it comes to matters of public duty, one must be **punctilious**."—*Appointment with Death*

Synonyms: assiduous, careful, conscientious, demanding, finicky, fussy, meticulous, painstaking, persnickety, precise, scrupulous, thorough

Scope of duties or responsibilities; range of authority; jurisdiction

Used in Context

"It is in my **purview** to make sure all my physicians are making the right choices for their patients and for the hospital."—*The X Files*, "I Want to Believe"

"Treaty compliance issues are the **purview** of the State Department."—"Pentagon Moves to Block Russian Spy Plane in American Skies," Eli Lake

"Clinton apparently made it clear that justice in a California courtroom was outside her **purview**."—"Outrage Over Polanski," Jacob Bernstein, Eric Pape

"Certain significant facts are within the **purview** of all but the very young and the comfortably blind."—*The Shadow On The Dial, and Other Essays*, Ambrose Bierce

"Secondly, while I'm here on active investigation, this division is under my **purview**."—*Fringe*, "Bound"

Synonyms: authority, boundary, compass, extent, periphery, responsibility

404. Pusillanimous
adjective (pyew•sil•*an*•eh•mus)

Lacking in courage and resolution

Example:
This word recently appeared in a *USA Today* article. It's good that writers are using sophisticated words without feeling the need to explain or define them; i.e., not talking down to the readers.

Used in Context

"Why, anyone can have a brain! That's a very mediocre commodity. Every **pusillanimous** creature that crawls on the earth or slinks through slimy seas has a brain!"— *The Wizard of Oz*

"The Marquess was the falsest, the most fickle, the most **pusillanimous**, of mankind."—*The History of England from the Accession of James II*, Thomas Babington Macaulay

"To remain where he was was certain death, and a shameful, **pusillanimous** death to boot."—*Patraas*, R. H. Busk

"That pink-livered, puerile, **pusillanimous** pip-squeak? Why, where I come from, we place critters like him on two slices of bread and eat 'em for sandwiches."—*Lost in Space*, "West of Mars"

Synonyms: afraid, chicken, cowardly, fainthearted, fearful, frightened, gutless, nervous, spineless, timid, timorous, lily-livered

Q

405. Qualm
noun (kwahm)

A sudden feeling of unease about something done, or to be done; a spasm of conscience, so to speak

Used in Context

"Yet I admit to feeling a **qualm** when I hear this phrase, 'moral defense.'"—"A Desperate Defense of Capitalism," David Frum

"He hated liars, he hated guys that were like this and studio people that would lie to you. He had no **qualm** about that."—*A Constant Forge*

"He felt that he could kill Bruce Browning without a **qualm** of conscience."—*Frank Merriwell's Cruise*, Burt L. Standish

"He had put her aside without a **qualm**; and now he met her announcement with approval."—*K*, Mary Roberts Rinehart

"Get you some of this Carduus Benedictus, and lay it to your heart. It's the only thing for a **qualm**."—*Much Ado About Nothing*, Williams Shakespeare

Synonyms: anxiety, apprehension, apprehensiveness, bad feeling, disquiet, doubt, foreboding, hesitation, misdoubt, misgiving, nervousness, pang, reluctance, scruple, trepidation, unease

406. Quell
verb (kwell)

To end something, such as a rebellion; to suppress revolt

Used in Context
"I depart for France to press our rights there. And I leave you here to **quell** this little rebellion."—*Braveheart*

"Police had done almost nothing to **quell** the violence, leading many to accuse the military of purposely turning a blind eye."—"Morsi Declares Emergency Amid Soccer-Ruling Chaos," Vivian Salama

"Few at home felt ready to offer up more blood and treasure to **quell** another in an apparently endless string of European wars."—"When America Said No to War," Marc Wortman

"He should be able to **quell** a mutiny, check a mob or stamp out a rebellion."—*Blood and Iron*, John Hubert Greusel

"That barely covers the cost of his room with nary a penny left over for appropriate treatments. Opiates to **quell** his temper. Restraints to chasten him when he misbehaves."—*Quills*

A popular topical treatment for head lice is called Kwell.

Synonyms: annihilate, conquer, crush, defeat, extinguish, overwhelm, pacify, put down, quash, quench, repress, shut down, stamp out, stifle, subdue, subjugate

407. Querulous
adjective (*kweer•uh•lus*)

Inclined to complain, to whine, to gripe

Used in Context

"The **querulous**, interconnected pamphlets printed in seventeenth-century Europe prefigure the culture of modern blogging."—"Social Media is So Old Even the Romans Had It," Nick Romeo

"Why the rush? Don't get so **querulous**, old man. It's bad for you."—*The Twilight Zone*, "Passage on the Lady Anne"

"I loved Sean's mind and his soul and every **querulous** and unpredictable moment with him."—*New Tricks*, "Dead Poets"

"On his face was an expression of **querulous** surprise as he reeled to the fall."—*The House of Pride*, Jack London

"I do not like my state of mind; I'm bitter, **querulous**, unkind. I hate my legs, I hate my hands, I do not yearn for lovelier lands."—*Mrs. Parker and the Vicious Circle*

Synonyms: argumentative, bemoaning, cantankerous, captious, carping, caviling, complaining, confrontational, critical, difficult, discontented, dissatisfied, faultfinding, grouchy, grousing, hot-tempered, irritable, lamenting, peevish, petulant, testy, whining

Inactive; at rest

Used in Context

"Captain, you are to be congratulated. Never before has Lokai been rendered so **quiescent**."—*Star Trek*, "Let That Be Your Last Battlefield"

"Maybe deep in our brains, a few bacteria are nestled near some **quiescent** virus and a touch of fetal DNA?"—"Scientists Find Bacteria Where It Isn't Supposed to Be: The Brain," Amanda Schaffer

"Jaded and thin, he lives a solitary and **quiescent** life, more sad and wild than ever."—*Reptiles and Birds*, Louis Figuier

"There may be a way to keep the captain **quiescent**, buy time till we can reclaim his soul."—*Sleepy Hollow*, "Awakening"

Synonyms: asleep, deactivated, dormant, fallow, idle, immobile, inert, inoperative, latent, motionless, passive, quiet, sluggish, slumbering, stagnant, still

409. Quintessential
adjective (kwin•teh•*sen*•shul)

The purest essence of a person or a thing

Used in Context

"But he was just being Vinny. He was being the **quintessential** Gambini."—*My Cousin Vinny*

"Charles Darwin, the **quintessential** rationalist, tried to use only logic to make such decisions."—"The Science of When to Get Married," Hannah Seligson

"Where the notion of doing so is simply ludicrous, you have **quintessential** poetry."—*Poetry for Poetry's Sake,* A. C. Bradley

"There are several **quintessential** moments in a man's life: Losing his virginity, getting married, fatherhood…and the right girl smiling at you."—*St. Elmo's Fire*

"Picture this: The **quintessential** family bakery, bringing a little slice of home to the big city."—*The Sweeter Side of Life*

Synonyms: archetypal, classic, definitive, exemplary, ideal, model, prototypical, standard, typical, ultimate

410. Quixotic
adjective (kwix•*ot*•ik)

Motivated by idealistic ideas that often overlook practical realities; romantic

Used in Context
"Rebuilding infrastructure utilizing the . . . anyway, my political aspirations are **quixotic** at best."—*Treme*, "This City"

"Even after Newtown, swarms of commentators warned that Obama would be a fool to take on such a **quixotic** cause."—"Gun Control Fight Finally Lays to Rest the Obama-as-Timid Meme," Peter Beinart

In Aaron Sorkin's HBO series *The Newsroom*, the main character, Will Mc-Avoy, is a big fan of the novel *Don Quixote* and has decided to model himself on Quixote's quest and throughout the series speaks frequently of his "mission to civilize."

"I stood by you with a fidelity that was nothing short of **quixotic**."—*The Convert,* Elizabeth Robins

"My massive manhood must have been sapping all the blood from my brain. That's the only way I could explain my acceptance of this retarded, **quixotic** quest."—*Eight Days a Week*

Synonyms: chimerical, chivalrous, dreamy, fanciful, fantastic, far-fetched, foolish, imaginary, impetuous, impracticable, impractical, impulsive, starry-eyed, unrealistic, utopian, visionary

411. Quotidian
adjective (kwoh•*tid*•ee•an)

Ordinary, everyday, daily

Used in Context

"I suppose that's what caught me up, too, with Astrid. Some notion of escaping the **quotidian**."—*The Sopranos*, "All Happy Families"

"The current GOP field, by contrast, finds itself hindered by detachment—even alienation—from the **quotidian** details of governance."—"GOP Presidential Contenders Are All Out of Office and as a Result Out of Touch," Michael Medved

"Videos uploaded by some mothers and fathers are less of a reach out than a simple continuation of their **quotidian** Internet habits."—"Parents of Stillborn Babies Post Hundreds of Memorials to YouTube," Brandy Zadrozny

"Yet what novelist has kept his ear so close to **quotidian** happenings, and with what dignity and charm in his crumbling cadences?"—*Unicorns*, James Huneker

"I care that you're asking me to take him to Chelsea. Part of our arrangement, you will recall, is that you assist with **quotidian** matters when I'm busy."—*Elementary*, "Bella"

Synonyms: commonplace, routine, trivial, usual

R

412. Raison d'etre
noun (ray•zon•*det*•ruh)

Reason for living; something that gives meaning and/or purpose for someone's existence

Used in Context

"The woman's **raison d'etre** is protecting children, yet she showed no sign of relief."—*Sleepy Hollow*, "Go Where I Send Thee"

"The discussion of this proposal seems to make plain the **raison d'etre** for the existence of the Sentinel."—*The Day of the Confederacy*, Nathaniel W. Stephenson

"The **raison d'etre** therefore for the book is convenience and arrangement."—*A Field Book of the Stars*, William Tyler Olcott

"Doing all six novels is the **raison d'etre** of the book club and it is the only reason I'm here."—*The Jane Austen Book Club*

"I've decided what I'm gonna do about Cuddy and Lucas. I'm going to break them up, of course. It's given me a purpose in life, a goal, a **raison d'etre**, albeit a selfish, mean-spirited, childish raison."—*House M.D.*, "Ignorance is Bliss"

Synonyms: basis, foundation, justification, justification for existing, logic, motivation, reason for existing, reasoning, reason why, underlying principle

413. Rancorous
adjective (*rank•or•us*)

Feeling bitter and long-lasting ill will, hatred, or resentment

Used in Context
"You could say that I'm intimately knowledgeable with the **rancorous** workings of the Mob."—*Career Opportunities*

"The **rancorous** debate ended on December 7, 1941, when the U.S. entered the war after the Japanese attacked Pearl Harbor."—"The Fight Over America's Entrance to WWII," Sandra McElwaine

"Smile in men's faces, smooth, deceive and cog, I must be held a **rancorous** enemy."—*Richard III*, William Shakespeare

Synonyms: acrimonious, bitter, embittered, frowning, grudging, implacable, merciless, offended, pitiless, resentful, ruthless, unforgiving, vengeful

414. Recalcitrant
adjective (ree•*kal*•sih•trent)

Resisting proper authority; difficult to deal with, control, or manage

Used in Context

"Your jacket reads like a bad detective novel. Volatile, **recalcitrant**. And the highest arrest record in the history of my field office."—*Sons of Anarchy*, "One One Six"

"These willfully ignorant, **recalcitrant** obstructionists are doing the country a tremendous service."—"Red States Respond To Obamacare With Angry Tea-Party Denial," Joe McLean

"The University was at first **recalcitrant** to my project of itself undertaking the process of heresy against Joan."—*The Executioner's Knife; Or, Joan of Arc* by Eugène Sue

"Don't be **recalcitrant**, Kevin. You know it brings out the worst in me."—*Supernatural*, "A Little Slice of Kevin"

"Recalcitrant" can also be used as a noun.

"Every signatory pledged to make sure the temperature wouldn't rise about that. The EU, Japan, Russia, China, countries that make their money selling oil like the United Arab Emirates, the most conservative, **recalcitrant**, reluctant countries on earth. Even the United States. If the world officially believes anything about climate changes it's that 2 degrees is too much."—*Do the Math*

"Though he was described as willing to talk, the C.I.A. moved him to a secret prison and immediately applied interrogation methods reserved for **recalcitrant** prisoners."—"How U.S. Torture Left a Legacy of Damaged Minds," Matt Apuzzo, Sheri Fink, James Risen

Synonyms: defiant, disobedient, fractious, insubordinate, intractable, obstinate, opposed, rebellious, refractory, resistant, resisting, stubborn, undisciplined, ungovernable, unmanageable, unruly, wayward, wild, willful

415. Recompense
noun (*reh*•kum•pens)

Payment for services rendered; compensation

Used in Context
"So you take the world I love as a **recompense** for your imagined slights?"—*The Avengers*

"These provisions materially reduce living expenses, and, in a way, **recompense** for the low salaries received."—*The School System of Norway*, David Allen Anderson

"I will not accept any **recompense**; but pray don't take offense."—*The Lost Child*, François Edouard Joachim Coppée

Synonyms: amends, atonement, damages, disbursement, emolument, pay, payment, reimbursement, remuneration, reparation, repayment, requital, reward, satisfaction, tip, wages

416. Rectitude
noun (*rek•*tih•tood)

Moral integrity, righteous principles, probity, character, correct judgment

Used in Context

"I invented moral fiber! Pappy was displaying **rectitude** when that egghead you work for was still messin' in his drawers!"—*O Brother, Where Art Thou?*

"Maybe it is his own reputation for **rectitude**, a reputation buttressed by the lack of scandals in his administration."—"Lousy Economy Won't Sink Obama," Peter Beinart

"Happily, it is not necessary they should try to, since you have returned to the path of **rectitude**."—*A Pessimist*, Robert Timsol

"You swore an oath to defend this country and behave with moral **rectitude**. Were you thinking of morals when you gave the go-ahead on Dorado Falls?"—Criminal Minds, "Dorado Falls"

"Now, every network has a censor, a guardian of moral **rectitude**, whose job is to ensure the viewing public is not corrupted by scenes of sex, violence or any other miscellaneous vulgarity."—*Millennium*, "Somehow Satan Got Behind Me"

Synonyms: correctness, decency, goodness, honesty, integrity, morality, righteousness, virtue

Having personal characteristics or traits worthy of respect or, in some cases, fear

Used in Context

"The door itself is of **redoubtable** Pittsburgh steel, when the casino closes, this entire underground complex is locked up, and the armed guard retreats to the casino's main entrance."—*The Ladykiller*

"Even the intelligence operations of the **redoubtable** New York City Police Department are under fire."—"The Second Oldest Profession is Here to Stay," Christopher Dickey

"The counsel for the defense felt he had been entrapped in attempting to be sarcastic with the **redoubtable** detective."—*The Big Bow Mystery*, I. Zangwill

"It's with surpassing pleasure and pride that I announce that Congress, just a short time ago, voted to confirm Robert Russell as the new Vice President of these United States; confirmed by unanimous vote, as befits this **redoubtable** choice."—*The West Wing*, "Han"

Synonyms: awesome, brave, courageous, fearsome, formidable, frightening, illustrious, imminent, terrible, valiant

418. Remonstrate
verb (ree•*mon*•strate)

To argue forcefully with someone; to passionately try to reason with someone

Used in Context
"And if you would take my advice, don't do as I did. Rage, **remonstrate**. Play the wounded wife."—*The Borgias*, "The Borgia Bull"

"They will expostulate, they will **remonstrate**, but they will not go to war with their own Colonies."—*Freedom's Battle*, Mahatma Gandhi

"I found it idle to **remonstrate** with the king about the indolence of his subjects."—*Captain Canot*, Brantz Mayer

"Well, I caught him by the arm to **remonstrate** with him and he shouted, 'Let me go. They'll kill him.'"—*Doctor Who*, "The Deadly Assassin, Part 2."

Synonyms: argue, bicker, blame, censure, challenge, combat, complain, criticize, decry, disapprove, disparage, dispute, fight, gripe, object, protest, recriminate, scold, sound off, squabble

419. Reproach
verb (ree•*proche*)

To criticize someone for making a mistake or doing something incorrectly; to feel ashamed for bad behavior

Used in Context
"Well be that as it may, General, it is the position of the President

that when our national security is at stake, no one is above **reproach**."—*Transformers: Revenge of the Fallen*

"Reproach" can also be used as a noun.

"As he moves towards a conclusion, he sounds an extended note of **reproach**."—"Samuel Johnson Pens an Erotic Love Letter," Ian McIntyre

"As we have seen above, all must participate that none may be in a position to **reproach** the rest."—*Folkways*, William Graham Sumner

"Oh! Is this about my wife? My wife is beyond **reproach**. She is, after all, my wife."—*Anna Karenina*

"And now nothing remains but for me to assure you in the most animated language of the violence of my affections. And no **reproach** on the subject of fortune will cross my lips once we're married."—*Pride & Prejudice*

Synonyms: accuse, blame, censure, chide, condemn, rebuke, reprimand, reprove, scold, scorn, upbraid

420. Reprobate
noun (*rep•row•bate*)

An immoral person; a person of vile reputation; a depraved person

Used in Context
"'Come out and show me this **reprobate**,' said the husband, rising."—*The Wreck of the Titan*, Morgan Robertson

"Reprobate" can also be used as an adjective.

"And he isn't a thief. You're the thief. You're nothing but a **reprobate**."—*Hugo*

"Alice would not condescend to join her **reprobate** brother, even in abuse of Adela."—*Demos*, George Gissing

"Reputation is everything in our society. Yours, my disinherited **reprobate**, has expired."—*Cloud Atlas*

Synonyms: black sheep, cad, criminal, degenerate, delinquent, deviant, good-for-nothing, lecher, miscreant, no-good, offender, outcast, pariah, rogue, scoundrel, tramp, troublemaker, wastrel, wretch, wrongdoer

421. Requisite
adjective (*rek•wiz•it*)

Necessary, indispensable

Used in Context
"If you're lucky, you have the **requisite** head shape and confidence to go out in sunglasses that are essentially a four-alarm fire on your face."—"Trying Snap's Spectacles: Live With the Look, Enjoy the View," Farhad Manjoo

"Voting three weeks from today is reduced to 182, which means 122 yes votes to reach the **requisite** two-thirds of the House."—*Lincoln*

"Evidence you gave your children the **requisite** amount of attention: they have no interest in being famous."—"How to Be Smart on Twitter," Alain de Botton

"Self-confidence is the first **requisite** to great undertakings."—*The Works of Samuel Johnson, LL.D. in Nine Volumes*, Samuel Johnson

"Which is why I think you've gotta wait the **requisite** three days before you call."—*The Vow*

Synonyms: basic, called for, condition, essential, mandatory, must, needed, obligatory, precondition, required, requirement, vital

Examples:
- "The requisite text for this course is *The Norton Field Guide to Writing.*"
- "The requisite equipment for playing baseball includes balls, bats, and gloves."

422. Res ipsa loquitur
noun (*ray*•ep•suh•*low*•kuh•tur)

Legal term; Latin for "The thing speaks for itself"

Used in Context
"Some suggest it was a fuel tank. Others, a faulty wire. Truth is, we don't know. **Res ipsa loquitur.** What that basically means is, the thing speaks for itself. The plane crashed. It speaks for itself."—*Ally McBeal*, "The Blame Game"

Something, usually negative, would not have happened without negligence and the evidence is so blatant, it speaks for itself.

"**Res ipsa loquitur.** She accepted what she had to have known were stolen goods on at least one occasion."—*Law & Order*, "Star Crossed"

"No doubt **res ipsa loquitur** gives a possible mode of treating cases where one maintains something likely to get out of hand and do injury."—*An Introduction to the Philosophy of Law*, Roscoe Pound

Synonyms: evidence, law, legal doctrine, rule of evidence, ruling

423. Risible
adjective (ris•ih•buhl)

Causing someone to laugh, oftentimes sardonically

Used in Context

"Cat and dog Warblers? I mean, the very question is **risible**. How about a student who's a skunk? Should it be allowed to become a Warbler?"—*Glee*, "Homecoming"

"Funny, but years ago the idea of seatbelts other than in an airplane or tobacco being deadly was **risible**."—"Stop Indulging, America," Margaret Carlson

"The argument depends on a number of **risible** and obviously untrue assumptions."—"Single Mothers Are Not America's Real Welfare Queens," Amanda Marcotte

"Mr. Trump's dwindling ranks of Republican apologists, including New Jersey Gov. Chris Christie and Carl Paladino, a one-time GOP gubernatorial candidate in New York, insist, against the evidence of the candidate's own words, that he never called for a total ban on Muslims coming to the United States. That **risible** assertion serves no other purpose than to confirm that his own allies realize that Mr. Trump's proposal was politically toxic."—"Mr. Trump's Gibberish on Muslims," *The Washington Post* Editorial Board

"It wasn't so very long ago that democracy itself sounded **risible**."—*37 Days: One Month in Summer*

Synonyms: amusing, comical, droll, funny, humorous, laughable, ludicrous

424. Rostrum
noun (*ros•trum*)

A raised platform, often used for public speaking

Used in Context

"The materials are gonna be on the **rostrum** only once before the print is made!"—*Talking Heads 2*

"Mr. Roosevelt is leaving the **rostrum** now on the arm of Captain James Roosevelt."—*The Winds of War*

"There is no mind wandering. I wish I could conduct the rest of my life like I do on the **rostrum**."—"Lorna Kelly Dies at 70; Left the Sotheby's Rostrum to Help the Poor," Margalit Fox

"It was hard not to get mixed messages from the **rostrum**, too."—"Fear and Loathing at the Republican Leadership Conference," David Freedlander

"Louise sat up on the **rostrum**, appointing the students to their parts."—*Hester's Counterpart*, Jean K. Baird

Synonyms: dais, lectern, podium, pulpit, reading stand, soapbox, stage, stand

425. Ruminate
verb (*roo•min•ate*)

To think long and carefully about an important subject or decision

Used in Context

"You don't realize what you got here. So why don't you **ruminate** while I illuminate the possibilities?"—*Aladdin*

"They post OOTDs (outfits of the day) and **ruminate** on body positivity."—"The Plus-Size Blogging Craze," Judy McGuire

"There are other, more contrived invitations to **ruminate**, such as the pendulum that hangs from the ceiling and trickles sand into a shallow box."—"Temples for the Literary Pilgrim," Drew Gardner, Samantha Quick, Maureen Towey

"Here our conversation ended, and I retired to **ruminate** on what had passed."—*Arthur Mervyn*, Charles Brockden Brown

"Hiking our skirts to Helena might put Yankton back on its heels. And as minutes turn to hours over the piss-pot, I wonder, should we **ruminate** publicly in loud voices over forming a new territory with an eye towards future statehood, or even our own republic?"—*Deadwood*, "Childish Things"

Synonyms: brainstorm, brood, chew over, cogitate, consider, deliberate, excogitate, meditate, mull over, muse, ponder, rack one's brain, reflect, stew about, think over, use one's head

S

Describes someone who is profoundly knowledgeable and whose expertise is based on a combination of intelligence, judgment, and education

Used in Context

"And according to my **sagacious** calculations, this is a big dog. At least 100 pounds."—*CSI*, "Justice Is Served"

"When storm clouds start to form, **sagacious** leaders deal with them before things get out of hand."—"Former Lobbyist Jack Abramoff On Congressional Travel Disclosure," Jack Abramoff

"The exhibition of the evidence showed how penetrating, how **sagacious**, as well as how industrious, malice can be."—*Deerbrook*, Harriet Martineau

"He was simply **sagacious** enough to see that all people must breathe."—*Big Jim MacLain*

Synonyms: apt, astute, canny, clever, discerning, erudite, insightful, knowing, learned, sage, savvy, sharp, smart, perceptive, wise, witty

427. Salient
adjective (*say•lee•ent*)

Noticeable; standing out conspicuously; relevant

Used in Context
"We know little of war, but much of vengeance. And the one **salient** point is this: vengeance is patient. It can wait a lifetime if necessary."— *The Borgias*, "Stray Dogs"

"The most **salient** poll of all—January's general elections—reflected no different tendencies."—"Beneath The Surface Of Israeli Content," Michal Levertov

Examples:
- A salient difference in productivity would mean that improvements made contributed to a noticeable increase in production.
- If an expert comments on something, his insight would be considered salient due to his credentials; he or she'd be credible.

"We can but skim the surface, and try to bring out the **salient** points."—*Expositions of Holy Scripture*, Alexander Maclaren

"What none of you glean is that the King is expressing a particularly **salient** view of the stage."—*Stage Beauty*

Synonyms: conspicuous, important, main, most important, notable, outstanding, prominent, remarkable, significant, striking, weighty

428. Salutary
adjective (*sal*•yoo•tair•ee)

Something that is good for you; something that promotes good health

Used in Context
"This drink has a very **salutary** effect. It's called 'Roadkill.' See if you like it."—*The L Word*, "Longing"

"But this **salutary** revolution, like so many revolutions, overstepped, and resulted in the Great Inversion."—"Why Can't We Talk About Culture?," Gil Troy

"In case of disease, this mode of exercise is sometimes one of the most **salutary** in the world."—*The Young Mother*, William A. Alcott

"I write this testament as a scientist and as a **salutary** lesson to those who would tamper with nature."—*Dr. Jekyll & Sister Hyde*

Synonyms: aiding, beneficial, constructive, healthful, helpful, nourishing, nutritious, restorative, salubrious, tonic, useful, valuable, wholesome

429. Sanguine
adjective (*san*•gwin)

Describes someone who is noticeably optimistic and cheerful

Used in Context

"The letter is **sanguine**. There is barely an oath in it from beginning to end."—*Persuasion*

"Why was his team so **sanguine** about its own polling, even though it often parted company with the publicly available data?"—"Was Romney Really Shocked to Lose?," Justin Green

"Nothing is lost; Antonelli is calm and **sanguine**, though, rest assured, there is no doubt about what I tell you."—*Lothair*, Benjamin Disraeli

"But before I answer any more questions what color was my smoke? Was it blue? If it was blue, it means that I am melancholy and **sanguine**. That means that I need more 'me' time."—*Arabian Nights*

Synonyms: animated, assured, buoyant, confident, enthusiastic, hopeful, lively, positive, self-assured, spirited, upbeat

430. Sardonic
adjective (sar•*don*•ik)

Bitterly sarcastic, grimly mocking

Used in Context

"This is the moment where she lets down her defenses. It's not dry, it's not **sardonic**, it's just honest and it's vulnerable."—*Dawson's Creek*, "Guerrilla Filmmaking"

"'Louie has a typical day'—that's the log line, **sardonic** and perfect."—"Why Is Louis C.K. So Funny? He Uses Humor as a Moral Compass," Andrew Romano

"The Doctor grinned at her with **sardonic** enjoyment of her predicament."—*When the Cock Crows*, Waldron Baily

"His new work is the Tobacco Project, a **sardonic** reflection on global capitalism and China's new cult of money."—*Art of China*

Synonyms: acerbic, arrogant, biting, caustic, contemptuous, derisive, disrespectful, ironic, mocking, mordant, nasty, offensive, sarcastic, scorching, scornful, sneering, taunting

> A sardonic comment has a much sharper edge to it than just plain sarcasm. There is an element of real insult in a sardonic remark.
> *Example:*
> "Regarding the assignment you asked me about, the directions explain what needs to be done . . . you can read, right?"

431. Satiate
verb (*say•she•ate*)

Satisfy completely

Used in Context

"To protect ourselves from the fear Death instills, to **satiate** our beings with pleasure, we create a paradise by and of ourselves."—*Neon Genesis Evangelion*, "The Fourth Child"

"And the not-so-subtle winks to Batman lore will be enough to **satiate** hungry fanboys for now."—"Batman Deserves Better Than *Gotham*," Sujay Kumar

"Must the flower of the world's manhood continue to be flung into the jaws of death to **satiate** the blood lust of militarism?"—*Our National Defense*, George Hebard Maxwell

"I think it's important to keep a safe distance, otherwise you will fully **satiate** me."—*Newlyweds*

Synonyms: fill, gratify, indulge, overfill, quench, sate, slake

432. Scintilla
noun (sin•*till*•uh)

A minute amount; an iota or trace

Used in Context

"They must believe beyond a **scintilla** of a doubt that she committed premeditated murder, or they acquit."—*Law & Order*, "The Wages of Love"

"How could anyone do all this without leaving behind a **scintilla** of microscopic evidence?"—"Stop Calling It Murder," Roy Black

A tiny, tiny amount that actually isn't measurable.
Examples:

- There isn't a scintilla of evidence that my client is guilty.
- Charles Manson has never shown even a scintilla of remorse.

"Not a **scintilla** of proof appeared that these men were spies."—*The Life of Jefferson Davis*, Frank H. Alfriend

"Why don't you use that newly acquired **scintilla** of power and influence to get Summer here to write an article about your man Robredo?"—*Definitely, Maybe*

Synonyms: dab, iota, particle, pinch, small quantity, smidgen, spot

433. Scurrilous
adjective (*scoor*•uh•lus)

Using rude, vulgar, slanderous language, often to defame

Used in Context

"These charges are **scurrilous**. It's a vain attempt to attack a fine young man."—*Oz*, "Exuent Omnes"

"The White House counsel was done in by a **scurrilous** leaks campaign."—"The Assassination of Greg Craig," Steve Clemons

"Did you never see a man who thought he was witty, when he was only **scurrilous** and impudent?"—*My Wife and I*, Harriet Beecher Stowe

"This fellow writes in the most **scurrilous** newspapers; you have told me so yourself."—*A Doll's House*, Henrik Ibsen

Synonyms: abusive, coarse, defamatory, filthy, foul, indecent, insulting, libelous, offensive, opprobrious, scandalous, slanderous, truculent, vituperative, vulgar

434. Seditious
adjective (suh•*dish*•us)

Being rebellious against a government

Used in Context

"Arrest warrant and automatic imprisonment for possession of materials considered **seditious**."—*Gandhi*

"He had not written, but had dared to print, a **seditious** pamphlet which justified the right of rebellion against the king."—"The Real Story of 'O,'" Robert McCrum

"But conservatives think liberals and Balzac are **seditious** and crazy."—"Romney's Worst Nightmare," Michael Tomasky

"Sedition" is the noun form of this adjective.

"The **seditious** magistrates were arrested and thrown into prison."—*Journal of a Voyage to Brazil*, Maria Graham

"Words like 'freedom' and 'peace' were seen as subversive and potentially **seditious** in certain quarters of the federal government, especially coming from a popular singer."—"Pete Seeger Delivered the News for Generations," Greg Kot

"Many messianic leaders of the time, most or all of them came to a bad end. Usually by crucifixion, because crucifixion was the Roman punishment for **seditious** activity."—*Caesar's Messiah: The Roman Conspiracy to Invent Jesus*

Synonyms: anarchistic, bellicose, defiant, disloyal, disobedient, dissident, factious, iconoclastic, insurgent, mutinous, radical, revolutionary, riotous, subversive, treasonous

435. Semantics
noun (suh•*man*•tix)

The study of how words and sentences create meaning

Used in Context

"The **semantics** make a difference, she said, because a voluntary evacuation will have a lower rate of compliance than one labeled mandatory."—"How to Get People to Evacuate? Try Fear," Christopher Mele

"Her disassociation with the feminist label and its negative connotations just boils down to **semantics**."—"Susan Sarandon Says She's Not a Feminist: Why She Dumped the Label," Lizzie Crocker

"Luntz refused to bite, remaining focused on policy when I was seeking to engage him on a matter of **semantics**."—"A Global Warming Conversion," Michael Smerconish

"I'm offering you my body, and you're offering me **semantics**."—*Clerks*

"This shouldn't be **semantics** or money. People will read this, and they'll believe us."—*The Paper*

Synonyms: connotation, definition, denotation, explanation, explication, exposition, interpretation, symbiology, symbolism

436. Simile
noun (*sim*•uh•lee)

A grammatical device in which you state that something is *like* something else: it uses "like" or "as" for comparison

Used in Context
"Stop the **simile**. No use in conjuring up imagery I'll only have to repress later."—*Frasier*, "Semi-Decent Proposal"

"The frame, to pursue our **simile**, is to the ship what ribs are to our bodies."—*All Afloat*, William Wood

<table>
<tr><td>

Examples:
- "I've been working like a dog."
- "He eats like a pig."
- "Her skin was as cold as ice."

</td><td>

"The **simile** striking her as original and clever, she made him a pretty compliment."—*Athalie*, Robert W. Chambers

"It's the creaking gate that gets oiled. A somewhat unfortunate **simile**."—*The Killing of King George*

</td></tr>
</table>

"An ordinary idiot can take a metaphor literally, but it takes a special kind of idiot to take a **simile** literally."—"Divide and Conquer," James Taranto

Synonyms: allegory, analogy, comparison, figure of speech, image, symbol

437. Sine qua non
noun (see•nuh•kwa•*noan*)

An indispensable thing without which something is not possible

Used in Context
"Not one to indulge a vain hope to the cost of lives. But then, everyone has his limits, '**sine qua non**,' as they say."—*Battlestar Galactica*, "Sine Qua Non"

"In the land of the industrial revolution, foreign ownership and management is the **sine qua non** of industrial success."—"Britain is in No Position to Rule the Waves," Noah Kristula-Green

"The **sine qua non** of all poetry is absolutely correct grammar and freedom from redundancy."—*Writings in the United Amateur, 1915–1922*, H. P. Lovecraft

"We are a corporate dating service. And if we want to find the right match, we have to understand the **sine qua non** of that person."—*Dead Like Me: Life after Death*

"That's not why I came here, although you are the **sine qua non** of my case."—*NYPD Blue*, "Steroid Roy"

Examples:
- Chocolate chips are the sine qua non of chocolate chip cookies.
- Wind is a sine qua non for flying a kite.

Synonyms: condition, demand, end product, end result, essential, main thing, must, must-have, necessary, necessity, need, needful, precondition, prerequisite, requirement, requisite, upshot

438. Specious
adjective (*spee•shus*)

Apparently right but not so in reality; appearing well at first view; plausible but false

Used in Context
"We'll contest this on the grounds that your request to the judge was based on a **specious** connection to the Snakebacks."—*CSI*, "Fight Night"

"While the public gasped at this **specious** statement, the defense took over for cross examination."—"Portrait of the Consummate Con Man," John Lardner

Examples:

- Several weight loss products on the market make specious claims as to their effectiveness.

- Because it was based on specious information, the study was flawed.

"Your argument is **specious**. Changing you will not result in the termination of all corporeal existence."—*Star Trek: Deep Space Nine,* "Prophet Motive"

"Let me stipulate in advance that I am not arguing or even hinting at any **specious** moral equivalence."—"The Case Against Serving in the Trump Administration," David Luban

Synonyms: baseless, bogus, deceptive, erroneous, fallacious, false, hollow, illogical, implausible, inaccurate, incorrect, misleading, phony, sham, spurious, unsound, untrue, wrong

439. Spurious
adjective (*spyur•ee•us*)

Phony, fake, a "fugazi"

Used in Context

"Once you've heard the evidence, I'm sure you'll agree with me that the charges against my client, Mr. Bartlett, are completely **spurious** and that you will find him not guilty."—*Ernest Goes to Jail*

"But what really stuck in my craw was that Pope mindlessly repeated a spate of **spurious** claims about ethanol and Brazil."—"How Wall Street Will Ruin the Environment," Robert Bryce

"Of course we're so guilty and scared, we end up subjecting this simple, lovely idea to every kind of **spurious** rationale."—*A Midnight Clear*

"At PUMAParty.com, people invented or repeated **spurious** claims about Obama, including the claim that he had been born abroad and was therefore ineligible to be President."—"Trump and the Truth: The Viral Candidate," Andrew Marantz

Synonyms: artificial, bogus, counterfeit, ersatz, fake, faked, false, feigned, forged, illegitimate, imitation, make-believe, mock, phony, sham, simulated, specious, substitute, unauthentic, ungenuine, unreal

440. Stasis
noun (*stay*•sis)

A steady state; a state when opposing forces balance each other

Used in Context
"Your mind and body are in a state of shock as a result of the **stasis**."— *Prometheus*

"Mars kind of went into a **stasis**, a cold, dry **stasis**. But could it happen on earth?"—The Universe, "Magnetic Storm"

"As to the meat of these reports, what they show over the past six months is that we have entered a realm of **stasis**."—"Unemployment Report: Why Job Growth Is Stalling," Zachary Karabell

"Cargo status stable. Life forms intact. **Stasis** uninterrupted."—*Alien: Resurrection*

"Constant commercials and interruptions by refs waving their arms do not produce 'appointment viewing'; rather, they produce punts, ties and **stasis**."—"Turned Off NFL Fans: 'Too Angry, Too Commercialized And Too Stupid Expensive,'" *Washington Post* Staff

Synonyms: balance, correspondence, counterbalance, equilibrium, equity, equivalence, evenness, harmony, parity, proportion, symmetry

441. Stoical
adjective (*sto•ih•kul*)

Unemotional and accepting

Used in Context
"We must remain **stoical** and display calm common sense."—*Cranford*, "November 1842"

"Watch Mr. Hurt's gruff, **stoical** Henry realizing that his girl has ditched him for his brother, with just a flicker of humiliation."—"Review: In *Love, Love, Love*, All You Need Is Selfishness," Ben Brantley

"Nancy bore the brunt of much criticism from people who were inclined but reluctant to assail her husband. She did not enjoy these slings and arrows, but she was shrewd enough to be **stoical** about her role as alternative target."—"Then Along Came Nancy," George F. Will

"I quite liked this hypothesis, which made my insomnia seem clear-eyed and **stoical** rather than blearily hysterical."—"How I Learned to Embrace My Insomnia," Will Self

Synonyms: calm, collected, composed, cool, enduring, impassive, imperturbable, in control, levelheaded, long-suffering, serene, steady, uncomplaining, unflappable, unflustered

442. Subjugate
verb (*sub*•juh•gate)

To bring someone or something, like a country, under control of the military or some other group; to make subservient

Used in Context

"I found myself on the planet Ogo. Part of an intellectual elite preparing to **subjugate** the barbarian hordes on Pluto."—*Twelve Monkeys*

"Fashion can summon the strange, can **subjugate** the body and render it alien just as readily as it can highlight every curve."—"Monsters of Fashion Exhibition Opens in Paris," Sarah Moroz

"She had several more boys to **subjugate** before she could establish herself."—*The Rainbow*, D. H. Lawrence

"I'd say this was Celtic. The Romans liked to build on top of Celtic sites of worship. **Subjugate** the people. Eradicate their heritage."—Bonekickers, "The Eternal Fire"

"Russian leaders fear that the West wants to **subjugate** or even destroy their nation, something President Vladimir V. Putin has at times said overtly."—"Donald Trump's Ambivalence on the Baltics Is More Important Than It Seems," Max Fisher

Synonyms: beat down, bring to knees, compel, conquer, crush, defeat, enslave, keep under thumb, overpower, overthrow, subdue, suppress, tame, quell, vanquish

443. Supercilious
adjective (soo•per•*sill*•ee•us)

Relating to speech that is lofty with pride; condescending speech

Examples:

- A supercilious woman demands special treatment for being pretty; a supercilious man demands special treatment because he's handsome.
- Supercilious people believe they are entitled for something they believe makes them superior.

Used in Context

"When I put my mind to it. I can memorize anything, and I don't need help from a dictatorial, truculent, **supercilious** gardener."—*Akeelah and the Bee*

"Gore comes off as a **supercilious** grandstander who gets swatted away dismissively by the brilliant Bill Clinton."—"The Quiet General Strikes Back," Lloyd Grove

"He never saluted me with other than what I regarded as a **supercilious** nod of the head."—*Wilfrid Cumbermede*, George MacDonald

"A lot of **supercilious** professors, slob professors shooting off their mouth about something, trying to teach me something they'd already failed at in life themselves."—*Life with Judy Garland: Me and My Shadows—A Behind-the-Scenes Look*

"It's also clear, as Schur acknowledges, that the first draft of that history was written in a **supercilious** tone and pockmarked with errors and omissions"—"Who Actually Won the *Moneyball* Revolution?," Josh Levin

Synonyms: arrogant, bossy, cavalier, cocky, condescending, contemptuous, disdainful, egotistic, haughty, high-and-mighty, imperious, insolent, lofty, nervy, overbearing, patronizing, pompous, scornful, snobby, snooty, stuck-up, superior, uppity, vainglorious

444. Superfluous
adjective (soo•*per*•floo•us)

More than is wanted or is sufficient; needless repetition

Used in Context

"It's just, I look around at you and Mom and everyone getting all ker-bobbled. Doesn't this all seem **superfluous**?"—*How the Grinch Stole Christmas*

"Of course, under the circumstances a personal encounter is **superfluous**."—*Iole*, Robert W. Chambers

"I didn't even have a cough. And I almost bought it. And I'm talking about a completely **superfluous** bottle of cough syrup."—*The Happening*

"Since no great naval power menaces the free world today, the Navy's overwhelming preponderance of surface ships seems to be **superfluous**."—*The Manchurian Candidate*

"Under the old feudalism, the peasants were exploited; under the new arrangement, they'll merely be **superfluous**."—"Our Automated Future," Elizabeth Kolbert

Examples:

- Advance warning—*a warning addresses something that will happen; thus, "advance" is intrinsic to its meaning.*

- Unexpected surprise—*a surprise is always unexpected; thus, "unexpected" is intrinsic to its meaning.*

Synonyms: excessive, exorbitant, extra, extravagant, gratuitous, in excess, not required, redundant, surplus, unessential, unnecessary, unneeded, unrequired

445. Surreptitious
adjective (sur•ep•*tish*•us)

Done in secret; clandestinely; done stealthily

Used in Context

"On matters of **surreptitious** romance, his skills went unquestioned."—*The Age of Innocence*

"But by 1953, with McCarthyism and the second Red Scare in full swing, the FBI moved from **surreptitious** research to direct contact." —"Inside Howard Zinn's FBI Files," Clark Merrefield

"But he did not complete his reference to last night's **surreptitious** conversation."—*The Martian Cabal*, Roman Frederick Starzl

"Why do I feel so conspiratorial about all this? **Surreptitious** meetings with the police, digging out the extra dream tapes, walking an ethical tightrope."—*Columbo*, "Murder: A Self Portrait"

"As much as we may yearn for a womb-like oneness with our spouses, our well-established right to privacy doesn't end in matrimony. Federal laws protect all of us from intrusive and **surreptitious** modes of spousal scrutiny."—"Do You Have a Right to Privacy in Your Marriage?," Stephanie Fairyington

Synonyms: clandestine, covert, furtive, furtively, hidden, hush-hush, on the down low, on the QT, private, secret, sly, sneaking, sneaky, stealthy, sub-rosa, unauthorized, undercover, underhanded, under the table, veiled

446. Sycophant
noun (*sik*•oh•font)

Someone who acts obsequiously toward someone rich, famous, or in a superior position, often with a self-seeking purpose

Used in Context

"He's a **sycophant**. Tells her what she wants to hear, keeps us away."—*Law & Order: Criminal Intent*, "Bombshell"

"However reactionary a **sycophant** to rich people and slasher of programs for others he might be, he is the governor."—"Conservatives and Rock and Roll," Michael Tomasky

"General Pervoyedov at last himself checked with dignity the disgusting officiousness of his **sycophant** in the grave."—*Short Stories*, Fyodor Dostoyevsky

"You have nothing in common. You are a genius, and he is a **sycophant** and a pervert."—*The Last Station*

"In any group, there are generally one or two people who believe the best way to get ahead is to be a **sycophant**."—"5 Signs Your Employees Think You're Awful," Erika Andersen

Synonyms: adulator, ass-kisser, back-scratcher, bootlicker, brownnoser, doormat, fawner, fawning parasite, flatterer, flunky, groupie, groveler, hanger-on, lackey, minion, puppet, servile flatterer, slave, toady, yes-man

447. Syllogism
noun (sil•oh•*jiz*•em)

A deductive argument consisting of a major premise, a minor premise, and a conclusion

Used in Context

"Fear causes inaction. Inaction causes pain. QED, fear causes pain. I'll grant it's a **syllogism**, but you get my meaning."—*Sleepy Hollow*, "For the Triumph of Evil"

"See, that's what we call a faulty **syllogism**. Just because you call Bill a dog, doesn't mean that he is a dog."—*House M.D.*, "Merry Little Christmas"

Examples:
- All mammals are warm-blooded. Dogs are mammals. Thus, all dogs are warm-blooded.
- All human beings have a heart. I am a human being. Thus, I have a heart.

"Watching him complete the **syllogism** in his head, and watching Juan's reaction, is heartbreaking."—"*Moonlight*: Is This the Year's Best Movie?," A. O. Scott

"The answers to such questions are complex, and these answers will also be slow-arriving. Complex because intelligence rarely tosses a tight **syllogism** at a policymaker, a series of incontrovertible 'statements' followed by some inevitable 'therefore.'"—"Intel, Obama and Walking Away from the Red Line in Syria," Mike Hayden

Synonyms: argument, conclusion, deduction, deductive argument, dialectic, line of reasoning, logic, reasoning

A relationship of mutual benefit or dependence

Used in Context

"We are not working at our full **symbiotic** potential. Late teens, early 20s. Completely devoid of flesh or odor."—*Bones*, "The Widow's Son in the Windshield"

"The **symbiotic** relationship between television and local officials played a huge role."—"A Hurricane of Hype," Howard Kurtz

"Menke was known for her **symbiotic** relationship with Tarantino."—"Sally Menke, Tarantino's Editor, Dies," Gina Piccalo

"I know a little something of the Leviathans and their **symbiotic** Pilots. Peaceful to a fault, if I recall."—*Farscape*, "The Peacekeeper Wars"

"The **symbiotic** relationship between superyacht owners and crew is not as one-sided as it might appear."—"Superyachts and Bragging Rights: Why The Super-Rich Love Their 'Floating Homes,'" David Batty

Examples:

- Humans and good bacteria: humans provide a host; good bacteria aid digestion.
- Dogs and humans: the dogs supply protection and companionship and the humans provide food and shelter.

Synonyms: collaborating, collaborative, collusive, combining, concerted, cooperative, coordinated, harmonious, in league, shared, synergetic, united

449. Syntax
noun (*sin*•tax)

The study of the rules whereby words are combined to form grammatical sentences

Used in Context

"Well, what's not to know? Your height, your body language, your **syntax**. You said 'in actuality.'"—*The Mentalist*, "Bleeding Heart"

"They never forget their **syntax**, children, when once they've been taught it."—*The Crown of Wild Olive*, John Ruskin

"Don't let the charming accent and my impeccable **syntax** mislead you. I live in the jungle, and in the jungle you either eat or be eaten."—*Transporter 2*

"And for the record, the correct **syntax** is: I'm the guy from whom you're trying to get away."—*The Big Bang Theory*, "The Staircase Implementation"

Syntax is the science that includes knowing whether or not to use an adjective or an adverb, how to use the apostrophe and possessives, which preposition and pronoun to use, which verb tense to use, etc.

"The **syntax**, in which sentences are composed in a continuous circle, is unlike anything she's ever seen. It shows a nonlinear understanding of time, as if all of creation were unfolding simultaneously."—"The Anti-*Gravity*: What *Arrival* Gets Right That Sandra Bullock's Space Odyssey Didn't," Nico Lang

Synonyms: grammar, language rules, order, pattern, sentence structure, structure, system

T

450. Tautological
adjective (tawt•oh•*loj*•ih•kul)

Refers to needless repetition of the same sense in different words; redundancy

Used in Context

"The report is full of sophistry and **tautological** thinking and is generally plagued by the kind of laziness and intellectual vanity which is native to the profiler profession."—*Elementary*, "The Adventure of the Nutmeg Concoction"

"A **tautological** sentence, perhaps, but one that nevertheless needs to be repeated and understood."—"Why Mitt Romney's Opportunity Tack Won't Work," Michael Tomasky

Unnecessary elaboration and using words that say the same thing.

Examples:

- She wrote her *autobiography* of *her own life* in just two weeks.
- *PIN number.*
- *Necessary require-ment.*

"The **tautological** blame always comes back to the claim that frivolous or even fraudulent lawsuits are commonplace."—"Scalding Takedown on Tort Reform," Gerald L. Shargel

"In truth, the statement that substance is permanent, is **tautological**."—*The Critique of Pure Reason*, Immanuel Kant

"It was a breathless and **tautological** remark, but it relieved her feelings."—*The Wishing-Ring Man*, Margaret Widdemer

"Reality competition shows and the pop industry share the **tautological** belief that success justifies itself: A winner is someone who wins."—"*American Idol* Ends With One Final Argument Over the Winner," James Poniewozik

Synonyms: iterating, not required, prolix, redundant, reiterating, reiterative, superfluous, surplus, unnecessary, unneeded

451. Temerity
noun (teh•*mair*•ih•tee)

Reckless confidence that could offend some people, sometimes described as "arrogance"

Used in Context
"And so, a quiet, humble, respectable Negro, who has had the unmitigated **temerity** to feel sorry for a white woman, has had his word put against two white people's."—*To Kill a Mockingbird*

"I accuse this man, Bishop Father, of arrogance, **temerity**, and disloyalty! I demand that you disregard every vile word."—The Tudors, "Look to God First"

"Should the caller have the **temerity** to ask where they were, the phone call would be quietly ended."—"The Bookstore That Bewitched Mick Jagger, John Lennon, and Greta Garbo," Felice Picano

"The curse began with your great-great-great grandmother, Genevieve Katherine Duchannes. She had the **temerity** to fall in love with a mortal, your ancestor, Ethan Carter Wate."—*Beautiful Creatures*

"Can I ask you a question? How the hell do you have the **temerity** to blackmail the president of the United States?"—*Nixon*

Synonyms: audacity, boldness, brass, cheek, effrontery, foolhardiness, forwardness, gall, impertinence, impudence, indiscretion, nerve, rashness, rudeness

452. Tenable
adjective (*ten*•uh•buhl)

Justified, possible, defensible, usually based on evidence and reason

Used in Context
"A sperm whale had been called into existence several miles above the surface of an alien planet. Since this is not a **tenable** position for a whale, this innocent creature had very little time to come to terms with its identity."—*The Hitchhiker's Guide to the Galaxy*

"Employee dumping is when employers find it **tenable** to pay the per-employee penalty for not providing health insurance."—"Five Things You Need to Know About the Health-Care Exchange Rollout," William O'Connor

"Truly, it is **tenable** that the world exists only in consciousness."—*The Mutiny of the Elsinore*, Jack London

"Both were so disheveled, so flushed, so hilarious, that only one supposition was **tenable**."—*The Furnace*, Rose Macaulay

"No view of God is **tenable** at the present day which regards Him as outside His own creation."—*Gloria Crucis*, J. H. Beibitz

"Your position is no longer **tenable**, regardless of how management is restructured. We will coordinate our statements to the least detriment of everyone."—*Network*

"I woke up in pain, facing another day—no project beyond breakfast seemed **tenable**. 'I can't go on,' I thought, and immediately, its antiphon responded, completing Samuel Beckett's seven words, words I had learned long ago as an undergraduate: 'I'll go on.' I got out of bed and took a step forward, repeating the phrase over and over: 'I can't go on. I'll go on.'"—*When Breath Becomes Air*, Paul Kalanithi

Synonyms: acceptable, arguable, doable, justifiable, maintainable, plausible, possible, rational, sound, viable, workable

453. Theist
noun (*thee•ist*)

Someone who believes a singular God created and rules all existence, based on faith, but who does not subscribe to the tenets of organized religion or the writings in sacred texts

Used in Context

"It forces the species to bond together and preserve the social structure, nothing more. The **theist** has a sound explanation as the why humans need more than to just survive."—*Blue Like Jazz*

"When the **theist** finds intention and design in nature he is but reading his own feeling and desires into nature."—*The Necessity of Atheism*, Dr. D. M. Brooks

What's the difference between a deist and a theist? A theist believes in a God based on faith; a deist believes in a God based on reason. Many of America's Founding Fathers were deists.

"I am a **theist** and an evolutionist, to be sure, but the combined term makes no sense to me."—"Meet the Prizewinning Catholic Biologist Creationists Can't Stand," Karl W. Giberson

"The world is not the same to the Christian **theist** and to the agnostic."—*Elementary Guide to Literary Criticism*, F. V. N. Painter

"This isn't just a problem for me, as a **theist**. Every human being walking the face of this Earth is aware of evil in the World."—*The Case for Faith*

"Mr. D'Souza dismissed Mr. Chapman as 'a wounded **theist**' in childish rebellion against the mean Sunday school teachers of the world. ('Are you angry at God?' Mr. Donvan asked Mr. Chapman. 'I'm angry at Dinesh,' he retorted.)"—"Have a Little Faith? At NYU, the Debate Rages On," Jennifer Schuessler

Synonyms: acolyte, advocate, believer, deist, supporter

454. Tonally
adverb (toe•nuh•lee)

The style or sensibility someone uses to say or create something; tone is used to suggest an aesthetic: dark, sad, questioning, happy

Used in Context

"It's just not the most aesthetically pleasing in the bunch, **tonally** speaking. It's got this irritating nasally quality."—*Moonlighting*, "Take a Left at the Altar"

"**Tonally** those two episodes remind me of the early episodes of the show."—"Resuscitation: A Q&A with the Creator of *Scrubs*," Miriam Datskovsky

"**Tonally**, however, it is very peculiar: It is undeniably Southern Gothic, but it has its own brand of off-beat humor."—"How Cormac McCarthy Changed My Life," James Franco

"We were very curious about these paintings. They could possibly be Medieval, but the colors were **tonally** wrong for this period."—*Horizon*, "Archimedes Secret"

"**Tonally**, the movie is continually shifting, and it's a credit to Lee that the whole thing doesn't give the viewer emotional whiplash."—"*Billy Lynn's Long Halftime Walk* Values Experimentation Over Emotion," Stephanie Merry

Synonyms: accent-wise, aesthetically, categorically, emphatically

455. Torpor
noun (tor•pour)

A pronounced lack of physical or mental energy; apathy; lethargy

Used in Context

"If not 'recession,' what word would the administration use? Slowdown, downturn, **torpor**?"—*The West Wing*, "Han"

"But it was first and foremost an attempt to wake up America from the **torpor** of the daily grind under its meritocratic overlords."—"Miley Cyrus's Smartest Tattoo," James Poulos

"She was the only one of his family who could rouse the old man from the **torpor** in which he seemed to live."—*My Antonia*, Willa Cather

"I didn't throw it at him. I picked up the board and dumped the pieces on his head as an object lesson to shake him out of his vegetable **torpor**."—*Whatever Works*

"The audience, mostly Russian-speaking from the conversations I heard around me before the show began, sat rapt throughout. I'm afraid I found it harder to engage, and while Brodsky's imagery is often darkly brilliant, a sense of **torpor** set in eventually."—"In *Brodsky/Baryshnikov*, One Friend Recalls Another," Christopher Isherwood

Synonyms: disinterest, dormancy, drowsiness, dullness, idleness, impassivity, inaction, inactivity, indolence, inertia, languor, lifelessness, listlessness, sloth, slowness, sluggishness, stillness, stolidity, stupor, torpidity

456. Transcendent
adjective (tran-sen-dent)

Existing outside the material world; also used to describe someone or something that achieves a pinnacle of excellence; i.e., "That mousse was transcendent."

Used in Context

"And it's very hard to describe the true magic of a group of guys singing in perfect harmony. It's **transcendent**."—*The Break-Up*

"While he was in a coma for seven days, his consciousness entered a series of **transcendent** realms."—"Eben Alexander Has a GPS for Heaven," Patricia Pearson

"A Europe which is no longer open to the **transcendent** dimension of life is a Europe which risks slowly losing its own soul."—"Pope's Blistering Attack on 'Haggard' Europe," Nico Hines

"When you were under the influence of the Rambaldi fluid, what you saw, was it not **transcendent**? Was it not divine?"—*Alien: Resurrection*

"Only one holiday song is worth a precious fraction of your rapidly dwindling time on earth: Dan Fogelberg's 1980 ballad 'Same Old Lang Syne,' a light-rock radio classic that deconstructs all the usual eggnog conventions and reassembles them into a proper work of art—something like a Raymond Carver story crossed with 'Escape (The Piña Colada Song)' crossed with T. S. Eliot's 'Four Quartets.' Like the holiday season itself, Fogelberg's song is simultaneously hilarious, sad, beautiful, corny and **transcendent**."—"Letter of Recommendation: Dan Fogelberg, 'Same Old Lang Syne,'" Sam Anderson

Synonyms: abstract, awe-inspiring, boundless, fantastic, inspirational, inspiring, magnificent, moving, otherworldly, peerless, sublime, supernatural, supreme, transcending, ultimate, uplifting

457. Transient
adjective (*tran•zee•ent*)

Lasting for a short period of time and then either changing or vanishing

Used in Context
"Apparently, Louis has murdered a **transient** and done things with the skin. We need his address and physical description."—*The Silence of the Lambs*

"If, however, our religion implicates itself in a political cause, it links its credibility to the most **transient** of moorings."—"The Illusory Promise of Apolitical Theology," David Sessions

"The storm was gone, unseasonable and **transient**, and only a broken remnant of its clouds hung about the western mountains."—*The Story of Old Fort Loudon*, Charles Egbert Craddock

"My mind is aglow with whirling, **transient** nodes of thought careening through a cosmic vapor of invention."—*Blazing Saddles*

"And it's become clear that, even as the number of our subscribers continues to grow, there has been less engagement with each issue; fewer downloads, fewer responses. It seems as though the format is

The word "transient" can also be a noun and be used to describe someone who doesn't stay in the same place very long.

too ephemeral, too **transient**; the very opposite of the letters that continue to arrive through our letterbox."—"From Me, With Love: The Lost Art Of Letter Writing," Jon McGregor

Synonyms: brief, changeable, ephemeral, evanescent, fleeting, flitting, impermanent, insubstantial, momentary, passing, provisional, short-lived, short-term, temporary, transitory

458. Treacly
adjective (*tree•klee*)

Ridiculously sentimental, cloying

Used in Context
"It avoids that **treacly**, touchy-feely ground on which Democrats so love to walk."—"With Joe Biden's Speech, The Democrats Finally Man Up," Michael Tomasky

"You've been out of ideas since Madonna week. Why don't you just embrace that lazy, horrible, **treacly** style of teaching and assign them a famous album?"—*Glee*, "Saturday Night Glee-ver"

"Another **treacly** truism, I think my sweet tooth is gonna start to ache."—*Dawson's Creek*, "Like a Virgin"

"The 1989 film *Dead Poets Society*, directed by Peter Weir, was full of the same 'carpe diem' hokum and misty uplift. But it had the saving grace of the performance by Robin Williams, whose charismatic strangeness usually gave a weird, anchoring conviction to **treacly** parts."—"Review: *Dead Poets Society*, Starring Jason Sudeikis as the Idealistic Teacher," Ben Brantley

Synonyms: clichéd, corny, cringeworthy, overwrought, saccharine, sweet, syrupy

459. Trope
noun (trope)

A word, phrase, or image used figuratively to make a rhetorical point

Used in Context

"Your prison mistress gave you a prison tat. You are turning into a **trope**."—*Orange is the New Black*, "Trust No Bitch"

"It has become a **trope** of the right to accuse Obama and the Democrats of trying to remake America in the image of Europe."—"How Republicans Screwed the Pooch," Paul Begala

"Visiting with the great figures of history is a familiar Allen **trope** of yore, and outwardly, *Midnight* is in that tradition."—"*Midnight in Paris*: I Loathe It," Richard Rushfield

"To have a sympathetic fictional character of a big-budget movie say that she hates jazz is a sign that the character is in on a long-running joke. The joke, years ago, became a **trope**, and then a screenwriter's cliché."—"Jazz Hate," Ben Ratliff

"It's an old **trope** but not without merit, the murderer returning to the scene of the crime to relive the glory of it."—*Penny Dreadful*, "Glorious Horrors"

"The idea of the Kennedy years as Camelot became an enduring **trope** and, for some, a maddening lie."—"*Jackie*: Under the Widow's Weeds, a Myth Marketer," Manohla Dargis

Synonyms: adumbration, allegory, analogy, conceit, device, euphemism, expression, image, manner of speaking, parable, stylistic device, turn of phrase

460. Truculent
adjective (*truk•yoo•lent*)

Belligerent, sullenly refusing to obey

Used in Context

"Hmm, a needy, **truculent** narcissist. I think it's been perfect training for parenthood."—*House M.D.*, "Gut Check"

"And it turns out those hard-charging characteristics are exactly what is needed to tangle with the **truculent** contenders."—"Candy Crowley, Martha Raddatz: Female Moderators Rocked the Boat in Debates," Lauren Ashburn

"His manner was **truculent**; indeed, verged almost upon the menacing."—*The Life of the Party*, Irvin Shrewsbury Cobb

"He's trying to get up. He is getting up. The whole stadium is standing.

He's up on his feet. Here's a guy who's normally very **truculent** with the media."—*Jerry Maguire*

"That **truculent** retreat handed responsibility for security in the Gulf and the Strait of Malacca to the United States."—"Global Trump," Steve Coll

Synonyms: abusive, aggressive, antagonistic, bad-tempered, belligerent, bullying, combative, confrontational, contentious, cruel, defiant, fierce, frightening, intimidating, mean, militant, ornery, pugnacious, quarrelsome, rebellious, savage, scrappy, scurrilous, surly, trenchant, violent, vitriolic

461. Truism
noun (*troo•ism*)

A statement that has become trite through repetition

Used in Context

"Power perceived is power achieved. I'd remember that little **truism**, Mr. Smith. It will assist you greatly in your teaching."—*The Substitute*

"Cases can be tied up for years, and the notion that 'rich people don't go to jail' is a **truism** in the minds of many Brazilians."—"Brazil's Soccer Star a Murderer?," Dom Phillips

Using truisms in writing is especially bad form because they will be perceived as the overused clichés they are. They lack originality and rarely will you catch a professional journalist or writer falling back on the use of a truism to make a point.

"'Like produces like' is a **truism** often quoted, but there are exceptions, and Boston terrier breeding furnishes an important one."—*The Boston Terrier and All About It*, Edward Axtell

"As they broke up, they passed on to us the one great **truism** that I think all humanity can understand. That in the end, the lunch you take is equal to the lunch you make."—*The Rutles 2: Can't Buy Me Lunch*

Synonyms: adage, aphorism, axiom, cliché, dictum, maxim, motto, platitude, proverb, saying

U

Being everywhere

Used in Context

"That's a technique that an artist uses. 'Ubiquitous gaze' or 'pursuant eyes' is the technical term. It's unnerving though, I'll give you that."—*Shanghai Knights*

"Giveaways in fast-food places, place mats, just all the different ways in which food marketing is ubiquitous."—*Super Size Me*

"But that changed in the 19th century, when two important developments helped make ice cream the ubiquitous snack it is today."—"An Investigation Into the Delicious Origins of Ice Cream," Andrew Romano

What is the single most ubiquitous piece of technology in today's society? The cell phone. In a sentence, "Today, cell phones are ubiquitous."

"With a new era of **ubiquitous** drones on the way, the company is flying some very friendly skies."—"Google Invests in Drone Company Airware," Leo Marani

"I could walk to the ruins and St. Dominic's from my hotel, but despite Macau's compact size, not everything is walkable. I would not recommend driving in Macau, nor riding one of the city's **ubiquitous** scooters."—"In Macau, Skipping the Casinos, but Embracing the Past," Lucas Peterson

Synonyms: all-pervading, ever-present, everywhere, omnipresent, pervasive, unavoidable, universal, wall-to-wall

463. Umbrage
noun (*um*•bridge)

Annoyance, resentment, or anger arising from a real or perceived insult or offense

Used in Context
"I offer the money, you'll play the man of honor and take **umbrage**."—*Serenity*

"I shall take no **umbrage** at the failure of my communications to call forth replies."—*An Ocean Tramp*, William McFee

"Please don't take **umbrage**, but in the plan that I have formulated, there's much more to it than just you and I making love."—*Cape Fear*

"Now. I've heard what you had to say. And forgive me, but I take **umbrage**. I take severe **umbrage**."—*Everybody Loves Raymond*, "Meeting the Parents"

"The groups opposing Trump have also gotten sympathy from people outside their respective causes. For example, Mormons in Utah take **umbrage** against Trump's proposal to ban Muslim immigration."—"A Common Enemy," Susan Milligan

Synonyms: annoyance, antagonism, displeasure, exasperation, grudge, high dudgeon, huff, indignation, ire, irritation, offense, pique, rage, resentment, sense of injury, vexation, wrath

464. Unabashed
adjective (un•uh•*basht*)

Not embarrassed or ashamed of something; not apologetic; confident in one's position

Used in Context
"Honey, wait. I want to tell you what really happened, the **unabashed** truth."—*King of the Hill*, "My Own Private Radio"

"We laugh at its **unabashed** sincerity, but secretly pine to express feelings so openly."—"Brit Wits Bash America," Sean Macaulay

"She knew that people were looking, but she felt brazen, **unabashed**, and happy."—*IT and Other Stories*, Gouverneur Morris

"Luck, it's got nothing with it. It's about talent, you know. Sheer, **unabashed** talent."—*Supernatural*, "Hell House"

"In fact, Rory and Lorelai's **unabashed** indulgence in food is so enjoyable for fans because it's just that—completely unconcerned with others' opinions."—"An Ode to the *Gilmore Girls'* **Unabashed** Love of Food," Cady Lang

Synonyms: audacious, blatant, bold, brash, brazen, cheeky, forthright, forward, hardened, overbold, presumptuous, shameless, unashamed, unblushing, unembarrassed

465. Unassailable
adjective (un•uh•*sale*•uh•buhl)

Something so accepted, strong, and established that it cannot be overtaken, replaced, or denied

Used in Context

"It's extremely difficult to access him remotely. His security measures are rigorous and virtually **unassailable**."—*Person of Interest*, "Search and Destroy"

"They foster courage, honesty and leadership. But most of all, an **unassailable** spirit of loyalty, comradeship and mutual responsibility."—*Chariots of Fire*

"Everyone always thought his control of these two companies was **unassailable**."—"The Buzzards Are Circling Around Sumner Redstone," Kim Masters

"Meanwhile, glam's **unassailable** cool allowed me to find a solid male identity within the rock aesthetic I already loved."—"Growing Up Gay to a Glam Rock Soundtrack," Jim Farber

Synonyms: absolute, bulletproof, conclusive, impregnable, incontestable, incontrovertible, indisputable, invincible, secure, sound, undeniable, undisputable, unquestionable, unshakeable

466. Unconscionable
adjective (un•*kon*•shin•uh•buhl)

Morally unacceptable; shocking and unreasonable

Used in Context

"And the fact that you bring Conrad into this juvenile game is **unconscionable**."—*The Game*

"For many black Americans, the Zimmerman verdict was an **unconscionable** nightmare."—"Why Do Black and White Americans See the Zimmerman Verdict So Differently?," Sophia A. Nelson

"He would have pitilessly repressed my **unconscionable** volubility." [See definition of "voluble" in this volume.]—*Faces in the Fire*, Frank W. Boreham

"But, as you know, I am a misanthrope. And that people do **unconscionable** things does not run counter to my normal view of humanity."—*Magic in the Moonlight*

"What she has said is **unconscionable**, and 'hurtful' barely scratches the surface."—"Acceptance and Denial," Mallory Orthberg

Synonyms: barbarous, excessive, extreme, immoderate, inordinate, outrageous, preposterous, uncivilized, unprincipled, unreasonable, unscrupulous, usurious, unwarranted, wanton, wicked

Excessively smug, pious, or faux-moralistic; oily; greasy

Used in Context

"It was an emotional speech, but a delightfully graceful, rather than **unctuous** and overblown, one." —"The Changing Color of the Oscars; *12 Years A Slave* Makes History' Tim Teeman

"A single, dispatched, putrid note to counterbalance all of the other sweet and **unctuous** scents in a fragrance. The ancient Mesopotamians used fish oil. The Greeks used animal matter." —Fringe, "A Short Story about Love'

"Mr. Tweedle had come to the desk and offered his hand in his usual conciliatory and **unctuous** manner." —Lost Fortune, Charles Ludley Wartler

"John Haverford is a selfish, **unctuous**, sleazy self-promoting, good-hearted, secretly kind and wonderful dry little person." —Park... Imagination, "Meet 'n Greet'

"The overconfident charm is the greasy, **unctuous** kind—to him to a studio is an insult to the make." —"Review: Denial the Bullying Mystery of Harry," Stephanie Zacharek

Synonyms: creepy, groveling, ingratiating, obsequious, phatic

468. Unequivocal
adjective (un•ee•*quiv*•uh•kul)

Definite, allowing no room whatsoever for questioning or doubt

Used in Context

"This is **unequivocal**. It is life or it is death."—*The Twilight Zone*, "The Bard"

"The religious messages in the April holidays are pointed, **unequivocal**, impossible to fudge."—"Why There's No 'War on Easter': Its Unequivocally Religious Message," Michael Medved

"Roosevelt's attitude toward the Indians as a race was **unequivocal**."—*Roosevelt in the Bad Lands*, H. Hagedorn.

"Look at that body language. Legs crossed towards each other. That's an **unequivocal** sex invite."—*Clueless*

"But the Mayor was **unequivocal** in his opposition to what Major Colvin did."—*The Wire*, "Mission Accomplished"

"The statement from the Van Gogh Museum was **unequivocal**. It said it had been aware of the claims for some time and, on the basis of looking at 56 high quality photographs, researchers and curators had agreed the drawings could not be attributed to Van Gogh."—"Newly Discovered 'Van Gogh' Drawings Labeled Imitations By Museum," Mark Brown

Synonyms: absolute, categorical, certain, clear, clear-cut, direct, explicit, incontestable, indisputable, indubitable, obvious, straightforward, undeniable, undisputable, unmistakable, unqualified,

469. Unilateral
adjective (yoo•nih•*lat*•er•uhl)

Involving only one side or ideological position, as in "a unilateral decision"

Used in Context

"If this was a legit op, and I can't possibly see how it could be, then so be it. But if this was someone's **unilateral** wet dream, then that somebody is going to prison."—*Enemy of the State*

"The Nevada Democrat would largely give President Obama **unilateral** power to boost the debt ceiling."—"Angry House Kills Reid Plan," Howard Kurtz

"Britain imposed an oil embargo on Rhodesia today after that country's **unilateral** declaration of independence."—*Good Morning, Vietnam*

Sometimes, if the president makes a decision without consulting the opposition party, people will criticize him for making as "unilateral" decision. Essentially, it means "without consulting those who have different views when making a decision or implementing an action."

"Throughout Europe, daily demonstrations demand **unilateral** nuclear disarmament."—*Octopussy*

"But let's be clear: 'America First' is not an isolationist policy but a **unilateral** one. It does not have America retreat from the world, but impose its will firmly upon it."—"Donald Trump's Foreign Policy Is a Black Box," Ian Bremmer

Synonyms: independent, one-sided

470. Unmitigated
adjective (un•*mitt*•ih•gay•ted)

Not eased or lessened in any manner; final; definitive

Used in Context

"This whole thing is an **unmitigated** disaster. I think act of God is a pretty decent excuse for a lousy date."—*Scott Pilgrim Vs. The World*

An extremely common usage of "unmitigated" in books, film, and on TV is the construct "unmitigated disaster."

"The British aristocracy is littered with stories of **unmitigated** spendthrifts who seem bent on self-destruction."—"The Secrets of Britain's Wildest Aristocrats," Tom Sykes

"Then came the second go-round under George W. Bush, and this of course was an **unmitigated** disaster."—"How Mitt Romney Finally Killed Reaganomics," Michael Tomasky

"Oh, Mr Bingley, it's so good to see you again so soon. First, I must tell you I've been the most **unmitigated** and comprehensive ass."—*Pride & Prejudice*

"If climate change continues **unmitigated**, global incomes are expected to fall 23 percent by 2100."—"Fantastic Beasts: Our Secret Weapon In Combating Man-Made Climate Change—Animals," Diane Stopyra

"You're an **unmitigated** madman! You don't have to tell me how weird you are. I know how weird you are! I'm the girl in your bed the past two months."—*Altered States*

Synonyms: absolute, clear-cut, complete, persistent, pure, total, unabated, unadulterated, undiluted, undiminished, unqualified, unrelieved, utter

471. Untenable
adjective (un•*ten*•uh•buhl)

Having no sound reasoning in terms of making an argument; indefensible

Used in Context

"Due to serious setbacks to our troops in Guantanamo and Santiago, my position in Cuba is **untenable**. I am resigning from office to avoid further bloodshed."—*The Godfather, Part II*

"They consider Leno ambitious, ego-driven, but a respectable guy who was put in an **untenable** position."—"Comedians Laugh as Leno Sinks," Gina Piccalo

"Suing him—and dragging their dealings and relationship into open court—is an **untenable** option."—"Bill Clinton's $20 Million Breakup," Kim Masters

"It is hard to bring such men to see how **untenable** their own position is."—*Pietro Ghisleri*, F. Marion Crawford

"The informant's position was becoming **untenable**. We were afraid she was in danger."—*Righteous Kill*

Synonyms: baseless, flawed, groundless, illogical, invalid, on shaky ground, questionable, shaky, unsound, unsustainable, weak

472. Usurp
verb (yoo•*surp*)

Take or use something without the right to do so; to seize something illegally

Used in Context

"Is it not also illegal to sit in the king's throne and **usurp** his power in his absence?"—*Robin Hood: Men in Tights*

"Makes you wonder why conservatives care so much who sits on the Supreme Court—since they seem determined to **usurp** its job."—"The Tea Party's Blind Spot," Peter Beinart

"Mightn't there be some benefit if I pay Princess Victoria a visit before Conroy has a chance to **usurp** her?"—*The Young Victoria*

"Or will you leave my mother's home and mine, and cease to **usurp** my rights?"—*Madeline Payne, the Detective's Daughter*, Lawrence L. Lynch

"No matter how popular or profitable certain college sports become, athletic associations should not **usurp** that role."—"The NCAA Isn't a Moral Arbiter—Nor Should It Be," John I. Jenkins

Synonyms: appropriate, arrogate, assume, commandeer, grab, high-jack, infringe upon, preempt, seize, swipe, take, wrest

V

473. Vacillate
verb (*vaa*•sil•ate)

To waver about something; to be indecisive

Used in Context

"You begin to **vacillate** between being repelled by touch and seeking it out in any form."—*Rectify*, "Plato's Cave"

"I kind of self-edit that out of the history, but they did **vacillate** for quite a while."—"David Chase on Tony Soprano's Fate, the State of TV, and Why He Couldn't Finish *True Detective*," Marlow Stern

"Long did he **vacillate** whether Tom Keane should not be arrested on suspicion."—*Roland Cashel*, Charles James Lever

"It's an imbalance of chemicals in the brain. And it means that your behaviors, they **vacillate** between euphoria and depression. Great highs and lows."—Necessary Roughness, "Dream On"

"That is largely thanks to Baker's yearning, slightly deranged vocal, which bounces around over woodwind riffs and guitars that **vacillate** between funk and fuzz."—"Mercury Rev-10 of the Best," Ben Cardew

Synonyms: be indecisive, change mind, dither, fence-straddle, fluctuate, hem and haw, hesitate, pussyfoot around, run hot and cold, think twice, waffle, waver

474. Vacuous
adjective (*vak•yoo•us*)

Having no ideas or intelligence; a moron

Used in Context
"We need an empty vessel. A shallow, dumb, **vacuous** moron."—*Zoolander*

"In America, however, there is a stubborn strain of **vacuous** unawareness that reflects no credit on American society."—"Ignorant America," Tunku Varadarajan

"The assumption that feminism comes in a neat, Xeroxable package is gravely outmoded and **vacuous**."—"Despite What You May Think, Miley Cyrus and Rihanna Are Feminists," Rawiya Kameir

"Those eyes were the shiny, **vacuous**, soulless eyes of a madman!"—*The Floating Island of Madness*, Jason Kirby

"Somewhere behind that **vacuous** face, that zombielike stare is a real human being, and I can bring it out."—*Zelig*

"Cable news has, this election cycle, had a vexed relationship with filling the air. For every unexpectedly juicy roundtable discussion, there's been one featuring **vacuous**, fact-light commentary rife with false equivalencies, or debates incendiary for their own sake."—"Here's What You Should Watch on Election Day," Daniel D'Addario

Synonyms: airheaded, birdbrained, blank, dim, dull, dumb, empty-headed, foolish, idle, inane, lamebrained, purposeless, shallow, stupid, superficial, uncomprehending, unintelligent, vacant, void

475. Vagary
noun (*vay*•guh•ree)

A change or a new idea that is difficult to predict; an erratic action

Used in Context
"You will purchase your keep with that voice intrusive and incessantly opinionated, no **vagary** of our past has yet stilled."—*Deadwood*, "A Two-Hearted Beast"

"What **vagary** had sent a girl who looked like this upon such a task!"— *Before the Dawn*, Joseph Alexander Altsheler

"Surely you do not mean to persist in that mulish **vagary**?"—*Bartleby, the Scrivener*, Herman Melville

"This common meaning for outrage actually grows out of a **vagary** of folk etymology."—"'Outrage' Is Not 'Rage,'" Katy Waldman

A common usage of "vagary" is the plural, as in, "the vagaries of the weather."

In the plural...

"But if you make a distinct product that is special, as I think I do, you are somewhat insulated from the **vagaries** of the economy."—"Luxury Condos: Dialing It Down," Julie Satow

"But due to the **vagaries** of the electoral system he was called upon to form a government."—"Him," Timothy Snyder

"You speak so eloquently of the human heart, Mama. You must be aware of its...**vagaries**."—*Downton Abbey*, "Episode 2.2"

Synonyms: caprice, crotchet, fool, humor, idea, impulse, inconsistency, notion, quirk, whim, whimsy

476. Valorous
adjective (*val•uh•rus*)

Showing courage and bravery, particularly during time of war

Used in Context
"However, this **valorous** visitation of a bygone vexation stands vivified and has vowed to vanquish these venal and virulent vermin vanguarding vice and vouchsafing the violently vicious and voracious violation of volition."—*V for Vendetta*

"Sometimes their **valorous** decoration or place of death is also listed." —"On Memorial Day, a Soldier Honors the Fallen," Jonathan Raab

"The history of the **valorous** and witty-knight-errant, Don-Quixote, of the Mancha."—*The Library of William Congreve*, John C. Hodges

"That was their leader, Sir Williams Glasdale, a most **valorous** knight."—*Personal Recollections of Joan of Arc*, Mark Twain

"I suppose the threat of death to someone with your **valorous** war record would mean nothing."—*Wild Wild West*

"President Truman, who felt he had shown a **valorous** decisiveness in ordering the bombs to be dropped, had no tolerance for retrospective moralizing."—*Big Science*, Michael Hiltzik

Synonyms: bold, brave, chivalrous, courageous, dauntless, fearless, gallant, gutsy, heroic, lionhearted, stalwart, stouthearted, strong, tough, unafraid, undaunted, valiant

477. Vapid
adjective (*va•pid*)

Lacking vitality; dull, lacking liveliness

Used in Context
"And Selwyn found himself drifting, mildly interested in the **vapid** exchange of civilities which cost nobody a mental effort."—*The Younger Set*, Robert W. Chambers

"There must be a moisturizer or an eye shadow somewhere that needs your **vapid** mush to flog it."—*Rush*

"Now they regard the phenomenon with bewilderment bordering on disgust, considering the content dumb and **vapid**."—"China Is in the Midst of a Live-Streaming Revolution," Hao Wu

"Grand language wrapped around a thin message produces only **vapid** blather."—"Why Inaugural Speeches Fail," David Frum

"The fruit of her labor was in her hands, but it was **vapid**, tasteless, unsatisfying."—*Madeline Payne, the Detective's Daughter*, Lawrence L. Lynch

"I acknowledge the pretense to civility in a man so brutally vicious as **vapid** and grotesque."—*Deadwood*, "Tell Him Something Pretty"

"All right, what do you want me to do?! You just want me to just keep dating these **vapid** Hollywood bimbos?"—*The Larry Sanders Show*, "The Prank"

Synonyms: boring, dead, dull, innocuous, insipid, lifeless, prosaic, spiritless, tasteless, tedious, tiresome, trite, unexciting, uninteresting, wishy-washy

478. Venal
adjective (*vee•nul*)

Corrupt, open to bribery, mercenary

Used in Context
"Well, I will not be judged by a kangaroo court of **venal** politicians."—*Public Enemies*

"On the *Daily Show*, Gates piled on, calling Congress 'venal and small.'"—"Rep. David Price Remembers When a Less Partisan Congress Actually Worked," Eleanor Clift

"Afterwards we find that meaner quill is replaced by **venal** quill; and the couplet about the rival translations is suppressed."—*Addison*, William John Courthope

"However, this valorous visitation of a bygone vexation stands vivified and has vowed to vanquish these **venal** and virulent vermin vanguarding vice and vouchsafing the violently vicious and voracious violation of volition."—*V for Vendetta*

"**Venal** and evil people are destroying the world you were born in."— *In the Electric Mist*

Synonyms: amoral, conscienceless, corrupt, corruptible, crooked, dishonest, evil, greedy, immoral, on the take, shady, unethical, unprincipled, vile

479. Verisimilitude
noun (*ver*•eh•sim•*il*•eh•tood)

Something that appears real or can be interpreted as true, sometimes incorrectly, sometimes accurately

Used in Context

"For there is no surer way of giving an air of **verisimilitude** to fiction than to mix with it some particles of truth."—*The Histories of Polybius*, Vol. II, Polybius

"From this day forward, our lives shall be filled with vim, vigor, and **verisimilitude**, lording over every living creature with fists of fury!"— *Pinky and the Brain*, "It's Only a Paper World"

"In fictional narration, **verisimilitude** is absolutely essential."—*Writings in the United Amateur, 1915-1922*, H. P. Lovecraft

"I am never tired of their bewitching absurdity, their inevitable defects, their irresistible touches of **verisimilitude**."—*Venetian Life*, William Dean Howells

"Ladies and gentlemen, we did use Oja's grandfather to lend **verisimilitude** to the reenactment of this story."—*F for Fake*

Synonyms: appearance, genuineness, plausibility, realism, resemblance, similarity, virtual reality

480. Verity
noun (*ver•eh•tee*)

Truth, fact

Used in Context

"Would you want me saying my first loyalty was to you, Mr. Hearst, or to **verity** instead of Mr. Swearengen?"—*Deadwood*, "A Two-Headed Beast"

"They are in **verity**, as worthless a Family as any other whatever."—*An Apology for the Life of Mrs. Shamela Andrews*, Conny Keyber

"When he looked at it directly and simply like that, there was nothing that could blur the **verity** of it."—*Michael*, E. F. Benson

"From globalization to migration, the willingness to sacrifice is weakening. But a better future cannot be reached without some sacrifice of the present. A society reluctant to accept this **verity** stagnates and, over the decades, consumes its substance."—"Out of the Brexit Turmoil: Opportunity," Henry A. Kissinger

Synonyms: accuracy, actuality, authenticity, certainty, exactness, genuineness, reality, truthfulness, veracity, verisimilitude

481. Vicariously
(adverb) (vy•*kar*•ee•us•lee)

Experienced secondhand, often through imagination

Used in Context

"Watching her on TV, people will have lived through her **vicariously**."—"Palin's Reality TV Makeover," Lee Siegel

"In the happy ending, the victim wins and you can **vicariously** enjoy her retaliation against the other woman."—"Wives Gone Wild!," Elizabeth Hayt

"As a representative of the American people, I received for my nation, **vicariously**, the stripes intended for many generations."—*Remarks*, Bill Nye

Roller coasters are a vicarious thrill. They allow us to feel what it's like to fall off a building without actually dying.

Virtual reality headsets are being built to allow everything from total immersion into a game, to realistic sexual experiences.

"Voilà! In view, a humble vaudevillian veteran cast **vicariously** as both victim and villain by the vicissitudes of fate. This visage, no mere veneer of vanity is a vestige of the *vox populi*, now vacant, vanished."—*V for Vendetta*

"Those of us who regard our fingernails as nature's Swiss Army Knives can only **vicariously** enjoy the majesty of a manicure masterpiece."—"Tokyo, Japan," Mary Elizabeth Williams

Synonyms: alternatively, by proxy, imagined, indirect, pretended, secondarily, substituted

482. Vicissitude
noun (*vis*•eh•tood)

An unexpected change in someone's life, especially financially

Used in Context

"But it is not good to look too long upon these turning wheels of **vicissitude**, lest we become giddy."—*Essays*, Francis Bacon

"But, on the whole, death and **vicissitude** had done very little."—*Fragments from The Journal of a Solitary Man*, Nathaniel Hawthorne

"So great a **vicissitude** in his life could not at once be received as real."—*The Scarlet Letter*, Nathaniel Hawthorne

"Your life will be full of peace and joy, and the home which you are establishing will abide through every **vicissitude**."—*The Shining Hour*

In the plural…

"In view, a humble vaudevillian veteran cast vicariously as both victim and villain by the **vicissitudes** of fate."—*V for Vendetta*

A common usage of "vicissitude" is in the plural, as in "the vicissitudes of life."

"You could have chosen any words in any order—there are no rules about that. So what's out there has your name on it, and it is purely authored by you. It's an expression of who you are. And so I think the ego is uniquely exposed in the writer to the **vicissitudes** of reality."—"Jonathan Franzen on Fame, Fascism, and Why He Won't Write a Book About Race," Isaac Chotiner

"Perhaps it's writing poetry, journaling, practicing religion, meditating or going for a long drive to cope with the **vicissitudes** of life."—"5 Key Characteristics of Successful Medical School Applicants," Sylvia Morris, M.D.

"The shadows, outlines and juxtaposition of elements that preoccupied him are things, he noted, that early man would have seen. They are the visual building blocks that toddlers see as they try to comprehend the **vicissitudes** of the physical world."—"Review: The Painter Ellsworth Kelly's Love Affair With Photography," Philip Gefter

Synonyms: alteration, correction, diversity, fate, flip-flop, fluctuation, karma, mutation, permutation, surprise, turn of events, uncertainty, ups and downs

483. Vilify
verb (*vil•uh•fy*)

To make vicious and defamatory statements about someone

Used in Context
"You can quote them, disagree with them, glorify or **vilify** them. About the only thing you can't do is ignore them."—*Jobs*

"But it remains a moral crime to **vilify** good cops who have made the city safe, saving thousands of lives."—"Protesters Slimed This Good Samaritan Cop," Michael Daly

"This is a story about a venomous rhino and his aggressive campaign to slander, **vilify**, defame, denigrate and villainize my good name!"—*Death to Smoochy*

> The noun form of "vilify" is "vilification."

> To make damning and libelous statements about someone is to vilify them.

"You know, **vilify** me if you want, Rachel, but I had a job to do, and I had every right to do what I did."—*Nothing But the Truth*

"'More and more of the electorate sees themselves as almost living in two separate worlds,' Zelizer said. 'And when this happens, you tend to **vilify** the opponent. It's not simply another view, it's an intolerable view.'"—"Good Riddance to a Campaign that Put the 'Ugh' in Ugly," Nancy Benac

Synonyms: abuse, asperse, assail, attack, bad-mouth, berate, blacken, calumniate, curse, cuss, damn, debase, decry, defame, denigrate, denounce, depreciate, disparage, dress down, give a black eye, knock, libel, malign, mistreat, mudsling, pan, put down, roast, run down, slander, slur, smear, speak ill of, tear down, tear into, vituperate

484. Virulent
adjective (*veer•uh•lint*)

Extremely toxic to living things; infectious; can also be used to describe a tone or sensibility

Used in Context
"There has been a perpetual and **virulent** lack of discipline upon my vessel. Why?"—*Pirates of the Caribbean: At World's End*

"Max Blumenthal says far right's **virulent** attacks are what really did him in."—"Did Women Beat the Right's Point Man?," Max Blumenthal

"In fact, once exposed to the elements, the organ became the site of **virulent** infections."—"Stop Pretending the War Is Over," Andrew J. Bacevich

"However, this valorous visitation of a bygone vexation stands vivified and has vowed to vanquish these venal and **virulent** vermin vanguarding vice and vouchsafing the violently vicious and voracious violation of volition."—*V for Vendetta*

"It was a **virulent** strain, fast-moving, because something else infected her in addition to the rust."—*Bones*, "The Heiress in the Hill"

"A public health approach to the epidemiology of hate crimes will enable an informed discussion of the character and volume of the problem and allow for preventive efforts in highly affected areas. When faced with the threat of pandemic, our public health systems are a fortress. Now, more than ever, they should be leveraged against our time's most **virulent** strain: hate."—"Donald Trump and the Epidemiology of Hate," Akash Goel, Andrew Goldstein

Synonyms: acerbic, baneful, dangerous, deadly, destructive, fatal, harmful, hostile, infective, injurious, malicious, malignant, noxious, poisonous, septic, spiteful, unhealthy, venomous, vicious

485. Visceral
adjective (vis•er•ul)

Coarse, base, instinctive

Used in Context

"Done to death, I know. But not like this. We strip it down, make it **visceral** and real."—*Black Swan*

"We wanted to have that **visceral** sort of 'screw you' moment of eye contact between Walt and Gus."—"*Breaking Bad*: Bryan Cranston, Vince Gilligan, Emmy Nominations," Maria Elena Fernandez

"The look of **visceral** satisfaction on his face was unmistakable."—*Makers*, Cory Doctorow

The source of the word is "viscera," which means the internal organs of the body.

Anything that stems from deep, inward feelings can be described as visceral.

"He was a civilized man, but when a homeless man spit on him, his visceral reaction was to beat the crap out of him."

"He stressed that he had learned powerful lessons from performing with pop stars. Never a natural performer, he saw firsthand the importance of connecting with the audience in a physical and **visceral** way."—"The Violinist Charlie Siem Strikes a High Note in Fashion," Elizabeth Paton

"Many in the audience had a personal and **visceral** response, which they communicated with cheers and finger snaps."—"Watching Postelection, So Much Feels Different," Alexis Soloski

Synonyms: animal, ingrained, inherent, innate, gutsy, instinctive, instinctual, primeval, reflex, rooted

To make faulty or imperfect; to reduce the effectiveness of something; to impair

Used in Context

"So long as the suspect understands the bare essentials of his Miranda Rights, no type of police deception will **vitiate** the waiver of those rights."—*Law & Order*, "Doubles"

"There is at least one error in the Symmes diary, which is however explainable, and need not **vitiate** the whole of it."—*The Life and Genius of Nathaniel Hawthorne*, Frank Preston Stearns

> Some government programs are constantly vitiated by bureaucratic red tape that prevents proper functioning of the system.

"Here's what we're going to do, my friend. We're going to **vitiate** that settlement, you're going to return the money, and in consideration, I will hold off moving for your immediate disbarment."—*Harry's Law*, "The Lying Game"

"She seems determined to run as a born-again populist who can emulate left-wing Democrats, such as Sen. Bernie Sanders or Sen. Elizabeth Warren. In the process, she adjusts positions in ways that **vitiate** her real advantage, which is that she's a strong, experienced, centrist politician."—"Bush and Clinton Should Embrace Their Brands," David Ignatius

"But let's be clear: a gargantuan proportion of medical resources has been devoted to developing pills, devices, and procedures to treat or

vitiate lifestyle diseases."—"Precision Medicine Approaches Peak Hype," Larry Husten

Synonyms: abrogate, damage, debauch, deflower, demean, impair, invalidate, mar, marginalize, misdirect, negate, nullify, pervert, quash, recant, revoke, ruin, subvert, sully, undermine, undo

487. Vociferous
adjective (vo•*sif*•er•us)

Making a loud outcry

Used in Context
"And they are in no way representative of the new, modern, improved British Navy. They are a small, **vociferous** minority."— *Monty Python's Flying Circus*, "The War Against Pornography"

Loud, boisterous, yelling; "The crowd protesting cuts to school lunch programs was vociferous."

"An awfully large number of people are beginning to think so, particularly among his most **vociferous** supporters on the left."—"Obama's Pretend Bipartisanship," Eric Alterman

"The cowboy subsided, then burst into **vociferous** demands for a bed."—*Roosevelt in the Bad Lands*, H. Hagedorn

"The attacks upon me stem from a **vociferous** minority which happens to control the press."—*Inherit the Wind*

"The Standing Rock Sioux tribe has waged a **vociferous** protest against the pipeline, which would run near its North Dakota reservation."—"Judge Denies Tribe's Request To Stop North Dakota Oil Pipeline Construction," Oliver Milman

Synonyms: boisterous, clamorous, distracting, enthusiastic, loud, loudmouthed, noisy, obstreperous, ranting, raucous, rowdy, shouting, shrill, strident, vocal, uproarious, vehement, vociferant

488. Volition
noun (voh•*li*•shun)

A person's will; a person's purpose and sense of action

Used in Context

"Jesus, nobody twisted your arm to be here. You're here of your own **volition**."—*Clerks*

"But then you have the women who go into the trade of their **volition**."—"A History of Sex in London: City of Lust?," Kevin Canfield

"An act of **volition** produces motion in our limbs, or raises a new idea in our imagination."—*An Enquiry Concerning Human Understanding*, David Hume

"He had resigned; but no resignation had ever appeared to have less of **volition** in it."—*The Bertrams*, Anthony Trollope

"However, this valorous visitation of a bygone vexation stands vivified and has vowed to vanquish these venal and virulent vermin vanguarding vice and vouchsafing the violently vicious and voracious violation of **volition**."—*V for Vendetta*

"The parents are denying that they forced their child to fast, saying she came to them of her own **volition** and requested permission."—"Indian Police Charge Parents of Girl Who Died Following a 10-Week Religious Fast," Dominique Rowe

Synonyms: choice, choosing, decision, desire, determination, discretion, election, option, preference, will, wish

489. Voluble
adjective (*vol*•yu•bull)

Describes someone who talks easily, and at some length

Used in Context
"In late 2007, the **voluble** Texas hedge-funder threw down $110 million against the subprime-mortgage market and made a killing."—"Wall Street's Biggest Players Avoiding Bets on Eurozone Financial Crisis," Alex Klein

"She was a **voluble**, untidy woman who made her own clothes and washed once a week in the water."—*The Falls*

"Those fears, combined with China's **voluble** online community, can sometimes lead to rumors. Last year, KFC, the fried-chicken chain popular in China, sued three Chinese internet companies over online accusations that it used genetically modified chickens with six wings and eight legs to feed its customers."—"In Push for G.M.O.s, China Battles Fears of 8-Legged Chickens," Amie Tsang, Cao Li

"A knave very **voluble**; no further conscionable than in putting on the mere form of civil and humane seeming."—*Othello,* William Shakespeare

"He was **voluble** in his welcome, talking partly in Spanish, partly in English."—*The Octopus,* Frank Norris

"She told me that they come in the night and stitch up your mouth if you use profanity or were otherwise **voluble**."—*CQ*

Synonyms: articulate, bigmouthed, chattering, chatty, fluent, full of hot air, gabby, garrulous, glib, long-winded, loquacious, mouthy, talkative, talky, prolix, rambling, verbal, verbose, vociferous, wordy

W

Describes being unable to make a committed
decision, or to shift from one position to another

Used in Context

"I'm sorry, I'm sorry, but that's far from **waffling**, that's just my way of
presenting a reasoned argument."—*Hustle*, "Picasso Finger Painting"

"His **waffling** on apologizing to Korean women who were sex workers in wartime Japan has enraged many."—"How Sexism Could Bring
Down Japan's Government," Angela Erika Kubo, Jake Adelstein

"Stop **waffling**. She deserved it. She was a home wrecker. She was a
man-eater. And she was a bad actress."—*Death Becomes Her*

"Did journalists create Trump? Of course not—they don't have that
kind of power. But they helped him tremendously, with huge amounts
of early, unfiltered exposure in the months leading up to the Republican primary season. With ridiculous emphasis put on every development about Hillary Clinton's email practices, including the **waffling**

of FBI Director James B. Comey."—"The Media Didn't Want To Believe Trump Could Win. So They Looked The Other Way," Margaret Sullivan

Synonyms: ambivalent, changing one's mind, contradictory, equivocating, flip-flopping, indecisive, uncertain, unsure, vacillating, yo-yoing

491. Wreak
verb (wreek)

To cause something destructive; to inflict violence or punishment on someone

Used in Context

"They can't just hop a ferry, scoot over to the mainland and **wreak** havoc."—*Shutter Island*

As you can tell from the quotes listed here, the most common form of construction using "wreak" is "wreak havoc." In fact, it's so commonplace, one might reconsider using it on the chance of deferring to a cliché.

"The media narrative by now is set in concrete: The voters are teed off, rising up, mad as hell and ready to **wreak** havoc."—"How the Media Blew the Midterms," Howard Kurtz

"Leading from the front, he has a cannonball of a shot and can **wreak** havoc from distance."—"World Cup Primer," Joshua Robinson

"He'll **wreak** havoc on our village if we let him wander free, so it's time to take some action, boys."—*Beauty and the Beast*

"You have your mission. Go forth, **wreak** havoc."—*Mallrats*

"Why didn't God empower the Israelites to **wreak** vengeance on their enemies who were evil people?"—"Passover, Non-Violence And Gun Control," Aryeh Cohen

"Nuclear weapons **wreak** destruction and menace the next generation."—"Shirley Hazzard, Novelist Who Charted Storm-Tossed Lives, Dies at 85," Helen T. Verongos

Synonyms: bring about, carry out, cause, create, do, effect, inflict, vent, visit, unleash, wreck

492. Wrought
verb (rawt)

To skillfully construct; to create

Used in Context
"Meanwhile, his countrymen must try to undo the damage that the madman has **wrought** over four decades."—"Gaddafi Goons Dig In," Babak Dehghanpisheh

"Is she not proud? Doth she not count her blest, unworthy as she is that we **wrought** so worthy a gentleman to be her bride?"—*Romeo and Juliet*

"But the maggot-infested underside of *News of the World* is a metaphor for what his whole tabloid operation has **wrought**."—"Murdoch's Dark Arts," Tina Brown

"Mrs. Latimer's sobs only roused his wrath at all the misery she had **wrought**."—*A Man of Two Countries*, Alice Harriman

"The miracles I have **wrought** out of fertilizer bills and cutlery invoices, but I had to."—*Lincoln*

"The challenge facing chief executives is compounded by the changes **wrought** by technology."—"Blockbuster Deals in a Race to Stay Ahead of the Competition," Steven Davidoff Solomon

Synonyms: crafted, created, elaborated, embellished, fashioned, formed, made, manufactured, produced, shaped, twisted

493. Wry
adjective (ry)

Refers to a mocking, ironic sense of amusement

Used in Context

"Not jokes so much, more sort of **wry**, little observations."—*One Day*

"The inscription is cheeky and modest, confident, **wry** and telling."—"Smithsonian's First Ladies Collection Offers More Intimate Look at History," Robin Givhan

"She had met Victoria on her home grounds twice, when Callista had invited her out to Shanesville with **wry** warnings."—*The Trial of Callista Blake*, Edgar Pangborn

"You're gonna meet a lot of terrific men in your life and, you know, I want you to enjoy me. My **wry** sense of humor and astonishing sexual technique, but never forget that you've got your whole life ahead of you."—*Manhattan*

"What's striking about the account isn't just its **wry** brilliance. It is that the man who defined the modern category of whistle-blower was the sort who gave career advice to Henry Kissinger."—"Daniel Ellsberg, Edward Snowden, and the Modern Whistle-Blower," Malcolm Gladwell

Synonyms: cynical, droll, dry, ironic, mocking, sarcastic, sardonic, twisted, warped

X

494. Xenophobia
noun (zeen•uh•*fo*•bee•uh)

Fear and/or hatred of foreign people, customs, beliefs, and culture

Used in Context

"Ideological purity, compromise as weakness, a fundamentalist belief in scriptural literalism, denying science, unmoved by facts, undeterred by new information, a hostile fear of progress, a demonization of education, a need to control women's bodies, severe **xenophobia**, tribal mentality, intolerance of dissent, and a pathological hatred of the US Government."—*The Newsroom*, "The Greater Fool"*

*This was the character Will McAvoy's assessment of the Tea Party on the Aaron Sorkin show *The Newsroom* (which was created and written by Sorkin). Will got into some hot water for saying this on the air during one of his broadcasts. It was during his editorial segment, though, not the main news segment, and he was Senior Editor and Anchor and could say whatever he wished. It's just that members of the Tea Party, as well as Tea Party–supported politicians didn't like it.

"At a time when **xenophobia** runs rampant in Egypt, foreigners are often met with distrust."—"Mysterious American Man Found Dead In Egyptian Jail," Sophia Jones

"By all indications, the Kes are a very progressive people. But the Prytt are not. They are reclusive to the point of **xenophobia**."—*Star Trek: The Next Generation*, "Attached"

"You know what it is? **Xenophobia**. That's what it is. Keep us living in fear."—*ER*, "The Gallant Hero & the Tragic Victor"

Synonyms: bias, bigotry, chauvinism, dislike of foreigners, fanaticism, intolerance, Luddite, narrow-mindedness, prejudice, racial intolerance

Z

495. Zeal
noun (zeel)

Passionate enthusiasm for a cause

Used in Context

"But which to us, summon up face after face, full of honesty and goodness, **zeal** and vigor and intellectual promise. The flower of a generation."—*Chariots of Fire*

"And he said no, he didn't need it, that he was quite warm. His **zeal** for King and Country kept him warm."—*Master and Commander: The Far Side of the World*

"Even as the ranks of culture warriors on the right diminish, their **zeal** seems to intensify."—"The Right Wing Screams for the Wambulance Over Gay Marriage Ruling," Walter Olson

"We have to be more than careful of Mrs. Goodhall. She has enough Christian **zeal** to start her own country."—*The Cider House Rules*

"When the company decided it wanted to reduce spam, it established a policy that limited its spread. If Facebook had the same kind of **zeal** about fake news, it could minimize its spread, too."—"Mark Zuckerberg Is in Denial," Zeynep Tufekci

Synonyms: alacrity, ardor, bustle, determination, devotion, drive, eagerness, enthusiasm, enthusiastic diligence, fanaticism, fervor, fire, gusto, keenness, mania, passion, spirit, support, zest

496. Zealot
noun (*zell•ut*)

Someone who expresses near-fanatical support for a cause, especially a religion or faith movement

Used in Context
"Clad in black, Al Pacino tells Gina Piccalo he loved playing Jack Kevorkian because he was a '**zealot.**'"—"Pacino's Best Performance in Years," Gina Piccalo

"I was sure the owner committed the cardinal sin of improperly storing his wine, and I smote him with all the fervor of a **zealot.**"—"The Myth About Old Wine," Keith Wallace

"The old man's voice was again the rapt and fiery utterance of the **zealot.**"—*The Roof Tree*, Charles Neville Buck

"You got me through my childhood. Then you go to Fort Lauderdale and you meet this fanatic, this **zealot.** He fills you full of superstition."—*Deconstructing Harry*

"As we have previously explained, it's certainly legitimate to sign up to volunteer as a poll watcher. Roaming free with a sidearm looking for 'people who can't speak American,' as one Trump **zealot** put it, is not that."—"Who Watches the Poll Watchers?," Dahlia Lithwick

Synonyms: activist, advocate, believer, bigot, crank, devotee, die hard, disciple, extremist, fanatic, fiend, maniac, militant, nut, radical

497. Zeitgeist
noun (*zite*•gyste)

The cultural sensibility of a certain time or era as expressed by its writings, religion, culture, values, and politics

Used in Context

"Judging by the pack of reporters outside, either ballet is ascendant in the **zeitgeist**, or it's leaked that a murder has occurred here."—*Elementary*, "Corpse de Ballet"

"Which just goes to show that if you wait long enough to reboot, the **zeitgeist** will eventually catch up with you."—"*Star Trek*: The Reboot," Tom Shone

"Where should I go for tea and for news of the workings of the **zeitgeist**?"—*The Convert*, Elizabeth Robins

"While on tour, Jimmy Page appeared onstage in full wizard costume. Even the beautiful Beatles tapped into the **zeitgeist** with John Lennon pushing for a film version of *The Lord of the Rings*."—*Ringers: Lord of the Fans*

"This country still yearning to escape its Nazi shadow is not known for its tolerance, and yet somehow, a bearded lady has seized the **zeitgeist**."—"Europe's Game-Changing Bearded Lady," Winston Ross

Synonyms: ambience, atmosphere, climate, disposition, feeling, flavor, inclination, leaning, milieu, movement, outlook, spirit, tendency, tenor, tone, trend

498. Zenith
noun (*zee•*nith)

The high point of something; the climax of something

Used in Context
"Yet even at the **zenith** of her pride and power, the Republic lay fatally stricken with a disease called human slavery."—*Spartacus*

"As summer reaches its **zenith**, these landscapes provide a welcome touchstone to seasons past."—"Van Gogh in Summer," Paul Laster

"In theory, Holbrooke should have been at the **zenith** of his diplomatic skills and career."—"Richard Holbrooke's Last Mission in Afghanistan," David Rohde

"Others question whether the parliament has already reached the **zenith** of its powers and will be further sidelined in the future."—"European Parliament Must Grapple With EU's Democratic Deficit," Laurence Norman

"Sometimes at the height of our revelries, when our joy is at its **zenith**, when all is most right with the world, the most unthinkable disasters descend upon us."—*A Christmas Story*

Synonyms: acme, apex, cap, capstone, culmination, eminence, height, high point, meridian, peak, pinnacle, roof, summit, tip-top, top

499. Zygote
noun (*zy•*goat)

An ovum that has been fertilized by a spermatozoon

Used in Context
"Willie, the girl was a **zygote** when you were in seventh grade."— *Beautiful Girls*

"But if the basis is not there, no amount of education can transform that **zygote** into a mathematician."—*Mendelism*, Reginald Crundall Punnett

"I raised you from when you were a **zygote**, okay? You got my DNA, all right? I can read you like a book."—*Rescue Me*, "Seven"

"If the mathematical faculty has been carried in by the gamete, the education of the **zygote** will enable him to make the most of it."— *Mendelism*, Reginald Crundall Punnett

"But here's the deal. In order for this **zygote** to stay firmly ensconced in my uterine wall, my doctor has put me on bovine hormones that are making me extremely nauseous."—*Glee*, "On My Way"

Synonyms: conception, egg, fertilized egg

ABOUT
THE AUTHOR

Stephen Spignesi is a writer, university professor, and author of more than seventy books on popular culture, TV, film, American and world history, the paranormal, and the American presidents.

He is considered an authority on the works of Stephen King (five books), The Beatles (three books), and the *Titanic* (two books).

Spignesi was christened "the world's leading authority on Stephen King" by *Entertainment Weekly* magazine and has worked with Stephen King, Turner Entertainment, the Margaret Mitchell Estate, Ron Howard, Andy Griffith, the Smithsonian Institution, George Washington's Mount Vernon, ITV, Viacom, and other personalities and entities on a wide range of projects.

Spignesi has also contributed short stories, essays, chapters, articles, and introductions to a wide range of books, his most recent being the short story "Lovely Rita" for the *Night of the Living Dead*–themed anthology *Rise of the Dead*. He is the author of four of the acclaimed "For Dummies" nonfiction reference books. He is also a novelist whose thriller *Dialogues* was hailed upon release as "reinventing the psychological thriller," and which he has adapted into a play.

Spignesi has appeared on CNN, MSNBC, the Fox News Channel, and many other TV and radio outlets. He also appeared in the 1998 E! documentary *The Kennedys: Power, Seduction, and Hollywood*, the A & E *Biography* of Stephen King that aired in January 2000, and the 2015 documentary *Autopsy: The Last Hours of Robin Williams*.

Spignesi's 1997 book *JFK Jr.* was a *New York Times* bestseller. Spignesi's *Complete Stephen King Encyclopedia* was a 1991 Bram Stoker Award nominee. Spignesi is a retired Practitioner in Residence at the University of New Haven in West Haven, Connecticut, where he was nominated for an Excellence in Teaching Award and taught English Composition and Literature and other literature courses, several of which were based on his books.

He lives in New Haven, Connecticut. His website is www. stephenspignesi.com.